# National Security and Free Speech

# National Security and Free Speech

## The Debate Since 9/11

Christopher M. Finan, editor

**International Debate Education Association**

New York, London & Amsterdam

Published by
The International Debate Education Association
105 East 22nd Street
New York, NY 10010

This book is published with the generous support of the Open Society Foundations.

Library of Congress Cataloging-in-Publication Data
National security and free speech : the debate since 9/11 /
Christopher M. Finan, editor.
    pages cm
  Includes bibliographical references.
  ISBN 978-1-61770-082-8
  1. Freedom of expression—United States.   2. National security—Law and legislation—United States.   3. Terrorism—Prevention—Law and legislation—United States.   I. Finan, Christopher M., 1953– editor of compilation.   II. International Debate Education Association, issuing body.
  KF4770.N38 2013
  342.7308'53—dc23                    2013025632


Composition by Brad Walrod/Kenoza Type, Inc.
Printed in the USA

 **IDEBATE Press**

# Contents

## Acknowledgments

I had a lot of help in preparing this book. Thanks to Jameel Jaffer, Joan Bertin, David Horowitz, Sharon Bradford Franklin, and Scott Roehm. At the Open Society Foundations and the IDEBATE Press, Lisa Magarrell, Martin Greenwald, Eleanora von Dehsen, and Jackson Tucker provided inspiration and guidance. Finally, thanks to Alex Finan for his research assistance.

# Introduction

In February 2003, high school junior Bretton Barber went to school wearing a T-shirt that displayed a picture of Pres. George W. Bush above the words "International Terrorist." Barber had been participating in protests against an American invasion of Iraq, and he was disappointed when none of his classmates asked about the T-shirt. He didn't hear any negative comments until an assistant principal approached him in the lunchroom. "He told me that it was 'promoting terrorism,' and that it was inappropriate," Barber said.[1] The vice principal told him to remove the shirt (he was wearing another underneath) or turn it inside out. But Barber was a member of the American Civil Liberties Union (ACLU) and was familiar with a U.S. Supreme Court decision that declares that students do not "shed their constitutional rights to freedom of speech or expression at the schoolhouse gate."[2] In that case, *Tinker v. Des Moines Independent School District* (1969), the Court had upheld the right of students to wear black armbands to protest American involvement in the Vietnam War. Barber refused to remove his T-shirt and was sent home. Later, he spoke to the school principal on the telephone:

> She immediately asked if I was familiar with the Supreme Court case, *Tinker v. Des Moines.* I said I was very familiar with it. She said it happened in 1969. And I said no, it happened in 1965, but it got decided in 1969. Then she quoted directly from the dissenting opinion, to say that the school has the right to control speech. I knew that wasn't how the case came out, but I didn't argue with her.[3]

He let the ACLU do the talking. It filed a lawsuit that charged school officials with violating Barber's First Amendment right to freedom of speech. He won. "It was ruled that Dearborn High School had violated my constitutional rights to free expression, and I am now able to wear the shirt as I please," Barber related.

By wearing a T-shirt, Bretton Barber joined a debate that has been under way between advocates of national security and defenders of free speech since the beginning of the American republic. The First Amendment to the Constitution promises us free speech. But just a few years after its adoption, at a time when it appeared that the United States might go to war with France, the government started throwing newspaper editors into jail for criticizing the policies of President John Adams. Ever since, national security and free speech have repeatedly clashed. During the Civil War, Clement Vallandigham, a northern critic of Pres. Abraham Lincoln, was sentenced to two years in prison for making a speech that might "demoralize the troops." During World War I, more than 1,000 Americans were convicted and sentenced to long prison terms for making statements that allegedly harmed the war effort. The cold war between the United States and Soviet Union in the 1940s and 1950s produced a government crackdown on anyone who appeared to share "communist" ideas, making people reluctant to advocate any reforms out of fear that they would be denounced as communists.

The terrorist attacks on Washington and New York on September 11, 2011, gave new urgency to the debate. Once again government leaders argued that the civil liberties that we enjoy in times of peace must be restricted when we face threats from abroad. They point out that American freedoms depend on the preservation of the American government. Civil libertarians reply that freedom of speech is not a privilege but a *right* that

2    NATIONAL SECURITY AND FREE SPEECH

must be respected even in the face of threats of violence. They insist that dissent is never more important than when wartime passions can blind us to errors by our leaders.

Yet, neither government officials nor civil libertarians hold absolutist views: almost everyone agrees on the importance of civil liberties and the danger of terrorism. We are all trying to come to grips with the consequences of how the world has changed since 9/11. It isn't easy to protect ourselves while preserving our hard-won liberties. Therefore, this book tries to give students an appreciation for the arguments that are being made on both sides of the debate about national security and free speech, drawing on a selection of speeches, press releases, and news stories. But, before we take up the current controversy, it is important to see how the debate over national security and free speech began.

## The Fight to Protect Free Speech

Pres. Woodrow Wilson faced a real problem in leading his country into war in 1917. Many Americans were strongly opposed to sending troops to Europe where Germany, England, and France had been involved in unprecedented slaughter since 1914. Millions had already died. Critics argued that the dispute had nothing to do with the United States. Millions of German immigrants supported the fatherland. The American Socialist Party, a significant political organization at the time, argued that workers of all nations had common interests and should not be fighting in a war that was enriching only capitalists.

Fearful that dissent would undermine the war effort, Wilson took steps to suppress his critics. He urged Congress to approve an Espionage Act that was directed at domestic opponents as much as at foreign spies. The first draft of the legislation provided a prison sentence of up to 10 years for anyone who published information that might possibly be useful to the enemy. This provision was dropped when the press complained that it would put the president in a position to prosecute newspapers anytime he disagreed with something they reported. Another section of the bill that became law in 1917 gave the post office broad new powers to exclude from the mails any material "advocating or urging treason, insurrection, or forcible resistance to any law of the United States."[4] The postmaster general immediately began excluding from the mail any material that was critical of the war.

The Espionage Act also provided a prison term of up to 20 years for anyone making "false statements with intent to interfere with the operation or success of the military forces." In a nation in the grip of war fever, almost any statement that didn't sound patriotic could be construed as interfering with the war effort. Thirty German Americans in South Dakota went to jail for sending a petition to the governor urging reforms in the draft laws. An Iowa man received a 20-year sentence for circulating a petition calling for the defeat of a congressman who had voted for the draft. Another Iowa man was sent to jail for a year for being present at a radical meeting, applauding, and contributing a quarter. More than 2,000 people were prosecuted for "disloyal" statements under the Espionage Act; half of them were imprisoned, including Eugene V. Debs, the four-time Socialist Party candidate for president. Debs was sentenced to 10 years for telling an audience of workers, "You need to know that you are fit for something better than slavery and cannon fodder."[5]

We normally look to the courts to protect our rights. But, during World War I, most judges agreed that criticism of the government is not allowed during wartime. When the first Espionage Act cases reached the U.S. Supreme Court, it gutted the First Amendment, unanimously upholding all of the convictions. When Debs ran for president for the fifth time, he was an inmate in the Atlanta penitentiary.

Even at the height of the war, however, a handful of individuals saw the danger in suppressing dissent. Zachariah D. Chafee, Jr., a professor at Harvard Law School, believed the country had made a mistake. "Under the pressure of a great crisis ... [j]udges ... have interpreted the 1917 Act so broadly as to make practically all opposition to the war criminal," he wrote in an article in *The New Republic*. As a result, the freedom at the core of democracy was threatened. "One of the most important purposes of society and government is the discovery and spread of truth on subjects of general concern. This is possible only through absolutely unlimited discussion."[6]

Chafee's article was published just days after the end of the war—few people paid any attention. But Justice Oliver Wendell Holmes, Jr., was willing to listen to what Chafee had to say. At 78, Holmes was the oldest justice on the Supreme Court. He was so old that he had fought and had been wounded in the Civil War. He even looked like an antique because he still cultivated the large mustache, now white, that had been popular in his youth. But, he was open to new ideas and was widely considered to be America's greatest jurist. One of the reasons critics of the Espionage Act were so disappointed in the Supreme Court's decision in *Debs. v. United States* (1919), which upheld Debs's conviction, was that Holmes was the author of the written opinion explaining the Court's thinking. In fact, we know today that Holmes had second thoughts about the case. In an unsent letter later found in his papers, he admitted, "I hated to have to write the Debs case and still more those of the other poor devils before us the same day. I think it is quite possible that if I had been on the jury I should have been for acquittal."[7] Over the next several months, Holmes corresponded with critics of the Espionage Act—he even had tea with Chafee. By the time the Supreme Court reviewed its next Espionage Act case, Holmes had changed his mind.

Holmes's fellow justices were shocked when he told them that he would write a dissenting opinion in the case of *Abrams v. U.S* (1919). Four radicals had been charged with distributing a pamphlet calling on workers to strike in protest over American policy toward the communists who had recently taken control of Russia. The justices viewed it as another effort to undermine the war effort, but Holmes saw something more important at stake. In his opinion, he wrote that by restricting free speech, government was denying a profound fact— nobody has a monopoly on the truth. People must be free to propose ideas and defend them in debate with those who disagree. Therefore,

> . . . . I think that we should be eternally vigilant against attempts to check the expression of opinions that we loathe and believe to be fraught with death, unless they so imminently threaten immediate interference with the lawful and pressing purposes of the law that an immediate check is required to save the country.[8]

Although Holmes did not say it in so many words, he clearly believed in protecting even speech calling for the violent overthrow of the government as long as it was not accompanied by violent acts. Only Justice Louis Brandeis voted with Holmes, but the old judge had presented an eloquent defense of and justification for free speech that would eventually be accepted by the Supreme Court.

## Communism, the Cold War, and the FBI

Even though the war had ended a year earlier, Americans weren't in a mood for pleas for free speech when Holmes delivered his opinion in November 1919. In the year since the war had ended, the country had grown increasingly fearful of the threat of communism. In 1917, revolutionaries overthrew the Russian czar. The most radical faction, the Bolsheviks, had taken control of the government and were proclaiming that the workers of the world would bury capitalism in a bloody revolt. This terrified many Americans. The country was full of immigrants, including some who advocated the overthrow of the existing order. And, the post-war period was a time of great turmoil. Industrial workers staged more than 3,600 strikes in 1919 in an effort to raise wages enough to keep pace with raging inflation. Employers portrayed the strikers as radicals, and the danger was driven home by a series of bombings, including one at the home of Attorney General A. Mitchell Palmer. The government responded by launching a series of raids, known as the Palmer Raids, that rounded up thousands of mostly Russian immigrants who belonged to radical political parties. Americans were as scared of radical ideas as they were by Russians. In New York, the legislature expelled four Socialist representatives for being disloyal to American values despite the fact that they were committed to achieving their goals through the political process.

The fear of communism subsided during the 1920s as the economy began to grow again, but it never disappeared entirely. In 1929, police in California arrested a 19-year-old counselor in a Communist Party summer camp for children. Yetta Stromberg was sentenced to five years in prison for raising a red flag every morning, violating a state law that banned the flag as a symbol of opposition to "organized government." In *Stromberg v. California* (1931), the Supreme Court created an important precedent when it overturned Stromberg's conviction as a violation of her right of free speech.

Fear of communism did diminish during World War II when the United States and the Soviet Union were allies. But it reemerged strongly as soon as the war was over. After repelling a German invasion, the Soviet Union had occupied much of Europe and showed no interest in restoring democracy in the countries it now occupied. In 1949, communists led by Mao Zedong established the People's Republic of China. Once again, it appeared that communism might achieve worldwide domination.

A new Red Scare began to grow in response to charges that members of the Communist Party had infiltrated the American government and were betraying the nation's secrets. Sen. Joseph McCarthy (R–WI) claimed that communists in the State Department were responsible for the "loss" of China. The response was a government campaign to eliminate employees suspected of disloyalty. In practice, this meant that any evidence of radical views—from the books people read to the paintings that hung on the walls of their homes—could be used against them. Individuals were fired for merely associating with anyone who had radical ties. The leaders of the American Communist Party were imprisoned, not for actually plotting the overthrow of the government, but for advocating it. The House Un-American Activities Committee conducted an investigation of Hollywood that cost many actors and directors their jobs. State and local government employees, including school teachers and college professors, were fired when they refused to sign statements swearing loyalty to the government. At a time when any criticism of government was attacked as communist propaganda, dissent nearly disappeared. Supreme Court Justice William O. Douglas was alarmed by what he called "the black silence of fear."

The government's most important weapon for fighting communists was the Federal Bureau of Investigation. Under the leadership of its director, J. Edgar Hoover, the FBI had developed a formidable capacity for spying on American citizens. Illegal wiretapping was augmented by the planting of secret microphones and break-ins that became so common that they were called "black bag jobs." The FBI also built a network of thousands of informants inside the Communist Party and organizations that were suspected of being communist "fronts." As result, the FBI was ready when the new Red Scare began. It had gathered information about tens of thousands of Americans whose political connections raised doubts about their loyalty. It supplied the background reports that cost thousands of government workers their jobs and helped heighten the anti-Red hysteria by feeding information to the congressional investigating committees. Because much of its information had been acquired illegally, the FBI often put it in "blind memos," which were printed on plain paper so they could not be traced back to the bureau.

The FBI's knowledge of the inside workings of dissident groups created an enormous temptation for Hoover and his agents to intervene directly in their affairs and attempt to disrupt them. FBI informants were often in a position to spread lies that would cause internal dissension, sometimes by raising suspicion about the loyalty of key leaders. In 1956, Hoover gave in to temptation and ordered the launch of a full-blown counterintelligence program (COINTELPRO). The program nearly succeeded in wiping out the Communist Party altogether as FBI agents and informants undertook nearly 1,400 actions intended to undermine the morale of their enemies. On one occasion, on learning that a party leader was homosexual, the FBI had him arrested for committing homosexual acts to embarrass the party. It even harassed a Cub Scout den mother by telling her neighbors that she was a communist; she was forced to resign. The FBI's control over a faction of the Communist Party grew so complete that Hoover considered allowing FBI informants to take over the party. It was hardly necessary. By the end of 1957, only 3,474 party members were left. Hoover was so impressed with the results of COINTEL-PRO that he soon turned it against other groups. In 1961, he targeted the Socialist Workers Party, a group that shared the Communist Party's desire to overthrow the capitalist system.

Hoover also feared the growth of a revolutionary movement among African Americans. In 1955, the Rev. Martin Luther King, Jr., led a boycott of the segregated bus system in Montgomery, Alabama, launching an aggressive campaign to win equal rights for blacks. Mainstream civil rights leaders were committed to nonviolence, but some radicals argued that blacks had to be prepared to defend themselves with force. Hoover saw the Black Panther Party as a potentially revolutionary force, and, in 1967, he added it to the list of groups targeted by COINTELPRO.

Hoover believed that Martin Luther King himself was a threat to the nation. As a Southerner, Hoover had been hostile to King from the beginning, but when he learned that one of the civil rights leader's closest advisers had been a high-ranking member of the Communist Party, he ordered King's telephone tapped and bugs planted in his hotel rooms. In the most notorious act of the COINTELPRO era, an assistant director of the FBI sent King an anonymous letter threatening to expose his extramarital affairs. King was in Sweden accepting the Nobel Peace Prize when the letter arrived at the Southern Christian Leadership Council's office, accompanied by a tape consisting of conversations and sounds of sexual activity that had been taped in King's hotel rooms. Not suspecting what it was, King's wife opened the package and listened to the tape. She called her husband. "They are out to break me," King said. "They are out to get me, harass me, break my spirit."[9]

The FBI also worked actively to undermine the movement that had emerged on college campuses in opposition to the Vietnam War. On May 23, 1968, a directive went out from Washington to all bureau offices ordering them to gather damaging information about student protesters in an effort to get them thrown out of school. "Every avenue of possible embarrassment must be vigorously and enthusiastically explored," the directive said.[10] It turned out that FBI agents could be very imaginative. One tactic was to send anonymous letters about student misbehavior to parents, neighbors, and employers. In the days before the Democratic National Convention in Chicago in August 1968, the FBI succeeded in disrupting plans antiwar activists had made for housing demonstrators. Agents in Chicago submitted 217 forms volunteering housing by people who didn't exist. As a result, many protestors were sent on wild goose chases, forced to make "long and useless journeys to locate these addresses," according to an FBI memo. "... [S]everal became incensed" at the organizers, who they held responsible. The organizers, in turn, began questioning the value of the legitimate offers of help they had received, which undermined their ability to house everyone they had promised to accommodate. FBI agents undertook nearly 1,000 actions against domestic political groups.[11]

## Let the Sunshine In

But the wall of government secrecy that was being used to shield efforts to suppress dissent was about to come crashing down. On June 13, 1971, the *New York Times* began publishing a secret government study of the Vietnam War, which became known as the Pentagon Papers. When Pres. Richard Nixon's Justice Department convinced a judge to block the publication of further installments in the series, the Supreme Court was faced with one of its most difficult decisions: whether the government's interest in protecting national security was more important than free speech. The Court would be considering the case in the middle of a war.

The owners of the *New York Times* knew that publishing the Pentagon Papers was going to cause trouble. The study had been commissioned by Secretary of Defense Robert McNamara in June 1967. Although McNamara was the architect of the American war effort, he had become convinced that the war was unwinnable, and he hoped that a study of American involvement in Vietnam since World War II would explain the policy mistakes that had led the United States into that quagmire. Over the next 18 months, a staff of 36 analysts wrote and assembled a 47-volume study that included 3,000 pages of historical interpretation and 4,000 pages of documents.

One of the authors, Daniel Ellsberg, a national security analyst who had become a passionate critic of the war, was convinced that making the Pentagon Papers public would end the war. During a two-year stay in Vietnam, Ellsberg had come to believe that America's leaders were being fooled by overly optimistic reports from the field. For example, American military commanders claimed that South Vietnamese troops were undertaking thousands of patrols. "Everyone in Vietnam knew that there had been no patrols—not one," Ellsberg said.[12] But, after reading the Pentagon Papers, Ellsberg concluded that the intelligence estimates given to the president were "remarkably accurate." It was America's leaders who had lied, particularly Pres. Lyndon B. Johnson, who had promised a swift and successful resolution to the war. For two years, Ellsberg tried to give the Pentagon Papers to antiwar leaders in Congress, but they were unwilling to accept responsibility for revealing classified information. Finally, he agreed to give them to Neil Sheehan, a reporter for the *Times*.[13]

The lawyers for the *Times* faced some formidable obstacles as the trial opened in the federal courthouse in Manhattan. The judge, Murray I. Gurfein, had just been appointed by Nixon, and this was his first case. In the opening session, Gurfein was obviously unsympathetic to the *Times*. The biggest problem faced by the newspaper, however, was the government's claim that the report included thousands of pages of classified documents that would harm national security if they were released. By the time they got to court, the government's lawyers were prepared to argue that the Pentagon Papers revealed secrets that would damage U.S. diplomatic relations, expose the nation's intelligence operations and operatives, and provide the enemy with useful information about military planning. During a closed hearing, government experts told Gurfein that the secret study would hamper the effort to obtain the release of American prisoners of war in North Vietnam. They also claimed that the reports would cause Australia, New Zealand, and Thailand to withdraw troops from South Vietnam, slowing the departure of American forces.

The government failed nonetheless. Gurfein lifted his injunction the next day, June 19, 1971, and, when the case reached the Supreme Court just two weeks later, it affirmed his decision. It was not that the judges doubted the government's claims. A majority of the Supreme Court justices said they believed that the Pentagon Papers contained material that would harm the nation, and several said they believed the government could prosecute the *Times* under the Espionage Act. But a majority of the justices agreed that the government had failed to prove that the harm was great enough to justify censoring the press.

The Supreme Court decision in *New York Times Co. v. United States* (1971) strengthened the power of the press to report on national security issues. It also helped precipitate a constitutional crisis that would force the resignation of President Nixon and expose decades of government wrongdoing. Just two weeks after the government lost its case in the Supreme Court, Nixon authorized the formation of an investigative unit within the White House and assigned it the job of cracking down on government whistleblowers, starting with Daniel Ellsberg. In September, probably with Nixon's knowledge, the "Plumbers" broke into the offices of Ellsberg's psychiatrist to get information to help convict Ellsberg, who had been indicted for violating the Espionage Act and theft of government property. The black bag job was only one example of the ways in which Nixon's men now imitated the tactics of the FBI's COINTELPRO program. Undertaking a campaign of what they called "rat-fucking," they also engaged in a series of dirty tricks to disrupt the campaigns of Democratic candidates who were vying to oppose Nixon in the 1972 presidential election.

On June 17, 1972, five members of the Plumbers were arrested in the act of burglarizing the Democratic National Committee offices in the Watergate building in Washington, D.C. Two years and an intensive investigation by the *Washington Post,* Federal District Court Judge John J. Sirica, and committees of the House and Senate were needed to reveal the truth: high officials in the Nixon administration had approved the burglary and the president himself had joined in covering up their role by authorizing the payment of hush money to the burglars. The White House also attempted to use FBI Director L. Patrick Gray to thwart his agency's investigation of the Watergate break-in. In July 1974, less than two years after Nixon won reelection in a landslide, the House Judiciary Committee approved three articles of impeachment. Two stemmed directly from the Pentagon Papers case: the formation of the Plumbers unit and the burglary of Ellsberg's psychiatrist. Nixon was forced to resign.

The Watergate scandal led to important reforms. Since the government had attempted to hide wrongdoing, Congress gave the press and the public broader access to government information. It had already approved a Freedom of Information Act (FOIA), establishing the principle that the public has a right to know what its government is doing. But the law was weakened by a number of exceptions that enabled government officials to successfully resist requests for documents. Soon after Nixon's resignation, Congress passed a series of amendments to the law that gave the public access to a wider range of documents as well as the power to force the government to comply with the law. Pres. Gerald Ford and his top advisers, including Chief of Staff Donald Rumsfeld and his deputy,

Richard Cheney, believed the measure would weaken national security by disclosing military and intelligence secrets and hamper law enforcement. However, Ford's veto of the bill was easily overridden. The strengthened Freedom of Information Act opened the federal government to wide-ranging scrutiny by journalists, scholars, and private citizens. Today, millions of FOIA requests are filed every year, and the information they provide is used in thousands of new stories.

Almost before the country could breathe a sigh of relief over the end of Watergate, however, it was shocked by new revelations of government wrongdoing. On December 22, the *New York Times* revealed that the CIA had been engaged in a massive campaign of spying on American citizens. Although forbidden by law to operate in the United States, the CIA had engaged in illegal break-ins, wiretaps, and mail openings to gather information on more than 10,000 antiwar protesters and other dissidents. The story was written by Seymour Hersh, a Pulitzer Prize–winning reporter. Over the next two weeks, Hersh and other *Times* reporters published 32 stories detailing the sins of the agency. The *Washington Post* joined in describing the misdeeds of the secret government. On January 19, 1975, it reported that the FBI had spied on members of Congress and collected information about their personal lives. A week later, the *Post* also revealed the first public evidence of the government campaign against Martin Luther King.

Congress worked quickly to follow up the charges made by the press. By the end of January, the Senate had established a special committee headed by Frank Church of Idaho and charged it with uncovering the operations of the "shadow government" created by the intelligence agencies. The Church Committee did not disappoint. It revealed that the CIA's computers contained the names of 1.5 million potentially "subversive" Americans. With the CIA, the FBI had secretly opened 380,000 letters, and it had investigated more than 500,000 dissidents without proving that any of them were guilty of committing a crime.

The Church Committee investigation produced a number of changes intended to rein in the government's power to suppress dissent. New limits were imposed on the ability of the government to conduct surveillance of citizens exercising their right to criticize the government. In March 1976, Attorney General Edward Levi imposed strict guidelines that prohibited the FBI from investigating any individual or group on the basis of activities protected by the First Amendment. The FBI could launch a preliminary investigation only when it had evidence of intent to break the law, and it could not continue for more than 90 days or involve the use of informants, wiretaps, and mail "covers" unless the preliminary investigation had identified "specific and articulable facts" supporting the suspicion of illegal intent. The Justice Department had to approve these investigations in advance and then review them annually to ensure that they were still justified. Congress also took steps to increase its oversight of the nation's intelligence agencies, both foreign and domestic. In May 1976, the Senate created a Select Committee on Intelligence; the House organized its own intelligence committee a couple of months later.

In the wake of the Church Committee investigation, reformers also succeeded in passing the Foreign Intelligence Surveillance Act (FISA) in 1978. The law recognized that the FBI needed to be granted authority to conduct wiretapping and secret searches in pursuit of foreign agents engaged in spying in the United States. In the past, the FBI had simply assumed it had this authority. However, FISA required the FBI to apply to a special court composed of federal judges who would review its applications to ensure that the primary purpose of the spying was to deter foreign espionage and not to evade the safeguards involved in normal criminal investigations. In a criminal investigation, the government must demonstrate that it has "probable cause" to believe that a person is engaged in criminal activity before it can obtain a search warrant or wiretap. Under FISA, however, it is only necessary to show that the person who is targeted is the "agent of a foreign power."

By the late 1970s, Vietnam, Watergate, and the intelligence scandals had helped create a movement for greater openness at all levels of government. State legislatures and many local governments passed legislation opening their records to public access for the first time. Many also enacted open meeting laws that strictly limited the amount of public business that could be transacted behind closed doors. Lawsuits often accomplished what public officials were unwilling to do voluntarily. The police in New York, Chicago, Los Angeles, and Memphis were sued for spying on dissidents in the 1960s. These cases were frequently resolved by agreements that barred similar conduct in the future. Sometimes politicians even took the lead in controlling the police. In 1979, the Seattle City Council responded to the news that its police department had spied on 750 residents by passing an ordinance setting strict limits to the department's intelligence gathering and providing for an auditor to ensure compliance. Appointed by the mayor, the auditor was given the responsibility of reviewing police files, issuing reports to the city council, and notifying citizens who may have been targets of illegal investigations. Not surprisingly, the police had opposed the ordinance, but they soon reconciled themselves to it. Although it was not required, the police chief opened his personal safe to the auditor.

The reforms of the Watergate era gave civil libertarians, the press, and citizens important new tools for monitoring government and preventing abuses of free speech and other civil liberties. But, as the memory of Watergate faded, the era of reform came to an end. Many government officials continued to believe that secrecy was essential for effective government, particularly in the area of national security. The world was still a perilous place, and threats from abroad strengthened their argument that the government needed greater powers to defend the homeland.

## 9/11: The Fight over Free Speech Resumes

Not since the Japanese attack on Pearl Harbor have Americans been as horrified as they were by the terrorism on 9/11. We were unified in our support for military efforts to strike back at al Qaeda and its Taliban allies in Afghanistan. Inevitably, some of this anger was directed at anyone who questioned the national security policies of Pres. George W. Bush. Comedian Bill Maher outraged Americans when he said on his television show that piloting airliners into the World Trade Center was braver than firing missiles into Afghanistan. Two columnists, Tom Gutting of the *Texas City Sun* and Dan Guthrie of the *Daily Courier* in Grants Pass, Oregon, were fired for writing that Bush was a coward because he did not immediately return to Washington after the attacks. The mood was ugly on college campuses as well. On the morning of the 9/11 attacks, Richard Berthold, history professor at the University of New Mexico, jokingly told his class, "Anyone who can blow up the Pentagon gets my vote."[14] Some of his students were appalled. So were university administrators. They promptly suspended him.

Conservative groups took advantage of the public mood by attacking professors and other dissenters who they had long suspected of disloyalty. In November 2001, the American Council of Trustees and Alumni denounced professors as "the weak link in America's response to terrorism" because they were pointing "accusatory fingers, not at the terrorists, but at America itself." They published a report that listed 117 allegedly anti-American statements made on college campuses in recent weeks, including calls for building "bridges and relationships, not simply bombs and walls" and for creating an international tribunal to try Osama bin Laden. Wasima Alilkhan of the Islamic Academy of Las Vegas was added to the list for saying "Ignorance breeds hate."[15]

As in the past, the greatest threat to free speech came not from individuals or private groups but from government. From the beginning, the Bush administration had been strongly inclined to expand the power of the Executive Branch in ways that undermined First Amendment rights. The 9/11 attacks gave administration officials a powerful rationale for expanding government secrecy, and they acted quickly to cloak crucial aspects of the newly declared "war on terror." They refused to release any information about the more than 1,000 Muslim men who had been arrested in the days after the attacks. Citizens of Arab countries, these men were arrested without warning, disappearing into jails all over the United States where they were sometimes beaten by prison guards who sought revenge against the "terrorists." Although many were later deported for visa violations, none was charged with terrorism. Nevertheless, the Justice Department refused to allow them to contact their families or hire lawyers. It also barred the press from attending the administrative hearings that would determine whether the men were to be expelled from the United States. On October 12, 2001, Attorney General John Ashcroft encouraged other federal government agencies to embrace secrecy. In a memo to the head of all federal departments and agencies, Ashcroft explained that while the administration was committed to "full compliance" with the Freedom of Information Act, it was "equally committed to protecting other fundamental values that are held by our society," including "safeguarding our national security, [and] enhancing the effectiveness of our law enforcement agencies, protecting sensitive business information and, not least, protecting personal privacy."[16]

Civil libertarians were not surprised by the efforts to bolster the power of the government. Only a few weeks after the 9/11 attacks, more than 150 civil liberties, civil rights, and human rights groups signed a statement urging Congress not to make the same mistake that had been made in previous crises by enacting policies that would erode free speech. Most of these groups looked to the ACLU for leadership. With a $50 million budget and a staff of 500, the ACLU was by far the largest civil liberties group in the country. In the immediate aftermath of the attacks, the ACLU offered a measured response to the hundreds of reporters who called hoping for dramatic quotes about the new threat to civil liberties. At first, the ACLU hoped to negotiate with the Bush administration. In late October, ACLU executive director Anthony Romero and members of his staff met with FBI director Robert S. Mueller, III in an effort to get answers about the hundreds of detainees who were being held by the government. Mueller's refusal to discuss any details of the detentions convinced Romero that the ACLU had to pursue a more aggressive strategy. A few days later, it joined with several other groups to file a request for the information under the Freedom of Information Act. It also began drafting a letter to the embassies of 10 Arab countries offering to help them secure the release of their countrymen. "We are particularly interested in highlighting instances of abuse by our government and in developing a systematic litigation to challenge its unconstitutional practices," it said.[17]

Some of the ambassadors were perplexed that an American organization would offer to sue its government on their behalf. Attorney General Ashcroft was outraged. He blasted civil libertarians in an appearance before the Senate Judiciary Committee. "We need honest, reasoned debate, and not fear-mongering," Ashcroft said.

> To those who pit Americans against immigrants and citizens against noncitizens, to those who scare peace-loving people with phantoms of lost liberty, my message is this: Your tactics only aid terrorists, for they erode our national unity and diminish our resolve. They give ammunition to America's enemies, and pause to America's friends. They encourage people of good will to remain silent in the face of evil.[18]

The ACLU fired back. Laura Murphy, the director of the national office, accused Ashcroft of "a blatant attempt to stifle growing criticism of recent government policy" and of "equating legitimate political dissent with something unpatriotic and un-American."[19]

A new battle over free speech had begun.

## The Debate Today

On April 15, 2013, two bombs exploded near the finish line of the Boston Marathon in downtown Boston, killing 3 and wounding 264. The bombs were packed with shrapnel that cost 16 of the injured an arm or a leg; 3 lost more than one limb. The bombers were soon identified as two Chechen-born brothers who were naturalized American citizens. The older brother, Tamerlan Tsarnaev, was killed in a shoot-out with police several days later. His brother, Dzhokar, was wounded and later captured. Dzhokar told police that he and his brother, both Muslims, planted the bombs as an act of revenge against the United States for its attacks on Muslims in Iraq and Afghanistan.

The Boston Marathon bombing was a terrifying reminder of the 9/11 attacks. Once again terrorists had killed American civilians on their own soil and shut down a major city as authorities searched for the bombers. Again demands were heard for the government to do more to defend against attacks. Government officials who had warned of the danger of terrorism by people living in the United States pointed to the bombing as justification for increasing surveillance of Muslims. Mayor Michael Bloomberg of New York City said that the attack proved the importance of the New York Police Department's extensive program of monitoring the Muslim community. Yet the new attack did not unsettle the country to the same extent as those in 2001. The killing of Osama bin Laden and government security measures appear to have reduced the chance that al Qaeda can launch a large-scale attack in the United States.

It may also reflect the fact the country has spent more than a decade debating how to balance measures to protect the nation with the need to maintain civil liberties. Repeated efforts have been made to add increased protection for civil liberties to the laws changed by the USA PATRIOT Act, which is an acronym for its full title—the Uniting and Strengthening America by Providing Appropriate Tools Required to

Intercept and Obstruct Terrorism. Drafted by Justice Department lawyers, the 342-page bill included a variety of changes that law enforcement officials had been seeking for years. Most of its provisions were not controversial, and it was overwhelmingly approved just six weeks after 9/11. However, parts of the PATRIOT Act dramatically expanded the government's ability to conduct surveillance.

Soon after the passage of the law, critics began to charge that it had freed the government to spy on American citizens without any proof that they were engaging in illegal acts. The press also touched off raging public debates with revelations that the Bush administration authorized the National Security Agency to violate the Foreign Intelligence Surveillance Act and ordered the CIA to operate a system of secret prisons where suspected terrorists were subject to "enhanced interrogation," which critics call torture. U.S. courts have validated a number of the claims of civil libertarians by declaring unconstitutional key provisions of laws passed since 9/11.

This book describes five issues that have emerged since 9/11 that potentially affect the First Amendment right to free expression. "Free speech" involves more than the right to stand on a street corner and say anything we want.

- Free speech is impossible if we are afraid that we are being spied on by the government. Does the PATRIOT Act threaten our right to read without worrying that the government is looking over our shoulder?

- Free speech is also in danger if the government can censor our speech. Should recipients of secret National Security letters be permanently gagged, even if that prevents them from protesting a potentially improper demand?

- We have seen that government secrecy has too often been used to hide conduct that the public has a right to examine and criticize. Should whistleblowers be prosecuted for violating laws designed to protect secrecy?

- We all want law enforcement to be vigilant in protecting public safety. When do police efforts to prevent terrorism cross the line and become spying and thus make people afraid to protest the actions of their government?

- Finally, what constitutes "material support" of terrorism? Do Americans have the right to express support for groups that advocate violence if they do not commit illegal acts themselves?

Americans have been fighting over free speech for almost the entire history of the United States. There will always be people who believe that some ideas are too dangerous to express. But, as Justice Holmes observed, debate is essential to democracy. Since no one has a monopoly of the truth, we must all decide for ourselves which ideas have merit; the only way to do that is to engage in dialogue with people who have a different opinion. Bretton Barber put on his T-shirt to encourage his classmates to argue. Now, it is your turn to search for answers. Can measures to protect national security go too far, threatening the freedom that is essential for democracy? Or have civil libertarians exaggerated the threat, weakening the government's ability to defend our freedoms?

### ENDNOTES

1. National Coalition Against Censorship, "Note from Courageous Resister Bretton Barber," http://www.refuseandresist.org/about/art.php?aid=1616.

2. *Tinker v. Des Moines Independent School District*, 393 U.S. 503 (1969).

3. Tamar Lewin, "High School Tells Student to Remove Antiwar Shirt," *New York Times*, Feb. 26, 2003.

4. Christopher M. Finan, *From the Palmer Raids to the Patriot Act: A History of the Fight for Free Speech in America* (Boston: Beacon Press, 2007), 8–9.

5. Ibid., 12.

6. Ibid., 31.

7. Ibid., 32.

8. Ibid., 33.

9. Richard Gid Powers, *Broken: The Troubled Past and Uncertain Future of the FBI* (New York: Free Press, 2004), 246–247.

10. Ibid., 279.

11. David Cunningham, *There's Something Happening Here: The New Left, the Klan, and FBI Counterintelligence* (Berkeley: University of California Press, 2004), 54.

12. Peter Schrag, *Test of Loyalty: Daniel Ellsberg and the Rituals of Secret Government* (New York: Simon & Schuster, 1974), 34.

13. Ibid., 44.

14. David Glenn, "The War on Campus," *The Nation*, Dec. 3, 2001, http://www.thenation.com/article/war-campus.

15. Emily Eakin, "On the Lookout for Political Incorrectness," *New York Times*, Nov. 24, 2001, 15.

16. John Ashcroft to Heads of All Federal Departments and Agencies, "Freedom of Information Act," Oct. 12, 2001, http://www.fas.org/sgp/foia/ashcroft.html.

17. William Glaberson, "A Nation Challenged: A Frustrated A.C.L.U. Tries to Guide Consulates Through a Thicket," *New York Times*, Jan. 2, 2002, 11.

18. William Glaberson, "A Nation Challenged: Excerpts from Attorney General's Testimony before Senate Judiciary, Dec. 7, 2001, B6.

19. ACLU press release, Dec. 10, 2001, http://www.aclu.org/freespeech/protest/10916prs20011210.html.

---

**PART 1**

# 9/11: The Day
# Things Changed

---

Americans felt fear in the aftermath of the attacks on September 11, 2001. Only a morning had been needed to kill 2,977 people on American soil. But more frightening than the terrible loss of life was the discovery that terrorists were ready, willing, and possibly able to inflict even worse carnage by using chemical and even nuclear weapons on civilians as they went about the normal business of their days. The feeling of those first weeks after the attacks is described by *Washington Post* reporter Robert O'Harrow in "Six Weeks in Autumn," an article published a year later. O'Harrow's piece also sets the stage for the battle to come between Pres. George W. Bush and critics who believed that the administration's "war on terror" threatened civil liberties, including freedom of speech.

Civil libertarians felt the same fear for their safety as other Americans, but they had an additional concern. They knew that some of the worst abuses of the rights of individuals had occurred during wartime and other periods when Americans feared attacks by foreigners. Soon after the 9/11 attacks, a coalition of more than 150 civil liberties, civil rights, and human rights groups issued a statement, "In Defense of Freedom," urging the president and Congress not to repeat the mistakes of the past by rushing to enact legislation that would erode the liberties and freedoms at the core of the American way of life.

Congress appeared to ignore this appeal by passing the USA PATRIOT Act, which dramatically expanded the investigative powers of the federal government, in October. Russell Feingold (D–WI), the only member of the Senate to vote against the PATRIOT Act, explained his opposition in a "Statement . . . from the Senate Floor" prior to the vote on October 25, 2001. Feingold urged his colleagues to recognize that they have a duty to protect civil liberties as well as ensure public safety. They must be careful not to deprive Americans of freedoms when expanding government powers. He said he would vote against the PATRIOT Act because it went too far in strengthening government. In the spring of 2002, members of the Free Expression Network outlined several threats to free speech ("The USA PATRIOT Act Six Months Later"): surveillance of American citizens without evidence of wrongdoing; new limitations on access to government information that would weaken democracy; and a growing intolerance for free discussion in critical venues, including newspapers, schools, colleges, and universities.

Most Americans, however, strongly supported the PATRIOT Act and other measures to strengthen national security. Writing five years after 9/11, Richard A. Posner, a federal judge, argued in *Not a Suicide Pact: The Constitution in a Time of National Emergency* (2006) that, despite improvements in national security, the country continues to face a grave and increasing danger of attack by terrorists using weapons of mass destruction. He criticizes civil libertarians for believing that individual rights are absolute and should not be restricted even during times of great peril to the country. He states that civil liberties have always been restored following previous crises. He also maintains that current restrictions are not severe.

In the spring of 2013, Pres. Barak Obama delivered a speech at the National Defense University that asked Americans to begin considering a new approach to global terrorism. The American war in Iraq is over and all U.S. troops will be withdrawn from Afghanistan by the end of 2014. Osama bin Laden is dead and al Qaeda's leadership appears to be unable to mount another major attack against the United States. This does not mean that terrorist attacks will cease, Obama said. But the threat has diminished to the point where we should end wartime measures like holding suspected terrorists without charging them with any crime at the military prison at Guantanamo Bay, Cuba. Although Obama did not say so, his call for rethinking our security measures could include reviewing laws adopted since 9/11 that affect free speech.

This section of readings provides historical background for understanding the debate about national security and free speech. As you read, consider the following questions:

- Why are civil liberties important?

- How did the government response to 9/11 affect freedom of speech?

- What role should civil libertarians play in shaping the nation's response to terrorism?

# Six Weeks in Autumn

*by Robert O'Harrow, Jr.\**

Assistant Attorney General Viet Dinh took his seat in La Colline restaurant on Capitol Hill and signaled for a cup of coffee. It was one of those standard Washington breakfasts, where politicos mix schmoozing and big ideas to start their days.

An intense foot soldier for Attorney General John Ashcroft, Dinh had been in his job for only a few months. He wanted to make a good impression on others at the session and craved the caffeine to keep his edge. As he sipped his fourth cup and listened to the patter of White House and Hill staffers, a young man darted up to the table. "A plane has crashed," he said. "It hit the World Trade Center."

Dinh and the rest of the voluble group went silent. Then their beepers began chirping in unison. At another time, it might have seemed funny. A Type-A Washington moment. Now they looked at one another and rushed out of the restaurant.

It was about 9:30 on September 11, 2001.

Dinh hurried back to the Justice Department, where the building was being evacuated. Like countless other Americans, he was already consumed with a desire to strike back. Unlike most, however, he had an inkling of how: by doing whatever was necessary to strengthen the government's legal hand against terrorists.

Jim Dempsey was sifting through e-mails at his office at the Center for Democracy and Technology on Farragut Square when his boss, Jerry Berman, rushed in.

"Turn on the TV," Berman urged. Dempsey reached for the zapper, and images came rushing at him. Crisp sunshine. Lower Manhattan glinting in the brilliance. A jetliner cutting through the scene.

Dempsey is a lanky and slow-speaking former Hill staffer who combines a meticulous attention to detail with an aw-shucks demeanor. Since the early 1990s, he has been one of the leading watchdogs of FBI surveillance initiatives, a reasoned and respected civil liberties advocate routinely summoned to the Hill by both political parties to advise lawmakers about technology and privacy issues.

As he watched the smoke and flames engulf the World Trade Center, he knew it was the work of terrorists, and the FBI was foremost in his mind. "They have screwed up so bad," he said to himself. "With all the powers and resources that they have, they should have caught these guys."

At the same moment, it dawned on him that his work—and the work of many civil liberties activists over the years to check the increasingly aggressive use of technology by law enforcement officials—was about to be undone. "We all knew well enough what it meant," Dempsey says now.

The car arrived at Sen. Patrick Leahy's house in Northern Virginia shortly after 9 a.m. The Vermont Democrat took his place in the front seat and, as the car coursed toward the Potomac, he read through some notes about the pending nomination of a new drug czar and thought about a meeting that morning at the Supreme Court.

Half-listening to the radio, Leahy heard something about an explosion and the World Trade Center. He asked the driver to turn it up, then called some friends in New York. They told him what they were seeing on television. It sounded ominous. The car continued toward the Supreme Court and a conference he was to attend with Chief Justice William Rehnquist and circuit court judges from around the country.

Leahy headed to the court's conference room, with its thickly carpeted floors and oak-paneled walls lined with portraits of the first eight chief justices. When Rehnquist arrived, Leahy leaned toward him and whispered, "Bill, before we start, I believe we have a terrorist attack."

As if on cue, a muffled boom echoed through the room. Smoke began rising across the Potomac.

Leahy's country was under attack. And soon enough, the five-term senator realized, he would be as well.

Leahy chaired the Senate Judiciary Committee, putting him at the center of an inevitable debate about how to fight back—a struggle that would subject him to some of the most intense political pressures of his career.

Leahy was more than a Senate leader; he was one of Congress's most liberal members, a longtime proponent of civil liberties who had always worked to keep the government from trampling individual rights. But Leahy was also a former prosecutor, a pragmatist who understood what investigators were up against in trying to identify and bring down terrorists.

He knew that conservatives were going to press him relentlessly for more police powers while civil libertarians would look to him as their standardbearer. Everyone would be watching him: party leaders, Senate colleagues, White House officials, editorial writers and cable commentators, his Vermont constituents.

Leahy wanted to strike the right balance. But after watching an F-16 roar over the Mall that afternoon, he also resolved to do whatever he could, as a patriot and a Democrat, to give law enforcement officials more tools to stop future attacks. "I was just thinking how angry I was," he recalls.

The attacks on the World Trade Center and Pentagon didn't just set off a national wave of mourning and ire. They reignited and reshaped a smoldering debate over the proper use of government power to peer into the lives of ordinary people.

The argument boiled down to this: In an age of high-tech terror, what is the proper balance between national security and the privacy of millions of Americans, whose personal information is already more widely available than ever before? Telephone records, e-mails, oceans of detail about individuals' lives—the government wanted access to all of it to hunt down terrorists before they struck.

For six weeks last fall, behind a veneer of national solidarity and bipartisanship, Washington leaders engaged in pitched, closed-door arguments over how much new power the government should have in the name of national security. They were grappling not only with the specter of more terrorist attacks but also with the chilling memories of Cold War red-baiting, J. Edgar Hoover's smear campaigns, and Watergate-era wiretaps.

At the core of the dispute was a body of little-known laws and rules that, over the last half a century, defined and limited the government's ability to snoop:

Title III of the Omnibus Crime Control and Safe Streets Act governed electronic eavesdropping. The "pen register, trap and trace" rules covered the use of devices to track the origin and destination of telephone calls. The Foreign Intelligence Surveillance Act, or FISA, regulated the power to spy domestically when seeking foreign intelligence information.

The White House, the Justice Department and their allies in Congress wanted to ease those restraints, and they wanted to do it as quickly as possible. Though put into place to protect individuals and political groups from past abuses by the FBI, CIA and others, the restrictions were partly to blame for the intelligence gaps on September 11, the government said.

The administration also wanted new authority to secretly detain individuals suspected of terrorism and to enlist banks and other financial services companies in the search for terrorist financing. What's more, law enforcement sought broad access to business databases filled with information about the lives of ordinary citizens. All this detail could help investigators search for links among plotters.

Dempsey and other civil libertarians agreed that the existing laws were outdated, but for precisely the opposite reason—because they already gave the government access to mountains of information unavailable a decade ago. Handing investigators even more power, they warned, would lead to privacy invasions and abuses.

By the time the debate ended—one year ago, with overwhelming approval of the USA Patriot Act by Congress, and its signing on October 26 by President Bush—the government had powers that went far beyond what even the most ardent law enforcement supporters had considered politically possible before the attacks.

How this happened—through backroom negotiations, political maneuvering and public pressure by Bush administration officials—is a largely untold tale with consequences that will reverberate for years to come.

They stared at a television in the bright sunroom of Dinh's Chevy Chase home, a handful of policy specialists from the Justice Department who wondered what to do next.

Only hours before, they had fled their offices, cringing as fighter jets patrolled Washington's skies. Now, as news programs replayed the destruction, they talked about their friend Barbara Olson, conservative commentator and wife of U.S. Solicitor General Ted Olson. She was aboard American Airlines Flight 77 when it crashed into the Pentagon.

Dinh couldn't believe Barbara was gone. He'd just had dinner at the Olsons' house two nights before, and she had been in rare form. Her humor was irrepressible. Dinh passed around a book of photography she had signed and given to him and the other dinner guests, Washington, D.C.: Then and Now.

It was hard to process so much death amid so much sunshine. Dinh and his colleagues tried to focus on the work head. They agreed they faced a monumental, even historic task: a long overdue reworking of anti-terrorism laws to prevent something like this from happening again on American soil.

Their marching orders came the next morning, as they reconvened in a conference room in Dinh's suite of offices on the fourth floor of Justice. Ashcroft wasn't there—he was in hiding along with other senior government officials. Just before the meeting, Dinh had spoken to Adam Ciongoli, Ashcroft's counselor, who conveyed the attorney general's desires.

"Beginning immediately," Dinh told the half a dozen policy advisers and lawyers, "we will work on a package of authorities"—sweeping, dramatic and based on practical recommendations from FBI agents and Justice Department lawyers in the field. "The charge [from Ashcroft] was very, very clear: 'all that is necessary for law enforcement, within the bounds of the Constitution, to discharge the obligation to fight this war against terror,'" he said.

Dinh's enthusiasm for the task was evident. At 34, he seems perpetually jazzed up, smiles often and speaks quickly, as though his words, inflected with the accent of his native Vietnam, can't quite keep up with his ideas. A graduate of Harvard Law School, he learned his way around Washington as an associate special counsel to the Senate Whitewater committee, and as a special counsel to Sen. Pete Domenici (R-N.M.) during the Clinton impeachment trial.

"What are the problems?" Dinh asked the group around the table.

For the next several hours—indeed, over the next several days—Dinh's colleagues catalogued gripes about the legal restraints on detective and intelligence work. Some of the complaints had been bouncing around the FBI and Justice Department for years.

Because of the law's peculiarities, it was unclear if investigators were allowed to track the destination and origin of e-mail the same way they could phone calls. They could obtain search warrants more easily for a telephone tape machine than for commercial voice mail services. And the amount of information that intelligence agents and criminal investigators were permitted to share was limited, making it much harder to target and jail terrorists.

All of this, the lawyers agreed, had to change. Now.

Dempsey was swamped. Reporters, other activists, congressional staffers—everyone wanted his take on how far the Justice Department and Congress would go in reaction to the attacks. "We were getting 50 calls a day," he recalls.

Like many attuned to the rhythms of Washington, Dempsey knew Congress would not have the will to resist granting dramatic new powers to law enforcement immediately. It was a classic dynamic. Something terrible happens. Legislators rush to respond. They don't have time to investigate the policy implications thoroughly, so they reach for what's available and push it through.

That was a nightmare for Dempsey. Looking for signs of hope that the legislative process could be slowed, even if it could not be stopped, he made his own calls around town.

He didn't find much support, even among longtime allies. "If you could get their attention," Dempsey says, "some members of the House and Senate were, 'Don't bother me with the details.'"

"A crisis mentality emerges, and there was clearly a crisis … The push for action, the appearance of action, becomes so great."

Within days of the attack, a handful of lawmakers took to the Senate floor with legislation that had been proposed and shot down in recent years because of civil liberties concerns. Many of the proposals had originally had nothing to do with terrorism.

One bill, called the Combating Terrorism Act, proposed expanding the government's authority to trace telephone calls to include e-mail. It was a legacy of FBI efforts to expand surveillance powers during the Clinton administration, which had supported a variety of technology-oriented proposals opposed by civil libertarians. Now it was hauled out and approved in minutes.

One of the few voices advocating calm deliberation, Dempsey says, was Leahy. But it was not clear what he would be able to do in such a highly charged atmosphere.

Across the city and across the country, other civil libertarians braced themselves for the fallout from the attacks.

Among them was Morton Halperin, former head of the Washington office of the American Civil Liberties Union and a former national security official in three administrations. Halperin, a senior fellow at the Council on Foreign Relations, is personally familiar with government surveillance.

While working as a National Security Council staffer in the Nixon administration, Halperin was suspected of leaking information about the secret U.S. bombing of Cambodia. To this day, Halperin has not addressed the allegations, but his house was wiretapped by the FBI, and the taps continued for months after he left the government.

Now, 24 hours after the attacks, he read an e-mail from a member of an online group that had been formed to fight a Clinton administration plan to make publishing classified materials a crime. The writer warned the plan would now be reprised.

Halperin had been anticipating this moment for years. More than a decade ago, he wrote an essay predicting that terrorism would replace communism as the main justification for domestic surveillance. "I sat and stared at that e-mail for a few minutes and decided that I could not do my regular job, that I had to deal with this," he says.

Halperin banged out a call to arms on his computer. "There can be no doubt that we will hear calls in the next few days for congress to enact sweeping legislation to deal with terrorism," he wrote in the e-mail to more than two dozen civil libertarians on September 12. "This will include not only the secrecy provision, but also broad authority to conduct electronic and other surveillance and to investigate political groups...We should not wait."

Within hours, Dempsey, Marc Rotenberg from the Electronic Privacy Information Center and others had offered their support. Their plan: to build on Halperin's call for legislative restraint, while striking a sympathetic note about the victims of the attacks. They started putting together a meeting to sign off on a civil liberties manifesto: "In Defense of Freedom at a Time of Crisis."

Underlying the discussion about how to respond to the terror attacks was the mid-1970s investigation, led by Sen. Frank Church (D-Idaho), into the government's sordid history of domestic spying. Through hundreds of interviews and the examination of tens of thousands of documents, the Church committee found that the FBI, CIA and other government agencies had engaged in pervasive surveillance of politicians, religious organizations, women's rights advocates, antiwar groups and civil liberties activists. At FBI headquarters in Washington, for example, agents had developed more than half a million domestic intelligence files in the previous two decades. The CIA had secretly opened and photographed almost a quarter-million letters in the United States from 1953 to 1973.

One of the most egregious intelligence abuses was an FBI counterintelligence program known as COINTELPRO. It was, the Church report said, "designed to 'disrupt' groups and 'neutralize' individuals deemed to be threats to domestic security." Among other things, COINTELPRO operations included undermining the jobs of political activists, sending anonymous letters to "spouses of intelligence targets for the purposes of destroying their marriages," and a systematic campaign to undermine the Rev. Martin Luther King Jr.'s civil rights efforts through leaked information about his personal life.

"Too many people have been spied upon by too many government agencies and too much information has been collected" through secret informants, wiretaps, bugs, surreptitious mail-opening and break-ins, the Church report warned.

Congress responded with a series of laws aimed at curbing government abuses. One was the Foreign Intelligence Surveillance Act of 1978, which gave broad powers for counterintelligence officials to monitor the agents of foreign countries.

Under FISA, authorities had to demonstrate, to the supersecret Foreign Intelligence Surveillance Court, that the principal purpose for their surveillance was foreign intelligence. But the law also restricted the use of those powers for domestic criminal investigations and prosecutions.

For all the secrecy surrounding FISA—and despite the fact the FISA court has never denied an application for electronic surveillance—civil libertarians consider the law one of the key safeguards against domestic spying.

But some conservatives have long contended that the law created unnecessary, even absurd, barriers between criminal and intelligence investigators. The Bush administration believed those barriers were getting in the way of uncovering terrorist cells operating here and abroad.

Law enforcement authorities also chafed at internal guidelines imposed by the Justice Department in response to the Church committee revelations. Agents weren't allowed to monitor religious services without evidence of a crime, for instance, which made it hard to investigate mosques that might be harboring terrorists. Ashcroft claimed that the rules even prohibited investigators from surfing the Web for information about suspects.

When Dinh and his team began taking stock of needed legal changes, the legacy of the Church committee loomed large. They saw a chance to turn back the clock. Standing in their way were people like Dempsey and Halperin.

Scores of people streamed into the ACLU's white stucco townhouse on Capitol Hill on the Friday after the attacks, responding to Halperin's e-mail and calls from ACLU lobbyists.

As with so many privacy battles, there were some strikingly strange bedfellows in attendance: Liberal immigration rights groups. Libertarians from the conservative Free Congress Foundation and Eagle Forum. Technology-savvy activists from the Electronic Privacy Information Center and the Center for Democracy and Technology.

They filled the main conference room downstairs, overflowing through French doors into a garden, and up the stairway to the ACLU's offices. The ACLU's headquarters, recently relocated downtown, has been the site of countless strategy meetings over the years on abortion rights, civil rights, freedom of speech and religious freedom.

Even so, "I had never seen that kind of turnout in 25 years," says Laura Murphy, director of the ACLU's national office. "I mean, people were worried. They just knew this was a recipe for government overreaching."

They also grasped the difficulty of their position. Here they were, trying to persuade Americans to hold fast to concerns about individual freedom and privacy, while the vast majority of people were terrified. Polls later showed that most people were more than willing to trade off civil liberties and privacy protections for more security.

Murphy and others also had reached out to Congress in an effort to head off any instant legislation. They found that normally privacy-minded lawmakers, including Sens. Dianne Feinstein (D-Calif.) and Charles Schumer (D-N.Y.), had no intention of questioning efforts to push a bill through quickly.

Even Rep. Bob Barr (R-Ga.), a conservative and dedicated privacy advocate, couldn't offer much hope. Barr and Murphy had worked closely together in recent years, though they come from different ends of the political spectrum. When she called him after the attacks, he confessed there was probably little he could do to temper the anti-terrorism fervor gripping Washington. "You could sort of hear the clutch in his voice: 'I don't know how we're going to do this,'" she recalls.

Murphy stood at the front of the room with Halperin, trying to win consensus from those assembled on language they would use to voice their concerns. Dempsey, who arrived late, was off to one side, a sinking feeling in his stomach. For all the numbers, the normally raucous group was subdued. Some in attendance owned up to their own fears about new attacks. Everyone "was a little overwhelmed by the magnitude of the task," Dempsey says.

After debate over how to express clear sympathy for the victims of the attack, the group worked out a 10-point statement. "We must have faith in our democratic system and our Constitution, and in our ability to protect at the same time both the freedom and the security of all Americans," read point No. 10.

The document was signed by representatives of more than 150 groups, including religious organizations, gun owners, police and conservative activists. A few days later, they released it at a press conference and posted it on a Web site.

What kind of impact did it have? Apparently not much. A year later, several key officials from the White House and Justice Department say they have never even heard of the appeal.

To say it was a trying time for Leahy is an understatement. He would later describe those days as among the most challenging and emotional of his 28 years in the Senate: "What made this the most intense were not just the issues, but the great sorrows I felt."

The senator was saddled with the responsibility of crafting the Senate proposal for anti-terrorism legislation. He didn't want to ram a bad law through Congress, but he also didn't want to be seen as an obstructionist. So he offered to negotiate a bill directly with the White House, avoiding the time-consuming committee-approval process. Now he had to come up with a way of maintaining meaningful privacy protections while expanding the government's surveillance powers.

As he worked to reconcile those competing interests, he took long walks around the Capitol and down to the Mall. Everywhere he went the mood was grim. "I saw the same faces as I did when I was a law school student [in the District] and President Kennedy had been killed," Leahy says. "I saw the same shock, and I wanted to make sure our shock didn't turn into panic."

It was crucial, Leahy thought, to take enough time with the legislation to get it right. Or as he put it to senior aide Beryl Howell, a former federal prosecutor: "Let's not do a knee-jerk reaction."

Leahy thought he could serve as a bridge between privacy advocates and the government. He was trusted by civil libertarians, but had a cordial enough relationship with Ashcroft, who was a former Senate colleague. Though Ashcroft was an ardent conservative loathed by many liberals, the two had worked together in Congress on encryption legislation. Even after Leahy voted against Ashcroft's confirmation as attorney general, he called Ashcroft afterward to pledge his cooperation. Since then they'd gotten along fine. In the weeks before September 11, they'd been consulting frequently on a major overhaul of the FBI, which was under fire for bungling a series of high-profile cases.

But the terrorist attacks quickly strained their amicable relations. Within days, Ashcroft held a press conference and called on Congress to approve the Justice Department's legislative plan in a week's time. Leahy was surprised—and irritated. The implication, Leahy says, was "we were going to have another attack if we did not agree to this immediately."

But if he balked, Leahy risked getting hammered as soft on terrorism—or so he and other Democrats feared. Leahy, backed by other Democrats, had begun working on his own anti-terrorism bill, a 165-page tome called the Uniting and Strengthening America Act.

On September 19, congressional, White House and Justice leaders gathered in an ornate room in the Capitol to exchange proposals.

Along with Leahy, Orrin Hatch (R-Utah), Richard Shelby (R-Ala.) and others were there from the Senate. House Majority Leader Richard Armey (R-Tex.), John Conyers Jr. (D-Mich.) and others represented the House. From the White House came counsel Alberto Gonzales. Ashcroft, Dinh and their entourage arrived from Justice.

As the meeting got started, Dinh made a beeline for a seat near the head of the conference table. Leahy and his colleagues raised their eyebrows and shook their heads. Only members of Congress were supposed to sit at the table, one of the senators told Dinh, asking him to sit with the rest of the staff.

Dinh wasn't too troubled by his faux pas. He and his staff were too focused on the 40-page proposal they'd brought with them, the fruit of several all-nighters at Justice. During the crash drafting effort, Dinh had slept on a black leather couch, beneath an American flag, not far from a worn paperback copy of the Federalist Papers.

He handed out copies of his proposal. Leahy did the same with his draft, stressing that he thought the group should move forward deliberately.

It turned out the proposals were similar in some key respects. Both bills called for updates to the pen register and trap and trace laws, clarifying how they applied to e-mail and the Internet. Both included provisions bolstering money-laundering and wiretap laws. They also proposed making it easier for authorities to get approval for wiretaps in spying and counterintelligence cases.

The administration proposal, however, went much farther. It called for indefinite detention of any noncitizen the attorney general "has reason to believe may further or facilitate acts of terrorism," as well as the unrestricted sharing of grand jury and eavesdropping data throughout the government. It permitted Internet service providers or employers to voluntarily allow the FBI to tap e-mail. And it made a small but important modification to the FISA law, changing the legal language so foreign intelligence had to be only "a" purpose of an investigation, rather than "the" purpose, to secure surveillance authority.

Leahy and some of the other lawmakers murmured about those last provisions. Giving criminal investigators unchecked access to FISA powers could break down constitutional safeguards against unreasonable searches and seizures, leading to abuses against U.S. citizens.

Armey, one of the most conservative members in Congress, also expressed concern. It was Armey, in fact, who was already discussing a "sunset" provision to the new law, placing time limits on how long parts of it would remain in effect. A sunset provision would guarantee that some of the most troubling new powers would be revisited by Congress, giving lawmakers an important check on executive authority.

"There were a lot of people in the room, both Republican and Democrat," Leahy says, "who were not about to give the unfettered power the attorney general wanted."

Armey also warned that it might take a few weeks to adopt a bill. In effect, he was urging Ashcroft to back away from his public pressure to approve a law in the next few days.

When the group emerged from the meeting, Ashcroft changed his tone slightly, telling reporters that he wanted to pass a bill as quickly as possible. Leahy likewise struck a conciliatory note. "We're trying to find a middle ground, and I think we can," he said that day. "We probably agree on more than we disagree on."

But Leahy also made it clear he would not be rushed into approving a bill. "We do not want the terrorists to win by having basic protections taken away from us," he said. It was a boilerplate rendering of a quotation from Benjamin Franklin that Leahy invoked repeatedly: "Those who would give up essential liberty to purchase a little temporary safety deserve neither liberty nor safety."

The truce between Leahy and Ashcroft didn't last long. Despite Ashcroft's shift in tone, the pressure to move quickly on legislation intensified. For Dempsey, it was depressing.

One afternoon in late September, he was invited by Howell, Leahy's adviser, to a legislative briefing. Howell wanted Justice Department officials and civil libertarians to describe to Senate staffers their thoughts about expanding law enforcement authority. The point was to give everyone involved more ideas.

Dempsey was eager to attend. "My hope was there could actually be some sort of debate," he says.

Then the Justice Department folks arrived. Howell hadn't told them they would be discussing their proposals with civil libertarians. "They were livid," Dempsey says. "They explicitly said, 'We don't think outsiders should be here, and we won't talk unless they leave the room.'"

Howell quickly brokered a deal. Dempsey and the other civil liberties advocates could stay to hear Justice's presentation, but there would be no back-and-forth discussion. As soon as the Justice delegation finished speaking about their proposals, "they got up and left," Dempsey says. "I was just in despair. I just thought we are never going to be able to work this out."

At the end of September, Leahy's staff and administration officials spent hours together thrashing out questions about civil liberties, the new police and intelligence powers, and oversight by courts and Congress.

[...]

On October 1, Leahy thought he had a final agreement in hand. He was so confident that he stopped by Senate Majority Leader Tom Daschle's office to assure him: "We have it all worked out."

Leahy left the Capitol that evening feeling satisfied. He'd done what he could to protect civil liberties by providing oversight for surveillance and domestic intelligence. But he had also moved quickly to bolster law enforcement and counter-intelligence operations. No one could accuse the Democrats of coddling terrorists.

The next morning Leahy sat in his office across a polished wood conference table from Ashcroft, Hatch, Michael Chertoff, chief of the Justice Department's criminal division, and Gonzales, the White House counsel. They'd come together to sign off on the deal. But Ashcroft was having second thoughts about some of [White House Deputy Counsel Timothy]

Flanigan's concessions. The agreement, he told Leahy, no longer held.

Leahy felt blindsided. He'd invested his prestige in these negotiations, and now it looked like he didn't count. "I said, 'John, when I make an agreement, I make an agreement. I can't believe you're going back on your commitment.'"

Ashcroft's support was critical to the bill's approval. The Senate and Bush administration had agreed to deliver a proposal together, and the process could not go forward without Ashcroft's imprimatur.

Flanigan downplays the dispute, saying it was only one of many disagreements in a tough series of talks that ebbed and flowed.

"There were several points in the negotiations at which they recognized that they had given up too much, and there were other times that we realized we hadn't asked for enough," Flanigan says. "It's understandable. It's the pace of the negotiations.

"You know, there'd be groans around the table and nobody was pleased to see an issue reopened. But I think it all was conducted in a spirit [of] we're all trying to get to a result here."

In any case, there was no hiding the growing animosity between Leahy and the administration. Ashcroft didn't even try. Not long after leaving Leahy's office, Ashcroft held a press conference with Hatch at his side.

"I think it is time for us to be productive on behalf of the American people," said the attorney general. "Talk won't prevent terrorism," Ashcroft said, adding that he was "deeply concerned about the rather slow pace" of the legislation.

"It's a very dangerous thing," Hatch agreed. "It's time to get off our duffs and do what's right."

Leahy was deeply distressed by the collapse of the deal. He felt the administration was intent on steamrolling over him. But there was frustratingly little he could do about it. He didn't even have the political leverage in the Senate to push for the same sunset provision being championed by Armey in the Republican-controlled House. Leahy knew he would have to rely on the House to fight that battle with the administration. He would have to do the same on securing court oversight of the government's new surveillance powers.

Court oversight would be especially important in light of a critical but unheralded portion of the new legislation: Section 215.

For many years, FISA gave investigators access to the commercial records of people under investigation in national security cases, but only from a small range of businesses, including hotels, storage facilities and car rental companies.

Section 215 of the bill would greatly expand that, allowing investigators to obtain records from Internet service providers, grocery stores, libraries, bookstores—just about any business. More importantly, it would remove the requirement that the target of the records search be "an agent of a foreign power."

Those changes were significant because of the data-collection revolution of the 1990s. Cheaper computing power and an ever-expanding Internet have enabled businesses to watch what was once unwatchable and glean meaning and profit from the ephemera of daily life. Never before has so much information been collected and parsed about so many of us—often in the name of giving us conveniences, discounts and other benefits.

Someone is likely monitoring us at work, recording what we buy, noting our whereabouts while we use our cell phones, scrutinizing our drug prescriptions. Marketers know our names, addresses, estimated incomes, the size of a family's house, the type of car we drive, the magazines we read, the beer we drink.

Libraries use computers to keep track of what we read. Hotels keep electronic records of when we come and go. Bookstores know what we buy. Many toll roads can say precisely when we have driven by.

The implications of giving the government access to so much personal information unnerved Dempsey and other civil libertarians, who were disappointed that Leahy and his allies couldn't do more to stand up to the administration. While Dempsey understood the political pressures on the senators, he worried that they didn't completely understand some of the compromises they were making. Leahy was also rueful about the outcome. His bill, introduced in the Senate two days after his acrimonious meeting with Ashcroft, gave Justice much more power than he had originally intended. But he was prepared to swallow hard and support it. To do anything else was politically impossible.

Late on October 11, the Senate assembled to vote. Leahy and Daschle knew every Republican would support the bill. They wanted Democrats to do the same. But Sen. Russell Feingold was refusing to go along.

A liberal who routinely bucks pressure from his own party, the Wisconsin Democrat had deep reservations about the bill hurtling through the Senate. He considered the provisions "some of the most radical changes to law enforcement in a generation" and was particularly worried that Section 215 gave the government way too much power to sift through people's lives. He wanted the Senate to vote on a series of amendments that would do more to protect privacy.

[...]

Feingold offered his amendments, and they were rejected. One month after the attacks, the bill passed the Senate, 96-1.

Lawmakers and legislative aides were lining up for nasal swabs and Cipro. Yellow police tape encircled the Hart Senate Office Building. The House had shut down for the first time in memory.

On October 17, the capital was confronting a new threat: anthrax. It was contained in a letter mailed to Daschle, and no one knew how many people might have been exposed. Were there more letters? Were anthrax spores floating through the Capitol's ventilation system? Suddenly, it became more urgent than ever to get the Patriot Act to the president's desk.

Amid the panic, Leahy, Daschle, Flanigan, Dinh and others gathered in House Speaker Dennis Hastert's office to smooth out the differences between the Senate and House versions of the bill. The House bill, which passed in the early morning hours of October 12, included sunset and court-oversight provisions Leahy had been unable to get in the Senate.

There was no longer any question that the Patriot Act would include some court oversight, though not as much as Leahy and Armey wanted. The key issue remaining for those in Hastert's office was how long the new law should be in effect. Leahy and Armey pressed for a four-year "sunset," which would force the White House to win congressional approval of the most controversial provisions of the law all over again in 2005. The administration wanted no time limit on its effect.

"We're feeling very strongly about the sunsetting," Flanigan told the lawmakers. "This is not a war of a fixed duration. And it will not change the culture of law enforcement and national security if we basically make this a short-term fix."

Daschle, who knew how badly Bush wanted to avoid any delay in signing the legislation, turned to the lawyer and smiled. "Mr. Flanigan, does this mean the president will veto the bill?" he asked.

"And then of course," Flanigan acknowledges now, "I had to say no."

They agreed on four years.

In the year since the Patriot Act was approved, the government has moved quickly to take full advantage of new and existing powers.

More than a thousand noncitizens were detained without being charged last fall, and their identities were kept secret. Hundreds of Muslim men—citizens and noncitizens—were placed under surveillance by federal investigators across the country. Their movements, telephone calls, e-mail, Internet use and credit-card charges are being scrutinized around the clock—a campaign that has resulted in criminal charges against 18 suspected al Qaeda operatives near Seattle, Detroit, Buffalo, N.Y., and Portland, Ore.

"We've neutralized a suspected terrorist cell within our borders," Ashcroft announced earlier this month at press conference about the indictments of six in Portland charged with conspiring to aid al Qaeda and the Taliban regime in Afghanistan. He called the indictments "a defining day in America's war against terrorism."

And it's clear that the war is just getting underway. The FBI is still building a data-mining system that will draw in huge amounts of commercial and governmental information and parse it for signs of terrorism. The Transportation Security Administration has begun work on a passenger-profiling system that some officials say would be the largest domestic surveillance system in the nation's history.

All of this makes Viet Dinh smile as he eats curry at a restaurant across from the Justice Department. The Patriot Act, he declares proudly, is making Americans safer, just as intended.

He dismisses criticism that Justice is using a heavy hand in its investigations, and that civil liberties are being compromised. While the government can peer into the lives of Americans as never before, he says, the Constitution is always there as a safeguard.

"It was very clear that we did not tell the American people just simply, trust us, trust law enforcement not to overstep their bounds. Rather we say, trust the law," Dinh says. "The attorney general said very clearly, 'Think outside the box, but not outside the Constitution.'"

Yet at least one federal judge, Gladys Kessler of the U.S. District Court for the District of Columbia, has already accused the government of overstepping its constitutional bounds by refusing to name more than 1,200 people detained since September 11. In response to a lawsuit by civil libertarians, Kessler ordered the Justice Department to release the names, saying that without the information it was impossible to know whether the government is "operating within the bounds of the law."

Kessler's ruling is being appealed by the government, which argues that the secrecy is necessary to avoid compromising its investigation into September 11 and future terror plots. The Justice Department is also challenging an extraordinary decision by the FISA court not to grant criminal investigators the authority to use FISA primarily for criminal prosecutions. The FISA court said earlier this year that, long before September 11, the government had misused the law and misled the court dozens of times in its requests for search warrants and wiretaps. Those warrants and wiretaps might not have been granted in criminal courts, which, unlike FISA, require evidence of probable cause. And if the FISA court won't let criminal investigators make wide use of FISA powers, the Patriot Act won't provide as much investigative muscle as the administration wants.

That would be just fine with Dempsey, who argues that the government already had all the power and information it needed to thwart terrorist attacks before September 11 and failed to make effective use of them.

Now, he says, "we are facing the risk of a fundamental redefinition of the role of government and the freedom of individuals . . . Look at this ocean of information that's available."

In his downtown office, he clacks away at the computer, drafting a legal brief in support of the FISA court's position on limiting the flow of information between intelligence and criminal investigators. The federal courts are the next battleground, Dempsey and other civil libertarians believe, in the clash between national security and privacy rights.

For Leahy, however, the battleground remains the Senate Judiciary Committee, where he and other panel members will be responsible for monitoring how the Justice Department uses its new powers. That won't be easy, given the secrecy involved in terrorism investigations and the administration's reluctance to share sensitive information with Congress. Even so, Leahy and his allies in the House and Senate have no intention of giving Justice a free ride on the Patriot Act. The potential for abuse is too great, they say, and the need for congressional oversight and scrutiny too strong. They'll be watching.

*Robert O'Harrow, Jr. is a reporter for the *Washington Post*. He is an expert on cybersecurity and has won multiple awards for his investigative journalism.

O'Harrow, Robert, Jr. "Six Weeks in Autumn (excerpts)." *Washington Post*, Oct. 27, 2002. http://www.washingtonpost.com/wp-dyn/content/article/2006/05/09/AR2006050900961.html.

# In Defense of Freedom
## Coalition Statement

1. On September 11, 2001 thousands of people lost their lives in a brutal assault on the American people and the American form of government. We mourn the loss of these innocent lives and insist that those who perpetrated these acts be held accountable.

2. This tragedy requires all Americans to examine carefully the steps our country may now take to reduce the risk of future terrorist attacks.

3. We need to consider proposals calmly and deliberately with a determination not to erode the liberties and freedoms that are at the core of the American way of life.

4. We need to ensure that actions by our government uphold the principles of a democratic society, accountable government and international law, and that all decisions are taken in a manner consistent with the Constitution.

5. We can, as we have in the past, in times of war and of peace, reconcile the requirements of security with the demands of liberty.

6. We should resist the temptation to enact proposals in the mistaken belief that anything that may be called anti-terrorist will necessarily provide greater security.

7. We should resist efforts to target people because of their race, religion, ethnic background or appearance, including immigrants in general, Arab Americans and Muslims.

8. We affirm the right of peaceful dissent, protected by the First Amendment, now, when it is most at risk.

9. We should applaud our political leaders in the days ahead who have the courage to say that our freedoms should not be limited.

10. We must have faith in our democratic system and our Constitution, and in our ability to protect at the same time both the freedom and the security of all Americans.

## Organizations in Defense of Freedom

Action LA, Los Angeles, CA

Advocates for Self-Government

Al-Fatiha Foundation, Washington, DC

Alchemind Society: International Association for Cognitive Liberties, Davis, CA

Alliance for Justice, Washington, DC

American-Arab Anti-Discrimination Committee, Washington, DC

American Association of Law Libraries, Washington, DC— statement (PDF)

American Association of University Women, Washington, DC—statement (PDF)

American Baptist Churches USA, Washington, DC

American Civil Liberties Union, Washington, DC

American Conservative Union, Alexandria, VA

American Federation of State, County and Municipal Employees, Washington, DC

American Friends Service Committee–Washington Office, Washington, DC

American Friends Service Committee's Central American Political Asylum Project, South Miami, FL

American Humanist Association, Washington, DC

American Immigration Lawyers Association, Washington, DC

American Liberty Foundation, Alexandria, VA

American Library Association, Washington, DC

American Muslim Alliance, Newark, CA

American Muslim Council, Washington, DC

American Policy Center, Warrenton, VA

Americans for Democratic Action, Washington, DC

Americans for the Preservation of Information Security, Baltimore, MD

Americans for Religious Liberty, Silver Spring, MD

Americans for Tax Reform, Washington, DC

Amnesty International-USA, Washington, DC—statement (PDF)

Arab American Institute, Washington, DC

Asian American Legal Defense and Education Fund, New York, NY

Asian Pacific American Labor Alliance, Washington, DC

Asian Pacific Islanders for Human Rights, Los Angeles, CA

Association for Competitive Technology, Washington, DC—statement (PDF)

Association of American Physicians and Surgeons, Tucson, AZ

Association of Research Libraries, Washington, DC—statement (html)

Baptist Joint Committee on Public Affairs, Washington, DC

Benton Foundation, Washington, DC

California First Amendment Coalition, Sacramento, CA

Campaign for America, Washington, DC

Catholic Vote.org, Washington, DC

Center for Constitutional Rights, New York, NY

Center for Democracy and Technology, Washington, DC

Center for Digital Democracy, Washington, DC

Center for Economic and Social Rights, Brooklyn, NY

Center for Media Education, Washington, DC

Center for National Security Studies, Washington, DC

Centre for Protection of Minorities and Against Racism and Discrimination in Bhutan, Nepal

Chinese for Affirmative Action, San Francisco, CA

Christ Covenant Metropolitan Community Church

Citizens and Immigrants for Equal Justice, Mesquite, TX

Citizens Committee for the Right to Keep and Bear Arms, Bellevue, WA

Citizens' Commission on Civil Rights, Washington, DC

Citizens' Council on Health Care, St. Paul, MN

Civil Rights Forum on Communications Policy, Washington, DC

Coalition for the Community of Reason, Charleston, SC

Coalition for Guarding Children's Media, Santa Fe, NM

Common Cause, Washington, DC—statement (PDF)

Common Sense for Drug Policy Legislative Group, Washington, DC

Competitive Enterprise Institute, Washington, DC—statement (PDF)

Computer Professionals for Social Responsibility, Palo Alto, CA

Consumer Action, San Francisco, CA

Council on American Islamic Relations, Washington, DC

Criminal Justice Policy Foundation, Washington, DC—statement (PDF)

Democracy Foundation, Ballwin, MO

Doctors for Disaster Preparedness, Tucson, AZ

Drug Police Alliance, Washington DC

Drug Reform Coordination Network, Washington, DC

Eagle Forum, Washington, DC

Eagle Forum of Alabama, Birmingham, AL

Electronic Frontier Foundation, San Francisco, CA

Electronic Privacy Information Center (EPIC), Washington, DC

Equality Mississippi, Jackson, MS

Ethics & Religious Liberty Commission of the Southern Baptist Convention, Nashville, TN

Families Against Mandatory Minimums Foundation, Washington, DC

Family Violence Clinic, Columbia, MO

Federation of American Scientists, Washington, DC

First Amendment Foundation, Washington, DC

Forfeiture Endangers American Rights

Free Congress Foundation, Washington, DC—statement (PDF)

Free the Eagle, Fairfax, VA

Freedom of Information Center, Columbia, MO

Friends Committee on National Legislation, Washington, DC

Freedom to Read Foundation, Chicago, IL

Fund for New Priorities in America, New York, NY

Fund for the Fourth Amendment, Washington, DC

Future Solutions, Nevada City, CA

Global Importune

Global Strategic Management, Annapolis, MD

God Bless America

Government Accountability Project, Washington, DC—statement (PDF)

Gun Owners of America, Springfield, VA

Harvard Information Infrastructure Project at Harvard University, Cambridge, MA

Health Privacy Project, Georgetown University, Washington, DC

Human Rights Campaign, Washington, DC

Human Rights Watch, Washington, DC

International Religious Liberty Association

Independent Institute, Oakland, CA

Intercommunity Center for Justice and Peace,
New York, NY

Islamic Institute, Washington, DC

James Madison Project, Washington, DC

Japanese American Citizens League, San Francisco, CA

Latina and Latino Critical Legal Theory, Inc.,
Coral Gables, FL

Lawyers Committee for Human Rights, Washington, DC

Leadership Conference on Civil Rights, Washington, DC

League for Programming Freedom

Legal Action Center, Washington, DC

Libertarian Party

LLEGO—The National Latina Latino Lesbian, Gay,
Bisexual & Transgender Organization, Washington, DC

MoveOn.org, Washington, DC

Multiracial Activist & Abolitionist Examiner,
Alexandria, VA

Muslim Public Affairs Council, Washington, DC

National Asian Pacific American Bar Association,
Washington, DC

National Asian Pacific American Legal Consortium,
Washington, DC

National Association for the Advancement of Colored
People, Board of Directors, Washington, DC

National Association of Criminal Defense Lawyers, Washington, DC

National Black Police Association, Washington, DC

National Coalition to Protect Political Freedom, Washington, DC

National Committee Against Repressive Legislation, Washington, DC

National Consumers League, Washington, DC

National Council of Churches of Christ, Washington, DC

National Council of La Raza, Washington, DC

National Gay and Lesbian Task Force, Washington, DC

National Immigration Project of the National Lawyers Guild, Boston, MA

National Lawyers Guild, New York, NY—statement (PDF)

National Legal Aid and Defender Association, Washington, DC

National Native American Bar Association, Birmingham, AL

National Youth Advocacy Coalition, Washington, DC

Net Action, San Francisco, CA

Network: A National Catholic Social Justice Lobby, Washington, DC

Nevada Concerned Citizens, Las Vegas, NV

North American Council for Muslim Women, Great Falls, VA

NOW Legal Defense and Education Fund, Washington, DC

Nuremberg Legacy Project, Washington, DC

OMB Watch, Washington, DC

OpenPrivacy.org

Patrick Henry Center for Individual Liberty, Fairfax, VA

Peacefire

PEN American Center, New York, NY

Pennsylvania Alliance for Democracy, Harrisburg, PA

People for the American Way, Washington, DC—statement
(PDF)

Philadelphia II, Washington, DC

Physicians for Human Rights, Washington, DC

Privacilla.org

Privacyactivism.org, Bellevue, WA

Privacy Digest, New York, NY

Privacy International, Washington, DC

Privacy Rights Clearinghouse, San Diego, CA

Privacy Times, Washington, DC

Progressive Jewish Alliance, Los Angeles, CA

Project On Government Oversight, Washington, DC

Republican Liberty Caucus, Fairfax, VA

Research & Policy Reform Center, Washington, DC

Rutherford Institute, Charlottesville, VA

Second Amendment Foundation, Bellevue, WA

Sentencing Project, Washington, DC

Sikh Mediawatch and Resource Task Force (SMART),
Germantown, MD

Sixty Plus Association, Arlington, VA

Society of American Law Teachers, Minneapolis, MN

Sovereign Society, Ltd., Baltimore, MD

Square One Media Network, Seattle, WA

StopCarnivore.org, Nevada City, CA

Stonewall Republicans Federation

Strategic Issues Research Institute, Arlington, VA

Students for a Free Tibet, New York, NY

Unitarian Universalist Association of Congregations, Washington, DC

United Church of Christ, Justice & Witness Ministries

United States Committee for Refugees & Immigration and Refugee Services, Washington, DC

USAction, Washington, DC

Washington Lawyers' Committee for Civil Rights and Urban Affairs, Washington, DC

WILD for Human Rights, San Francisco, CA

Women of Reform Judaism, New York, NY

Women's International League for Peace and Freedom, US Section, Washington, DC

World Organization Against Torture USA, Washington, DC

Yale Social Justice Network, New Haven, CT

In Defense of Freedom Coalition. Statement. September 20, 2001. http://www.indefenseoffreedom.org and http://www.indefenseoffreedom.org/organizations.html.

# Statement on the Anti-Terrorism Bill from the Senate Floor

*by Russ Feingold\**

Mr. President, I have asked for this time to speak about the anti-terrorism bill before us, H.R. 3162. As we address this bill, we are especially mindful of the terrible events of September 11 and beyond, which led to the bill's proposal and its quick consideration in the Congress.

This has been a tragic time in our country. Before I discuss this bill, let me first pause to remember, through one small story, how September 11th has irrevocably changed so many lives. In a letter to The Washington Post recently, a man wrote that as he went jogging near the Pentagon, he came across the makeshift memorial built for those who lost their lives there. He slowed to a walk as he took in the sight before him—the red, white and blue flowers covering the structure, and then, off to the side, a second, smaller memorial with a card.

The card read, "Happy Birthday Mommy. Although you died and are no longer with me, I feel as if I still have you in my life. I think about you every day."

After reading the card, the man felt as if he were "drowning in the names of dead mothers, fathers, sons and daughters." The author of this letter shared a moment in his own life that so many of us have had—the moment where televised pictures of the destruction are made painfully real to us. We read a card, or see the anguished face of a grieving loved one, and we suddenly feel the enormity of what has happened to so many American families, and to all of us as a people.

We all also had our own initial reactions, and my first and most powerful emotion was a solemn resolve to stop these terrorists. And that remains my principal reaction to these events. But I also quickly realized that two cautions were necessary, and I raised them on the Senate floor the day after the attacks.

The first caution was that we must continue to respect our Constitution and protect our civil liberties in the wake of the attacks. As the chairman of the Constitution Subcommittee of the Judiciary Committee, I recognize that this is a different world with different technologies, different issues, and different threats. Yet we must examine every item that is proposed in response to these events to be sure we are not rewarding these terrorists and weakening ourselves by giving up the cherished freedoms that they seek to destroy.

The second caution I issued was a warning against the mistreatment of Arab Americans, Muslim Americans, South Asians, or others in this country. Already, one day after the attacks, we were hearing news reports that misguided anger against people of these backgrounds had led to harassment, violence, and even death.

I suppose I was reacting instinctively to the unfolding events in the spirit of the Irish statesman John Philpot Curran, who said: "The condition upon which God hath given liberty to man is eternal vigilance."

[...]

I have approached the events of the past month and my role in proposing and reviewing legislation relating to it in this spirit. I believe we must redouble our vigilance. We must redouble our vigilance to ensure our security and to prevent further acts of terror. But we must also redouble our vigilance to preserve our values and the basic rights that make us who we are.

The Founders who wrote our Constitution and Bill of Rights exercised that vigilance even though they had recently fought and won the Revolutionary War. They did not live in comfortable and easy times of hypothetical enemies. They wrote a Constitution of limited powers and an explicit Bill of Rights to protect liberty in times of war, as well as in times of peace.

There have been periods in our nation's history when civil liberties have taken a back seat to what appeared at the time to be the legitimate exigencies of war. Our national consciousness still bears the stain and the scars of those events: The Alien and Sedition Acts, the suspension of habeas corpus during the Civil War, the internment of Japanese-Americans, German-Americans, and Italian-Americans during World War II, the blacklisting of supposed communist sympathizers during the McCarthy era, and the surveillance and harassment of antiwar protesters, including Dr. Martin Luther King Jr., during the Vietnam War. We must not allow these pieces of our past to become prologue.

[…]

In 1917, the Postmaster General revoked the mailing privileges of the newspaper the Milwaukee Leader because he felt that some of its articles impeded the war effort and the draft. Articles called the President an aristocrat and called the draft oppressive. Over dissents by Justices Brandeis and Holmes, the Supreme Court upheld the action.

During World War II, President Roosevelt signed orders to incarcerate more than 110,000 people of Japanese origin, as well as some roughly 11,000 of German origin and 3,000 of Italian origin.

[...]

Now some may say, indeed we may hope, that we have come a long way since the days of infringements on civil liberties. But there is ample reason for concern. And I have been troubled in the past six weeks by the potential loss of commitment in the Congress and the country to traditional civil liberties.

As it seeks to combat terrorism, the Justice Department is making extraordinary use of its power to arrest and detain individuals, jailing hundreds of people on immigration violations and arresting more than a dozen "material witnesses" not charged with any crime. Although the government has used these authorities before, it has not done so on such a broad scale. Judging from government announcements, the government has not brought any criminal charges related to the attacks with regard to the overwhelming majority of these detainees.

[...]

Of course, given the enormous anxiety and fears generated by the events of September 11th, it would not have been difficult to anticipate some of these reactions, both by our government and some of our people. Some have said rather cavalierly that in these difficult times we must accept some reduction in our civil liberties in order to be secure.

Of course, there is no doubt that if we lived in a police state, it would be easier to catch terrorists. If we lived in a country that allowed the police to search your home at any time for any reason; if we lived in a country that allowed the government to open your mail, eavesdrop on your phone conversations, or intercept your email communications; if we lived in a country that allowed the government to hold people in jail indefinitely based on what they write or think, or based on mere suspicion that they are up to no good, then the government would no doubt discover and arrest more terrorists.

But that probably would not be a country in which we would want to live. And that would not be a country for which we could, in good conscience, ask our young people to fight and die. In short, that would not be America.

Preserving our freedom is one of the main reasons that we are now engaged in this new war on terrorism. We will lose that war without firing a shot if we sacrifice the liberties of the American people.

That is why I found the antiterrorism bill originally proposed by Attorney General Ashcroft and President Bush to be troubling.

[...]

As I will discuss in a moment, I have concluded that this bill still does not strike the right balance between empowering law enforcement and protecting civil liberties. But that does not mean that I oppose everything in the bill. Indeed many of its provisions are entirely reasonable, and I hope they will help law enforcement more effectively counter the threat of terrorism.

[...]

In the end, however, my focus on this bill, as Chair of the Constitution Subcommittee of the Judiciary Committee in the Senate, was on those provisions that implicate our constitutional freedoms. [...]

[...]

I am also very troubled by the broad expansion of government power under the Foreign Intelligence Surveillance Act, known as FISA. When Congress passed FISA in 1978 it granted to the executive branch the power to conduct surveillance in foreign intelligence investigations without meeting the rigorous probable cause standard under the Fourth Amendment that is required for criminal investigations. There is a lower threshold for obtaining a wiretap order from the FISA court because the FBI is not investigating a crime, it is investigating foreign intelligence activities. But the law currently requires that intelligence gathering be the primary purpose of the investigation in order for this lower standard to apply.

This bill changes that requirement. The government now will only have to show that intelligence is a "significant purpose" of the investigation. So even if the primary purpose is a criminal investigation, the heightened protections of the Fourth Amendment won't apply.

It seems obvious that with this lower standard, the FBI will try to use FISA as much as it can. And of course, with terrorism investigations that won't be difficult, because the terrorists are apparently sponsored or at least supported by foreign governments. This means that the Fourth Amendment rights will be significantly curtailed in many investigations of terrorist acts.

The significance of the breakdown of the distinction between intelligence and criminal investigations becomes apparent when you see the other expansions of government power under FISA in this bill. One provision that troubles me a great deal is a provision that permits the government under FISA to compel the production of records from any business regarding any person, if that information is sought in connection with an investigation of terrorism or espionage.

Now we're not talking here about travel records pertaining to a terrorist suspect, which we all can see can be highly relevant to an investigation of a terrorist plot. FISA already gives the FBI the power to get airline, train, hotel, car rental and other records of a suspect.

But under this bill, the government can compel the disclosure of the personal records of anyone—perhaps someone who worked with, or lived next door to, or went to school with, or sat on an airplane with, or has been seen in the company of, or whose phone number was called by—the target of the investigation.

And under this new provision all business records can be compelled, including those containing sensitive personal information like medical records from hospitals or doctors, or educational records, or records of what books someone has taken out of the library. This is an enormous expansion of authority, under a law that provides only minimal judicial supervision.

Under this provision, the government can apparently go on a fishing expedition and collect information on virtually anyone. All it has to allege in order to get an order for these records from the court is that the information is sought for an investigation of international terrorism or clandestine intelligence gathering. That's it. On that minimal showing in an ex parte application to a secret court, with no showing even that the information is relevant to the investigation, the government can lawfully compel a doctor or hospital to release medical records, or a library to release circulation records. This is a truly breathtaking expansion of police power.

[...]

Another provision in the bill that deeply troubles me allows the detention and deportation of people engaging in innocent associational activity. It would allow for the detention and deportation of individuals who provide lawful assistance to groups that are not even designated by the Secretary of State as terrorist organizations, but instead have engaged in vaguely defined "terrorist activity" sometime in the past. To avoid deportation, the immigrant is required to prove a negative: that he or she did not know, and should not have known, that the assistance would further terrorist activity.

This language creates a very real risk that truly innocent individuals could be deported for innocent associations with humanitarian or political groups that the government later chooses to regard as terrorist organizations. Groups that might fit this definition could include Operation Rescue, Greenpeace, and even the Northern Alliance fighting the Taliban in northern Afghanistan. This provision amounts to "guilt by association," which I believe violates the First Amendment.

And speaking of the First Amendment, under this bill, a lawful permanent resident who makes a controversial speech that the government deems to be supportive of terrorism might be barred from returning to his or her family after taking a trip abroad.

[...]

We must maintain our vigilance to preserve our laws and our basic rights.

We in this body have a duty to analyze, to test, to weigh new laws that the zealous and often sincere advocates of security would suggest to us. This is what I have tried to do with this anti-terrorism bill. And that is why I will vote against this bill when the roll is called.

Protecting the safety of the American people is a solemn duty of the Congress; we must work tirelessly to prevent more tragedies like the devastating attacks of September 11th. We must prevent more children from losing their mothers, more wives from losing their husbands, and more firefighters from losing their heroic colleagues. But the Congress will fulfill its duty only when it protects both the American people and the freedoms at the foundation of American society. So let us preserve our heritage of basic rights. Let us practice as well as preach that liberty. And let us fight to maintain that freedom that we call America.

I yield the floor.

*__Russ Feingold__ was U.S. senator (D–WI) from 1993 to 2011. He was the only member of the Senate to oppose the USA PATRIOT Act during the first vote on the proposed legislation.

Feingold, Russ. "Statement by U.S. Senator Russ Feingold on the Anti-Terrorism Bill from the Senate Floor." October 25, 2001. 107th Congress. http://epic.org/privacy/terrorism/usapatriot/feingold.html.

# The USA PATRIOT Act
# Six Months Later

*by Members of the Free Expression Network\**

Historically, in times of crisis in the United States, an understandable desire to protect the nation has led to efforts to curtail civil liberties, particularly the freedom of speech. In hindsight, these efforts have invariably proved to be both unwise and unnecessary. The issue is not just of historical interest. In response to the events of September 11, 2001, the USA PATRIOT Act was passed with little debate, and dramatically expanded the investigative powers of the federal government at the expense of Constitutional freedoms. Today, six months after its enactment, is an appropriate moment to pause and consider whether the erosion of legal principles and individual rights is justifiable.

Under the PATRIOT Act and other recent government actions, there have been many instances where the flow of information to the public about government policies and activities has been restricted, debate on important matters suppressed, dissent chilled, and individuals threatened with legal sanction solely for their views or associations.

While the undersigned members of the Free Expression Network support legitimate law enforcement activities designed to bring to justice the perpetrators of the September 11 attacks and to prevent future threats to our security, we oppose doing so in ways that fundamentally threaten democracy, by allowing government broad power to monitor and investigate the personal opinions of its residents, and by restricting the free flow of information beyond the need to protect national security. We also condemn all efforts to demonize or punish dissent.

We list below some of the events that collectively form a troubling pattern, reminiscent of past judgment errors committed in the name of a worthy cause:

## Government Surveillance

With the passage of the USA PATRIOT Act, the federal government has assumed broad powers to investigate the opinions of individuals suspected of being a threat, creating the danger that Americans will be afraid to communicate freely over the Internet, to purchase the books they want to read, or to use libraries to obtain information they need.

Government investigators can now obtain court orders to monitor online communications upon an extremely low legal standard—with only a government official's assertion of relevance—and without effective judicial oversight.

Investigators can also obtain orders compelling booksellers or librarians to turn over private information about their customers and patrons; a bookseller can be ordered to turn over a list of the books a customer has purchased; a librarian can be compelled to report what books a patron has borrowed and, if the library has computers, what Web sites he or she has visited. These orders can be issued following secret hearings at which a special court hears only the government's case. The law also forbids booksellers and librarians to make public even the fact that they have received such orders. The Colorado Supreme Court recently addressed the free speech implications of government searches of book purchases, and recognized the general "right to purchase books anonymously, free from governmental interference."

On October 30, 2001, the Attorney General issued regulations permitting warrantless monitoring of attorney-client communications without judicial review under certain circumstances in cases involving terrorism.

## Access to Government Information

Citing national security concerns, the government has restricted access to a wide range of information. The drive for government secrecy, moreover, is part of a much larger effort to insulate government decision-making from the press and public scrutiny.

By memorandum dated October 12, 2001, the Attorney General restricted public access to documents under the Freedom of Information Act. Federal officials handling FOIA requests are now under instructions to deny requests on any "sound legal basis"; previously, information could only be withheld if government officials could show that disclosure would cause "substantial harm."

Information previously readily available in the public domain is now being withheld at the sole discretion of federal agencies. The Government Printing Office has ordered over one thousand libraries that serve as federal depositories to destroy government records that federal agencies say could be "sensitive," and at least 15 government agencies have removed information from the Internet.

On November 1, 2001, President Bush blocked the release of presidential papers, despite the mandate of the Presidential Records Act of 1978; although this dispute began before September 11, the President is now defending his action in part based on the need to protect "national security."

Homeland Security Director Tom Ridge has consistently refused to testify before Congress, and other members of the Bush Administration have invoked executive privilege or other secrecy claims in situations unrelated to national security. For example, the General Accounting Office, Congress' investigative arm, sued the White House over its refusal to provide documents relating to the energy task force overseen by Vice President Cheney, and the *LA Times* recently reported that the Justice Department is refusing to turn over documents to Congress relating to Attorney General Ashcroft's stated desire to have the FBI destroy records of all gun sales within 24 hours, rather than the current 90 day period, a change in policy which a GAO report indicates may allow illegal gun purchases to go undetected.

Administration officials have openly limited the ability of the press to cover the war and prevailed on the news media to censor statements by Osama bin Laden and other information; and the Defense Department disbanded a planned Office of Strategic Information only after a government employee revealed publicly the intent to use the office to disseminate false information to the American people, and America's allies as well as its enemies.

An estimated 1200 people were initially detained in connection with the investigation of terrorist activity, and an undetermined number are being held now. Many have been held in virtual secrecy, without disclosure of their identities or the grounds for detention. Government officials have vigorously opposed disclosure of information about detainees in several pending lawsuits. The government also asserts that national security justifies keeping immigration proceedings involving detainees closed to the press and public.

Under the rules governing military tribunals, certain information deemed to implicate national security may be kept secret even from defendants, jeopardizing their ability to mount an effective defense.

## Freedom of Association

Since September 11, a wide range of lawful political association has been deemed suspect and subject to government scrutiny. Ill-defined grounds for suspicion will likely lead to a repetition of past abuses of investigative authority.

Lawful aliens who associate with members of "terrorist" organizations are subject to deportation; the definition of terrorism is so broad that a member of Congress has proposed that the Justice Department investigate two AIDS activists who allegedly harassed and threatened health officials for "terrorism" under the provisions of the USA PATRIOT Act.

The Attorney General reportedly wants to relax the standards governing investigation of domestic political activities, which have been in place since the 1970s, and were adopted to prevent abuses connected with the then-routine surveillance of civil rights groups and anti-war protestors.

## Suppression of Speech and Dissent

These governmental acts have also created a climate chilling to speech, debate, and dissent in the very places intended to foster discussion and dialogue—schools, colleges and universities, and newspapers. On college campuses, and in high schools and even elementary schools, students and teachers face discipline if they question official US policy in response to terrorism. Sidewalk speakers have been attacked, journalists fired, and writers and entertainers publicly chastised for being insufficiently "patriotic," *i.e.* for expressing a dissenting opinion.

In the immediate aftermath of the September 11 attacks, colleges and universities disciplined faculty members for speech deemed inappropriate or unpatriotic, including Sami Al-Arian, a tenured professor at the University of South Florida whose dismissal is sought because of comments he made on a television show, Prof. Kenneth Hearlson of Orange Coast College in California, who was suspended and officially reprimanded, and Prof. Richard Berthold, who was subjected to disciplinary action at University of New Mexico.

Three newspaper editors have lost their jobs for criticizing American policy. In September, Tom Gutting, the city editor of the Texas City Sun, and Dan Guthrie, a columnist for the Grant's Pass Dial in Oregon, were dismissed for writing columns that criticized President Bush for not returning to Washington immediately after the September 11 attacks. In February, Tim McCarthy, editor of the weekly Courier in Littleton, N.H., was fired over his criticism of the Bush administration's war on terrorism.

Other voices openly call for the suppression of discussion and debate on college campuses, by characterizing anyone who questions government policies as "unpatriotic." The American Council of Trustees and Alumni issued a report in November, 2001, listing 117 allegedly anti-American statements made on college campuses following the terrorist attacks. The report called professors "the weak link in America's response to the attack." In March, 2002, the Americans for Victory Over Terrorism released its list of "objectionable" statements from professors, legislators, and writers who, it claims, "misunderstand ... [American] ideals and their practice." Among others, former President Jimmy Carter is criticized for his comment that President's Bush's use of the phrase "axis of evil" was "overly simplistic and counter-productive." While entitled to express their views about these statements, ACTA and AVOT appear more interested in suppressing criticism of the government than hearing dissenting opinions and encouraging discussion and dialogue. Since both organizations have close ties to the Administration, the appearance of government coercion and power is also of concern.

The pattern of these events shows significant erosion of fundamental rights and legal principles, not always confined to any realistic claim of necessity for national security purposes. These rights and principles are essential to our system of government, and the best advertisement for democracy outside our borders. We call on our political leaders to resist proposals that unduly and unwisely restrict the very freedoms that we as a nation now collectively seek to preserve. The hasty measures that were taken in the immediate wake of the attacks of September 11 should now be reconsidered, and we should reaffirm the right to free expression, open government, discussion and debate that have kept us strong and free for more than two hundred years.

## Endorsing Organizations:

American Booksellers Foundation for Free Expression

American Civil Liberties Union

Electronic Frontier Foundation

Electronic Privacy Information Center

Feminists for Free Expression

First Amendment Project

National Coalition against Censorship

Online Policy Group

Peacefire

PEN American Center

People for the American Way

Washington Area Lawyers for the Arts

*The **Free Expression Network** is an alliance of organizations that aims to protect free speech and other forms of expression. Members include the American Civil Liberties Union and the Association of American Publishers.

Free Expression Network. "The USA PATRIOT Act Six Months Later." April 26, 2002. http://ncac.org/FEN/The-USA-PATRIOT-Act-Six -Months-Later.

Used by permission.

# Not a Suicide Pact: The Constitution in a Time of National Emergency

*by Richard A. Posner\**

## Introduction

[...]

[...] Now, in the early years of the twenty-first century, the nation faces the intertwined menaces of global terrorism and proliferation of weapons of mass destruction. A city can be destroyed by an atomic bomb the size of a melon, which if coated with lead would be undetectable. Large stretches of a city can be rendered uninhabitable, perhaps for decades, merely by the explosion of a conventional bomb that has been coated with radioactive material. Smallpox virus bioengineered to make it even more toxic and vaccines ineffectual, then aerosolized and sprayed in a major airport, might kill millions of people. Our terrorist enemies have the will to do such things and abundant opportunities, because our borders are porous both to enemies and to containers. They will soon have the means as well. The march of technology has increased the variety and lethality of weapons of mass destruction, especially the biological, and also, critically, their accessibility. Aided by the disintegration of the Soviet Union and the acquisition of nuclear weapons by unstable nations (Pakistan and North Korea, soon to be joined, in all likelihood, by Iran), technological progress is making weapons of mass destruction ever more accessible both to terrorist groups (and even individuals) and to hostile nations that are not major powers. The problem of proliferation is more serious today than it was in what now seem the almost halcyon days of the Cold War; it will be even more serious tomorrow.

I am not a Chicken Little, and I agree with those who argue that our vigorous campaign against al-Qaeda and our extensive if chaotic efforts at improving homeland security have bought us a breathing space against terrorist attacks on U.S. territory. But how long will this breathing space last? The terrorists, their leadership decimated and dispersed, may be reeling, but they have not been defeated. In January 2006 Osama bin Laden declared that there would be further terrorist attacks on the United States; it would be reckless to dismiss his declaration as idle boasting. This is not the time to let down our guard.

[...]

The research that I have been conducting for the past several years on catastrophic risks, international terrorism, and national security intelligence has persuaded me that we live in a time of grave and increasing danger, comparable to what the nation faced at the outset of World War II.

[...]

## How Does National Security Shape Constitutional Rights

[…]

The sharpest challenge to the approach that I am sketching will come from civil libertarians. In a broad sense, almost all Americans are civil libertarians, that is, believers in a large sphere of freedom from government intrusion. But I denote by the term the adherents to the especially capacious view of civil liberties that is often advanced in litigation and lobbying by the American Civil Liberties Union.

Civil libertarians so defined are reluctant to acknowledge that national emergencies in general, or the threat of modern terrorism in particular, justify *any* curtailment of the civil liberties that were accepted on the eve of the emergency. They deny that civil liberties should wax and wane with changes in the danger level. They believe that the Constitution is about protecting individual rights rather than about promoting community interests, a belief that some civil libertarians ground in a quasi-religious veneration of civil liberties coupled with a profound suspicion of the coercive side of government—police, prosecutors, the military, the intelligence community. [ … ] They base their suspicion on a belief, urged most recently in Geoffrey Stone's book *Perilous Times*, that past curtailments of civil liberties were gratuitous responses to hysterically exaggerated fears. They believe that government always errs on the side of exaggerating threats to national security. And so they believe that the current threat—the terrorist threat—is exaggerated, perhaps deliberately by the Bush administration to promote its political fortunes, and that the laws and institutions in place on September 11, 2001, required no changes in order to be adequate to cope with the current threat. [...] Implicitly they deny that the counterterrrosim measures taken since 9/11 may be among the reasons that we haven't been attacked since.

Some civil libertarians [...] believe that any curtailment of civil liberties in time of emergency will continue when the emergency passes; they believe, in other words, that there is a civil liberties ratchet that might cause a succession of national emergencies to culminate in tyranny. [...]

[...]

Civil libertarians are not always careful about history. [...] History does not confirm the existence of a civil liberties ratchet, a "slippery slope" on which the first step toward curtailing civil liberties precipitates an uninterrupted and perhaps accelerating decline. Every time civil liberties have been curtailed in response to a national emergency, whether real or imaged, they have been fully restored when the emergency passed—and in fact before it passed, often long before. [...]

[...]

This pattern is no accident. At the outset of an emergency, the government is uncertain about its gravity, and on the principle that it is better to be safe than sorry reacts on a worse-case assumption. As more is learned about the danger, response measures are scaled down from worse case to best estimate. Most of the terrorist suspects, mainly illegal immigrants, rounded up and detained in urgent sweeps that followed 9/11 were released after it became apparent that the 9/11 hijackers were not members of a vast internal network of suicide terrorist and their supporters. National security programs adopted by the president and Congress in the wake of the 9/11 attacks were, four years later, under siege.

[...]

More important than the one-sidedness of the civil libertarians' historical narrative is their assumption that the past is a good guide to the future. [...] The past does not include attacks on the United States by terrorists wielding nuclear bombs, dirty bombs, biological weapons capable of killing millions of people, or other weapons of mass destruction; the future may well include such attacks. We must not emulate the Bourbon kings, who learned nothing and forgot nothing. Or, as another saying goes, if we want things to stay the same, things will have to change. Those who believe that since we survived decades of confrontation with the Soviet Union unscathed we have nothing to fear from a handful of terrorists [who] are looking backward rather than forward. [...]

[...]

Civil libertarians are right to be concerned about the personal costs and potential political consequences of national security measures.

[...]

But the relevant question is not whether curtailing civil liberties imposes costs, to which the answer is obvious; it is whether the costs exceed the benefits. Civil libertarians tend to exaggerate the costs (how many innocent U.S. citizens in a population of 300 million have experience real hardship as a result of the post-9/11 security measures?) and to ignore or slight the benefits. Most civil libertarians, and almost all their leaders are lawyers. They are comfortable defending liberties recognized by law but uncomfortable assessing threats to national security, about which they know little and don't want to learn more. [ ... ]

[ ... ]

*Richard A. Posner is a judge on the United States Court of Appeals for the Seventh Circuit and a professor at the University of Chicago Law School. He is the author of many books on jurisprudence, law, and economics.

Posner, Richard A. *Not a Suicide Pact: The Constitution in a Time of National Emergency.* New York: Oxford University Press, 2006, pp. 2–3, 41–51. By permission of Oxford University Press, USA.

---

## PART 2

# Reader Privacy

---

One of the first free speech fights after 9/11 targeted Section 215 of the 2001 PATRIOT Act. Prior to the passage of this legislation, the government was required to demonstrate to a court that there was probable cause to believe a crime was being committed before it could obtain a search warrant. Section 215 permitted the government to apply to a secret court to obtain an order allowing it to review any records that it believed were somehow relevant to a terrorism investigation. The government was not required to provide any evidence (probable cause) that the person under investigation was involved in criminal activity or that he or she was connected to a foreign power.

Section 215 alarmed the nation's librarians and booksellers because it allows the government to find out what people are reading. They believed that library patrons and bookstore customers would no longer feel free to read material that the government might consider suspicious. Section 215 also gags librarians and booksellers, forbidding them to reveal the order to the person whose records have been targeted. The American Library Association (ALA) had declared privacy as essential to free speech as early as 1939 and reasserted its stance in its 2002 statement, "Privacy: An Interpretation of the Library Bill of Rights."

In October 2002, Vermont librarians and booksellers sent an "Open Letter to Vermont's Congressional Delegation" urging its members to introduce legislation restoring the protections for reader privacy that the PATRIOT Act had eliminated. Rep. Bernie Sanders (Ind.) of Vermont took up the challenge and, at a March 2003 press conference, announced the introduction of a bill that would amend the act to exempt libraries and bookstores from Section 215 ("Comments on the 2003 Freedom to Read Protection Act"). Sanders argued that allowing the FBI to search the records of anyone "relevant" to an investigation made it too easy to spy on people who were not suspected of engaging in criminal acts. The book and library community rallied behind Sanders by issuing a "Book and Library Community Statement Supporting the Freedom to Read Protection Act" in which they argued that freedom of speech depends on the freedom to explore ideas privately. The ALA put itself at the forefront of the movement to protect reader privacy by approving a "Resolution on the USA PATRIOT Act and Related Measures That Infringe on the Rights of Library Users." Some librarians even posted signs warning patrons that the government might search their records ("Liberty in the Balance: Librarians Step Up").

Defenders of the PATRIOT Act denied that the government had any interest in spying on what Americans were reading. In a 2003 speech, "The Proven Tactics in the Fight against Crime," Attorney General John Ashcroft ridiculed the concerns expressed by the librarians as hysteria and hyperbole while asserting that the right of law enforcement to examine business records, including library records, was an important, and successful, tool in the "war on terror." Safeguards in the PATRIOT Act prevented government abuse, he maintained. During a House debate on the Sanders's legislation in July 2004, Republican representatives Howard Coble (NC) and Christopher Shays (CT) argued that if the FBI could not monitor libraries, they might become terrorist sanctuaries ("Debate on Sanders Amendment"). Democratic representative Jerrold Nadler (NY) responded that the government could use a subpoena to obtain library records whenever it could show evidence that the person whose records were sought was engaged in criminal acts. The Sanders amendment was narrowly defeated.

Section 215 was reauthorized in 2005 for four years. During public debate over reauthorization in 2009, Rep. James Sensenbrenner (R–WI) gave a speech at the University of Wisconsin, "Speech on the USA PATRIOT Act," defending the PATRIOT Act and insisting that many safeguards against abuses of Section 215 were in place. In 2011, Congress reauthorized Section 215 for another four years. However, Attorney General Eric Holder promised that the administration will apply a higher standard in seeking library and bookstore records, using Section 215 only if there is evidence that the person whose records are sought is a terrorist, spy, or someone known to be associated with a terrorist or spy. This promise partly restores the safeguards for the privacy of reader records that existed before passage of the PATRIOT Act.

A new controversy about Section 215 erupted in June 2013 when a journalist revealed that a Section 215 order had been secretly issued to Verizon requiring it to turn over information about the telephone calls of all its business subscribers in the United States. President Obama defended the order, which does not allow the government to listen to calls. But Sen. Mark Udall (D–CO) said that the order did not appear to have helped identify any terrorist plots. He called for renewed debate of Section 215. At the same time, journalists revealed a second program, Prism, that the government has been using to conduct surveillance of foreigners by monitoring the Internet data of companies like Facebook and Skype. Government officials said the program helped prevent a terrorist attack on the New York City subway, but civil liberties groups expressed concern that data about American citizens was being collected as well.

As you read the articles in this section, think about the following questions:

- Is the privacy of reader records a free speech issue?
- Are the concerns and fears of librarians and booksellers exaggerated?
- Are adequate safeguards in place to prevent abuses of Section 215?

# Privacy: An Interpretation of the Library Bill of Rights

*by the American Library Association\**

## Introduction

Privacy is essential to the exercise of free speech, free thought, and free association. The courts have established a First Amendment right to receive information in a publicly funded library.[1] Further, the courts have upheld the right to privacy based on the Bill of Rights of the U.S. Constitution.[2] Many states provide guarantees of privacy in their constitutions and statute law.[3] Numerous decisions in case law have defined and extended rights to privacy.[4]

In a library (physical or virtual), the right to privacy is the right to open inquiry without having the subject of one's interest examined or scrutinized by others. Confidentiality exists when a library is in possession of personally identifiable information about users and keeps that information private on their behalf.[5]

Protecting user privacy and confidentiality has long been an integral part of the mission of libraries. The ALA has affirmed a right to privacy since 1939.[6] Existing ALA policies affirm that confidentiality is crucial to freedom of inquiry.[7] Rights to privacy and confidentiality also are implicit in the *Library Bill of Rights'* guarantee of free access to library resources for all users.[8]

## Rights of Library Users

The *Library Bill of Rights* affirms the ethical imperative to provide unrestricted access to information and to guard against impediments to open inquiry. Article IV states: "Libraries should cooperate with all persons and groups concerned with resisting abridgement of free expression and free access to ideas." When users recognize or fear that their privacy or confidentiality is compromised, true freedom of inquiry no longer exists.

In all areas of librarianship, best practice leaves the user in control of as many choices as possible. These include decisions about the selection of, access to, and use of information. Lack of privacy and confidentiality has a chilling effect on users' choices. All users have a right to be free from any unreasonable intrusion into or surveillance of their lawful library use.

Users have the right to be informed what policies and procedures govern the amount and retention of personally identifiable information, why that information is necessary for the library, and what the user can do to maintain his or her privacy. Library users expect and in many places have a legal right to have their information protected and kept private and confidential by anyone with direct or indirect access to that information. In addition, Article V of the *Library Bill of Rights* states: "A person's right to use a library should not be denied or abridged because of origin, age, background, or views." This article precludes the use of profiling as a basis for any breach of privacy rights. Users have the right to use a library without any abridgement of privacy that may result from equating the subject of their inquiry with behavior.[9]

## Responsibilities in Libraries

The library profession has a long-standing commitment to an ethic of facilitating, not monitoring, access to information. This commitment is implemented locally through development, adoption, and adherence to privacy policies that are consistent with applicable federal, state, and local law. Everyone (paid or unpaid) who provides governance, administration, or service in libraries has a responsibility to maintain an environment respectful and protective of the privacy of all users. Users have the responsibility to respect each other's privacy.

For administrative purposes, librarians may establish appropriate time, place, and manner restrictions on the use of library resources.[10] In keeping with this principle, the collection of personally identifiable information should only be a matter of routine or policy when necessary for the fulfillment of the mission of the library. Regardless of the technology used, everyone who collects or accesses personally identifiable information in any format has a legal and ethical obligation to protect confidentiality.

## Conclusion

The American Library Association affirms that rights of privacy are necessary for intellectual freedom and are fundamental to the ethics and practice of librarianship.

Adopted June 19, 2002, by the ALA Council.

## NOTES

1. Court opinions establishing a right to receive information in a public library include *Board of Education. v. Pico,* 457 U.S. 853 (1982); *Kreimer v. Bureau of Police for the Town of Morristown,* 958 F.2d 1242 (3d Cir. 1992); and *Reno v. American Civil Liberties Union,* 117 S.Ct. 2329, 138 L.Ed.2d 874 (1997).

2. See in particular the Fourth Amendment's guarantee of "[t]he right of the people to be secure in their persons, houses, papers, and effects, against unreasonable searches and seizures," the Fifth Amendment's guarantee against self-incrimination, and the Ninth Amendment's guarantee that "[t]he enumeration in the Constitution, of certain rights, shall not be construed to deny or disparage others retained by the people." This right is explicit in Article Twelve of the Universal Declaration of Human Rights: "No one shall be subjected to arbitrary interference with his privacy, family, home or correspondence, nor to attacks upon his honour and reputation. Everyone has the right to the protection of the law against such interference or attacks." See: http://www.un.org/Overview/rights.html. This right has further been explicitly codified as Article Seventeen of the "International Covenant on Civil and Political Rights," a legally binding international human rights agreement ratified by the United States on June 8, 1992. See: http://www.unhchr.ch/html/menu3/b/a_ccpr.htm.

3. Ten state constitutions guarantee a right of privacy or bar unreasonable intrusions into citizens' privacy. Forty-eight states protect the confidentiality of library users' records by law, and the attorneys general in the remaining two states have issued opinions recognizing the privacy of users' library records. See: State Privacy Laws.

4. Cases recognizing a right to privacy include: *NAACP v. Alabama,* 357 U.S. 449 (1958); *Griswold v. Connecticut* 381 U.S. 479 (1965); *Katz v. United States,* 389 U.S. 347 (1967); and *Stanley v. Georgia,* 394 U.S. 557 (1969). Congress recognized the right to privacy in the Privacy Act of 1974 and Amendments (5 USC Sec. 552a), which addresses the potential for government's violation of privacy through its collection of personal information. The Privacy Act's "Congressional Findings and Statement of Purpose" state

in part: "the right to privacy is a personal and fundamental right protected by the Constitution of the United States." See: http://caselaw.lp.findlaw.com/scripts/ts_search.pl?title=5&sec=552a.

5. The phrase "Personally identifiable information" was established in ALA policy in 1991. See: Policy Concerning Confidentiality of Personally Identifiable Information about Library Users. Personally identifiable information can include many types of library records, for instance: information that the library requires an individual to provide in order to be eligible to use library services or borrow materials, information that identifies an individual as having requested or obtained specific materials or materials on a particular subject, and information that is provided by an individual to assist a library staff member to answer a specific question or provide information on a particular subject. Personally identifiable information does not include information that does not identify any individual and that is retained only for the purpose of studying or evaluating the use of a library and its materials and services. Personally identifiable information does include any data that can link choices of taste, interest, or research with a specific individual.

6. Article Eleven of the *Code of Ethics for Librarians* (1939) asserted that "It is the librarian's obligation to treat as confidential any private information obtained through contact with library patrons." See: Code of Ethics for Librarians (1939). Article Three of the current Code (1995) states: "We protect each library user's right to privacy and confidentiality with respect to information sought or received and resources consulted, borrowed, acquired, or transmitted." See: http://www.ala.org/alaorg/oif/ethics.html.

7. See these ALA Policies: Access for Children and Young People to Videotapes and Other Nonprint Formats; *Free Access to Libraries for Minors; Freedom to Read* (http://www.ala.org/alaorg/oif/freeread.html); *Libraries: An American Value;* the newly revised Library Principles for a Networked World; Policy Concerning Confidentiality of Personally Identifiable Information about Library Users; *Policy on Confidentiality of Library Records; Suggested Procedures for Implementing Policy on the Confidentiality of Library Records.*

8. Adopted June 18, 1948; amended February 2, 1961, and January 23, 1980; inclusion of "age" reaffirmed January 23, 1996, by the ALA Council. See: http://www.ala.org/work/freedom/lbr.html.

9. Existing ALA Policy asserts, in part, that: "The government's interest in library use reflects a dangerous and fallacious equation of what a person reads with what that person believes or how that person is likely to behave. Such a presumption can and does threaten the freedom of access to information." Policy Concerning Confidentiality of Personally Identifiable Information about Library Users.

10. See: *Guidelines for the Development and Implementation of Policies, Regulations and Procedures Affecting Access to Library Materials, Services and Facilities.*

\*The **American Library Association** is a nonprofit organization that supports libraries and library education worldwide. It opposes some provisions of the PATRIOT Act and has tried to work with Congress to change federal law.

American Library Association. "Privacy: An Interpretation of the Library Bill of Rights." June 19, 2002. http://www.ala.org/Template .cfm?Section=interpretations&Template=/ContentManagement/ ContentDisplay.cfm&ContentID=8613.

Used with permission from the American Library Association.

# Open Letter to Vermont's Congressional Delegation

*by the Vermont Library Association**

We, the undersigned librarians and booksellers, implore Senators Leahy and Jeffords and Congressman Sanders to introduce legislation to eliminate provisions in the USA PATRIOT Act that undermine Americans' Constitutionally guaranteed right to read and access information without governmental intrusion or interference. The Act—passed with virtually no Congressional debate—gives law enforcement officials broad authority to demand that libraries or booksellers turn over books, records, papers, and documents—in fact "any tangible things." The government, for example, can subpoena records of books that individuals have borrowed or purchased, as well as the establishment's computer hard drives. And the bookseller or librarian is prohibited from telling anyone that an investigation is underway. It also allows the government—without showing probable cause—to install devices to monitor Internet use within a library, no matter who is using the computers. The monitors can sweep up vast amounts of information about people who are not suspected of a crime.

We understand the need for sufficient government authority to protect Americans from real danger of terrorist acts. But these new provisions are unnecessary. Laws already existed, prior to the passage of the USA PATRIOT Act, giving law enforcement ample power to use warrants, subpoenas, or wiretaps to obtain confidential information about individuals. The important difference is that these laws conformed to the Constitution. Access to Americans' private lives required probable cause and was subject to judicial oversight.

The freedom to read is one of the cornerstones of democracy. Our professions are founded on principles that encourage the free expression of ideas and the right of a citizenry to access those ideas free of censorship, violations of privacy, or the threat of governmental intrusion. We consider ourselves front-line defenders of the First Amendment.

It is especially crucial for a free society to remain vigilant against threats to its liberties during periods of national stress and crisis, when those liberties are most at risk. We do not have to reach back far to know that our concerns are not abstract. Internments of Japanese-Americans during World War II, the destruction of innocent lives during McCarthy's anti-communist crusade—lawmakers at the time considered these policies to be rational, reasonable responses to perceived threats. Now, of course, those moments are shameful to us.

Let us do what is right so that Americans will look back at this time with pride, rather than shame.

These provisions of the USA PATRIOT Act do not protect us from terrorism. Rather, they cast a wide net of suspicion and surveillance over the community of readers, researchers, and information-seekers. They are dangerous steps toward the erosion of our most fundamental civil liberties. Please present your colleagues in Congress with a bill to repeal these provisions now.

We thank you on behalf of all who treasure the right to read, speak, and think as free Americans under our Constitution.

Signed,
Executive Board, The Vermont Library Association

*The **Vermont Library Association** comprises Vermont's librarians and library employees and seeks to improve library services in the state. It cosponsors an annual spring conference and publishes a bimonthly newsletter.

Vermont Library Association. "Open Letter to Vermont's Congressional Delegation." Letter. October 21, 2002. http://www.vermont libraries.org/publications/patriot.

Used with the permission from the Vermont Library Association.

# Comments on the 2003 Freedom to Read Protection Act

*by Bernie Sanders\**

Good afternoon, and thank you for joining us here today to announce the introduction of the Freedom to Read Protection Act—legislation which will protect libraries, bookstores and their patrons from unjustified government surveillance into what books Americans are reading and buying, and what Web sites they may be visiting when using a library computer.

Let me begin by thanking the Members of Congress who have joined me here today. I also want to thank Chris Finan, president of the American Booksellers Foundations for Free Expression, and Emily Sheketoff, executive director of the American Library Association's Washington Office, for joining us. I am also delighted that Trina Magi—a librarian from the University of Vermont—and Linda Ramsdell, a bookstore owner from Hardwick, Vermont, who is the President of the New England Booksellers Association, are here with us today.

Let me also congratulate the 62 cities and towns all across this country that have passed resolutions on this issue—and that number is growing rapidly. That effort is being coordinated by the Bill of Rights Defense Committee, which understands that civil liberties and constitutional rights are not only a national issue, but also a local issue. I also want to thank the editorial boards of the many newspapers all over this country who have spoken out on this freedom to read issue—including the Los Angeles Times, the Detroit Free Press, the Honolulu Observer, the Providence Journal—Bulletin, the Caledonia Record, and the Valley News.

The tri-partisan legislation we are introducing today— called the Freedom to Read Protection Act—would protect the privacy and First Amendment rights of American citizens against unnecessary government intrusion. Specifically, this legislation will exempt libraries and bookstores from Section 215 of the so-called "Patriot Act." The Freedom to Read Protection Act is being introduced by 24 members of Congress including Republican Ron Paul of Texas, and Congressman John Conyers, the Ranking Member of the House Judiciary Committee. They are both unable to join us today, but I do want to recognize their support and leadership in protecting civil liberties. I am confident that in the days and weeks to come we will add many more cosponsors.

One of the cornerstones of our democracy is the right of Americans to criticize their government, and to read printed materials without fear of government monitoring and intrusion.

Yes, all of us are concerned about terrorism and all of us are determined to do all that we can to protect the American people from another terrorist attack. But, the threat of terrorism must not be used as an excuse by the government to intrude on our basic constitutional rights. We can fight terrorism, but we can do it at the same time as we protect the civil liberties that have made our country great.

Unfortunately, the Patriot Act has changed all that. Section 215 of the Patriot Act greatly expanded the FBI's ability to get records from all businesses, including libraries and booksellers, without meeting the traditional standard needed to get a search warrant in the United States.

This is a very dangerous situation. Today, all the FBI has to claim is that the information they want is somehow relevant to an investigation to protect against international terrorism. This is an extremely low threshold for government intrusion, and average Americans should be extremely concerned.

The reason they should care is that Section 215 does not just apply to terrorists, or even foreigners or agents of foreign powers. Under Section 215 of the Patriot Act, the person whose records are being searched by the FBI can be anyone. The FBI doesn't even have to say that it believes the person is involved in criminal activity or that the person is connected to a foreign power.

Even more frightening, the FBI can investigate American citizens based in part on an American's exercise of his or her First Amendment rights, such as writing a letter to the editor of a newspaper or reading books the government may not approve of.

And the traditional legal protections, which have been embodied in our Constitution for hundreds of years, no longer apply. The government can gain access to our reading records through the secret FISA court, which was created by the Foreign Intelligence Surveillance Act in 1978, and which is off limits to the public. There's no way to know how many times the FBI has spied on library or bookseller records or whose records they have reviewed.

In fact, Section 215 prevents librarians and booksellers from telling their customers that their privacy has been violated. Who would have thought that in 21st century America, the government could gain access to library circulation records and bookseller customer records with no evidence that the person whose records they are getting is involved in any wrongdoing, that all of this would be handled through a secret government court, and that the librarians and booksellers would be compelled by the law not to let anyone know that the government had swooped in to get their records?

Now, some may ask how the federal government is using this new power. Members of Congress on both sides of the aisle are also interested in that question and have pressured the Justice Department to show how they are using these new powers. The information they have received after months of badgering the Department is inadequate. The Justice Department claimed most of the information regarding libraries and bookstores was "confidential," and could not be provided. This past October, several national organizations, including the American Booksellers Association, filed a Freedom of Information Act request to get statistical information, such as how many times the government has used its expanded surveillance authority under the Patriot Act. In January, a very limited amount of information was released to these groups, and they are continuing to push for a more complete disclosure.

Importantly, an anonymous survey done by the University of Illinois found that over 175 libraries across the county have been visited by federal authorities since the September 11 attacks. How is the Congress and the public supposed to make sure that these new powers are not being abused when we do not even know how often they are being invoked and the types of institutions that are being investigated?

For many people who cannot afford to buy books or have the Internet at home the library is critical to their ability to access information. Many librarians and booksellers now fear that patrons have begun to self-censor their library use and book purchases due to fears of government surveillance. We need to remove libraries and booksellers from Section 215 so that Americans know their freedom to access information won't be improperly scrutinized by federal agents.

Let us be clear. The FBI would still be able to gain access to library or bookseller records as part of an investigation into illegal activity. All our bill does is restore the traditional protections that Americans expect and deserve. If the FBI has probable cause to believe that information in a library or bookseller's records or computers is connected to an ongoing criminal investigation or terrorism investigation, they can go to court and get a search warrant.

In addition, the bill requires that the Justice Department provide more detailed information about its activities under Section 215 so we can determine how the FBI is using its new powers under Section 215.

Let me conclude by saying that all of us support protecting Americans from terrorism. But we do not win against terrorists by abandoning our most basic civil liberties. We cannot be an example of freedom for the world when our own government is spying on what Americans are reading.

*__Bernie Sanders__ is a United States senator from Vermont. He previously served in the House of Representatives and is the longest-serving independent congressman in American history.

Sanders, Bernie. "Comments on the 2003 Freedom to Read Protection Act." Press conference, March 6, 2003. http://www.bookweb.org/news/rep-sanders-comments-freedom-read-protection-act-2003.

# Book and Library Community Statement Supporting the Freedom to Read Protection Act (H.R. 1157), the Library and Bookseller Protection Act (S. 1158), and the Library, Bookseller and Personal Data Privacy Act (S. 1507)

*by Campaign for Reader Privacy**

Our society places the highest value on the ability to speak freely on any subject. But freedom of speech depends on the freedom to explore ideas privately. Bookstore customers and library patrons must feel free to seek out books on health, religion, politics, the law, or any subject they choose, without fear that the government is looking over their shoulder. Without the assurance that their reading choices will remain private, they will be reluctant to fully exercise their right to read freely.

Section 215 of the USA PATRIOT Act threatens bookstore and library privacy. FBI agents do not need to prove they have "probable cause" before searching bookstore or library records: they can obtain the records of anyone whom they believe to have information that may be relevant to a terrorism investigation, including people who are not suspected of committing a crime or of having any knowledge of a crime. The request for an order authorizing the search is heard by a secret court in a closed proceeding, making it impossible for a bookseller or librarian to object on First Amendment grounds prior to the execution of the order. Because the order contains a gag provision forbidding a bookseller or librarian from alerting anyone to the fact that a search has occurred, it would be difficult to protest the search even after the fact.

The organizations listed below strongly support federal legislation that addresses this problem: the Freedom to Read Protection Act (H.R. 1157), the Library and Bookseller Protection Act (S. 1158) and the Library, Bookseller and Personal Data Privacy Act (S. 1507). These bills strengthen protections for the privacy of bookstore and library records without preventing the FBI from obtaining crucial information. Under H.R. 1157 and S. 1158, the courts would exercise their normal scrutiny in reviewing requests for bookstore and library records. S. 1507 allows the FBI to follow the procedures authorized by Section 215 but limits searches to the records of "foreign agents" engaged in acts of terrorism or espionage.

We applaud the authors of these bills, U.S. Representative Bernie Sanders (H.R. 1157), Senator Barbara Boxer (S. 1158) and Senator Russell D. Feingold (S. 1507) as well as the Democratic and Republican sponsors and co-sponsors of this legislation. They have shown great courage by defending civil liberties during a time of crisis.

## Associations

American Association of Law Libraries

American Booksellers Association

American Booksellers Foundation for Free Expression

American Library Association

American Society of Journalists and Authors

Antiquarian Booksellers Association of America

Association of American Publishers

Association of American University Presses

Association of Booksellers for Children

Association of Research Libraries

Authors Guild

California Association of Library Trustees and Commissioners

California Library Association

Children's Book Council

Comic Book Legal Defense Fund

Florida Publishers Association

Freedom to Read Foundation

Great Lakes Booksellers Association

Illinois Library Association

Independent Online Booksellers Association

Medical Library Association

Mid-South Independent Booksellers Association

Minnesota Library Association

Montana Library Association

Mountains and Plains Booksellers Association

National Association of Independent Publishers
    Representatives

New Atlantic Independent Booksellers Association

New England Booksellers Association

New York Library Association

Northern California Independent Booksellers Assn.

Pacific Northwest Independent Booksellers Assn.

PEN American Center

PEN New England

PEN USA West

Publishers Association of the West

Publishers Marketing Association

Publishing Association of the South

Science Fiction and Fantasy Writers of America

Small Press Center

Small Publishers Association of North America

Society of Children's Book Writers and Illustrators

Southeast Booksellers Association

Southern California Booksellers Association

Special Libraries Association

Upper Midwest Booksellers Association

Virginia Library Association

## Companies

2nd Look Books

96 Inc.

ABEBooks.com

Academy Chicago Publishers

Accurate Writing & More

Aesop's Room

Akashic Books

Aliform Publishing

A. Pankovich Publishers

Arte Público Press

Arundel Books

Authors & Artists

Avalon Publishing Group

Avocet Press Inc.

Baker & Taylor

Barnes & Noble Booksellers

Bay Street Trading Company

Beacon Press

Book Connection

BookFinder.com

Books+, Inc.

Borders Group Inc.

Burke's Book Store

Capital Books

Cargo Publishing Company

Cat's-paw Press

Center for Thanatology Research & Education, Inc.

Chicory Blue Press

Cold Spring Harbor Laboratory Press

Cornell Maritime Press & Tidewater Publishers

Darwin Press

Devenish Press

Duke University Press

Fact & Fiction

Fact & Fiction Bookshop

The Feminist Press at the City University of New York

Fine Print Book Store

First Books & Inkwater Press

FoulkeTale Publishing

Four Walls Eight Windows

Fugue State Press

Fulcrum Publishing

George Braziller, Inc.

Gival Press, LLC

Green Map System

Grove/Atlantic, Inc.

Holtzbrinck Publishers

Houghton Mifflin

Humanics Publishing Group

Hyde Brothers Booksellers, Inc

I Love a Mystery Bookstore

In The Alley Bookshop

Independent Booksellers Consortium, Inc.

Ingram Book Group

Inkwell Books

Innerlit Stone

Island Press

International Publishers Co., Inc.

John Wiley & Sons, Inc.

KingChamp Books

Lee Stookey Books

Left Bank Books

Lynne Rienner Publishers

Maria's Bookshop

MCJ Global Resources, Inc.

Mountain Empire Publications

Mountaintop Books

New York University Press

Nolo Bookstore

North Country Books

North Star Books

Oblong Books & Music

Patria Press, Inc.

Peak Publications

Pelican Island Publishing

Penguin Group USA

Penington Press

Pocahontas Press

Portrait of a Bookstore

Plum Branch Press

Princeton University Press

PublishingGame.com/Peanut Butter and Jelly Press

Rainbow Books, Inc.

Random House, Inc.

Readmore Books

The Reader's Loft

Red Dust, Inc.

Red Rock Press

Rexdale Publishing Company

SassyJacks Books

Scholastic, Inc.

Sem Fronteiras Press

Seven Stories Press

Shambling Gate Press

Simon & Schuster

Snake Nation Press

Southern Illinois University Press

Spankstra Press

Square One Publishers

Star Bright Books

Stein Software Corporation

Surrey Books

Turtle Books

Trafalgar Square

University Book Store, Inc., Seattle, WA

University Press of Colorado

Used Book Haven

VaiVecchio Press

Vashon Island Books

Village Books

Viveca Smith Publishing

Walker & Company

Wesleyan University Press

West Edge Media

Wild Horizons Publishing, Inc.

Wildcat Press

Winged Willow Press

The Winstead Press Ltd.

Workman Publishing

Yale University Press

*The **Campaign for Reader Privacy** was created in 2004 to restore the protections for reader privacy that were elimination by the PATRIOT Act. It is a joint initiative of the American Booksellers Association, the American Library Association, the Association of American Publishers, and PEN American Center.

Campaign for Reader Privacy. "Book and Library Community Statement Supporting the Freedom to Read Protection Act (H.R. 1157), the Library and Bookseller Protection Act (S. 1158), and the Library, Bookseller and Personal Data Privacy Act (S. 1507)," May 27, 2005.

Used by permission.

# Resolution on the USA PATRIOT Act and Related Measures That Infringe on the Rights of Library Users

*by the American Library Association**

WHEREAS, The American Library Association affirms the responsibility of the leaders of the United States to protect and preserve the freedoms that are the foundation of our democracy; and

WHEREAS, Libraries are a critical force for promoting the free flow and unimpeded distribution of knowledge and information for individuals, institutions, and communities; and

WHEREAS, The American Library Association holds that suppression of ideas undermines a democratic society; and

WHEREAS, Privacy is essential to the exercise of free speech, free thought, and free association; and, in a library, the subject of users' interests should not be examined or scrutinized by others; and

WHEREAS, Certain provisions of the USA PATRIOT Act, the revised Attorney General Guidelines to the Federal Bureau of Investigation, and other related measures expand the authority of the federal government to investigate citizens and non-citizens, to engage in surveillance, and to threaten civil rights and liberties guaranteed under the United States Constitution and Bill of Rights; and

WHEREAS, The USA PATRIOT Act and other recently enacted laws, regulations, and guidelines increase the likelihood that the activities of library users, including their use of computers to browse the Web or access e-mail, may be under government surveillance without their knowledge or consent; now, therefore, be it

RESOLVED, That the American Library Association opposes any use of governmental power to suppress the free and open exchange of knowledge and information or to intimidate individuals exercising free inquiry; and, be it further

RESOLVED, That the American Library Association encourages all librarians, library administrators, library governing bodies, and library advocates to educate their users, staff, and communities about the process for compliance with the USA PATRIOT Act and other related measures and about the dangers to individual privacy and the confidentiality of library records resulting from those measures; and, be it further

RESOLVED, That the American Library Association urges librarians everywhere to defend and support user privacy and free and open access to knowledge and information; and, be it further

RESOLVED, That the American Library Association will work with other organizations, as appropriate, to protect the rights of inquiry and free expression; and, be it further

RESOLVED, That the American Library Association will take actions as appropriate to obtain and publicize information about the surveillance of libraries and library users by law enforcement agencies and to assess the impact on library users and their communities; and, be it further

RESOLVED, That the American Library Association urges all libraries to adopt and implement patron privacy and record retention policies that affirm that "the collection of personally identifiable information should only be a matter of routine or policy when necessary for the fulfillment of the mission of the library" (ALA Privacy: An Interpretation of the Library Bill of Rights); and, be it further

RESOLVED, That the American Library Association considers sections of the USA PATRIOT Act are a present danger to the constitutional rights and privacy rights of library users and urges the United States Congress to:

1. provide active oversight of the implementation of the USA PATRIOT Act and other related measures, and the revised Attorney General Guidelines to the Federal Bureau of Investigation;

2. hold hearings to determine the extent of the surveillance on library users and their communities; and

3. amend or change the sections of these laws and the guidelines that threaten or abridge the rights of inquiry and free expression; and, be it further.

RESOLVED, That this resolution be forwarded to the President of the United States, to the Attorney General of the United States, to Members of both Houses of Congress, to the library community, and to others as appropriate.

Adopted by the ALA Council, January 29, 2003

*The **American Library Association** is a nonprofit organization that supports libraries and library education worldwide. It opposes some provisions of the PATRIOT Act and has tried to work with Congress to change federal law.

American Library Association. "Resolution on the USA PATRIOT Act and Related Measures That Infringe on the Rights of Library Users." January 29, 2003. http://www.ala.org/Template.cfm?Section= ifresolutions&Template=/ContentManagement/ContentDisplay .cfm&ContentID=11891.

# Liberty in the Balance: Librarians Step Up

*by Sam Stanton and Emily Bazar\**

Tucked behind the circulation desk at the library on the campus of California State University, Sacramento, there is a simple red binder labeled "Search Warrant Procedures."

Inside are copies detailing exactly how library workers are to respond if the FBI shows up asking for information about the reading habits of library patrons.

In Santa Monica this summer, the city libraries posted signs: "Attention library patrons: The FBI has the right to obtain a court order to access any records we have of your transactions in the library, a right given to them by Section 215 of the USA Patriot Act."

South Pasadena has done the same, as has Santa Cruz. In Seattle, librarians hand out bookmarks warning patrons that their reading habits may fall into the hands of federal agents.

Across the nation, librarians and bookstore owners have taken to warning patrons that their records are vulnerable to FBI searches under the USA Patriot Act, and many have joined local groups in condemning the law's reach.

"If I read about terrorism, am I a terrorist?" asked Rhonda Rios Kravitz, a librarian at CSUS who is spearheading a whole-sale review of the school's policies on patron privacy. "Should a student's records be subject to subpoena just because they happen to be from Iran or Iraq?"

With the help of a nationwide campaign by the American Civil Liberties Union and other groups, people are asking those questions in metropolitan areas as well as farming communities such as Woodland, where the city library bought a shredding machine in July to dispose of certain records, including sign-up sheets for Internet access.

The impetus is Section 215 of the Patriot Act, which gives the FBI authority to seek a subpoena from the secretive federal anti-terrorism court to obtain virtually any record a library has of readership habits or computer use. Under the provision, the FBI can declare that agents need the information simply as part of a criminal investigation.

"The FBI is not required to show probable cause—or any reason—to believe that the target of the order is a criminal suspect or foreign agent," the ACLU charges in a lawsuit challenging Section 215.

The resulting subpoena can be used in a variety of ways, including seeking library records, banking files, medical information and information from bookstores on what patrons have purchased.

Federal officials say the provision is rooted in the notion that a would-be terrorist seeking information on bomb-making would not use his own computer, but instead would turn to seemingly anonymous terminals and bookshelves in public libraries.

Supporters of the law say the concerns have been blown out of proportion and that Section 215 is being exploited by groups opposed to the Patriot Act.

"The ACLU has done a brilliant job with this," said Larry Brown, the No. 2 official in the U.S. attorney's office in Sacramento. "They're spreading misinformation about it just like they did with the death penalty and 'three strikes.'"

Attorney General John Ashcroft said last week that the "hysteria and hyperbole" over the provision had reached such a pitch he had decided to declassify information on how many times the section has been used.

"The number of times Section 215 has been used to date is zero," Ashcroft wrote in a memo to FBI Director Robert S. Mueller.

Librarians contend, nonetheless, that law enforcement has sought information from them repeatedly since the Sept. 11 attacks. Across the nation, they have joined with bookstore owners, city councils and other local groups struggling to deal with the Patriot Act.

While the law has been roundly criticized by liberal and conservative groups alike, the most controversial part so far has been the power it gives federal agents to probe library records. Section 215 makes it a crime for a librarian even to divulge the fact that agents have delivered a subpoena.

To get around that, some libraries have taken odd steps. In Santa Cruz, for instance, library director Anne Turner has devised this method:

"When I'm reporting to the board, in my standard oral report to the board, I say we've not been contacted by the FBI in the last month," Turner said. "The month I don't say it, the board will know I have been contacted because, of course, I'm not allowed to tell them."

Many librarians say flat out they've never been asked for records, while some others, such as Sacramento Public Library Director Anne Marie Gold, say the law precludes her from even answering the question.

Federal officials say that, in any case, there's no army of agents sifting through your library records or the hard drives of library computers peeking at what you read.

"During my tenure, we have not approached any library for anything," said Michael Mason, who until August was special agent in charge of the Sacramento FBI field office, which oversees an area from the Oregon state line to Bakersfield.

There is a long history of the FBI using information from libraries to conduct probes. The American Library Association and many librarians note that the "Library Awareness Program" was used by agents in the 1970s and 1980s to ferret out information on potential Soviet supporters. Agents routinely would ask for records without a court order.

More recent approaches also have been made, including during the Unabomber probe, when FBI agents visited libraries in the Bay Area and elsewhere seeking names of patrons who might have checked out books named in the bomber's so-called manifesto.

Within a week of the Sept. 11 attacks, someone from the U.S. Air Force visited the Berkeley Public Library and said he was investigating a hacking attempt on Air Force computers by someone using the library's computers, said library director Jackie Griffin.

Griffin said library officials told the Air Force they would be happy to cooperate, but needed a subpoena. The official pressed the case, noting the nation was in the midst of an emergency, but the library would not comply without the subpoena.

"They never came back," Griffin said.

The insistence on officials having some sort of court order to obtain library records is not a whim of librarians.

Forty-eight states have laws protecting the confidentiality of library records, while there are legal opinions in the other two—Kentucky and Hawaii—that say those states' records are confidential also, said Deborah Caldwell-Stone of the American Library Association.

The concern over library records has sparked a bill in Congress by Rep. Bernie Sanders, Ind-Vt., to exempt libraries and bookstores from Section 215.

"One of the cornerstones of our democracy is our right as Americans to criticize our government and to read printed material without fear of government intrusion," Sanders said at a Washington press conference announcing his bill in March. "That's a basic American right."

So far, the measure has attracted 135 co-sponsors, including many who originally voted for the Patriot Act.

Concern over library privacy has spread across the nation, with libraries in unlikely spots taking steps to protect patrons.

In Woodland, for instance, librarian Marie Bryan has been ripping up records by hand as her stand against the Patriot Act. In July, the library received a new shredder to help keep records out of federal hands; its use is legal until the library receives a subpoena seeking information.

"For me, it has been like waiting for the other shoe to drop," Bryan said. "When is someone going to be knocking on the door with search warrants? There have been no requests for information yet. That's a relief, but that doesn't mean it won't happen."

The government has made it clear it believes citizens have no right to expect their library usage or bookstore purchases to be private matters.

In response to questions from the Senate last year about how far the government can go, Assistant Attorney General Daniel J. Bryant said citizens give up certain rights when they check out or buy a book.

"Any right of privacy possessed by library and bookstore patrons in such information is necessarily and inherently limited since, by the nature of these transactions, the patron is reposing that information in the library or bookstore and assumes the risk that the entity may disclose it to another," Bryant wrote in response to the Senate queries.

Nationwide, at least 545 libraries were visited by federal or local law enforcement officials seeking patrons' records in the year after Sept. 11, 2001, according to a University of Illinois study.

In 209 of the libraries, staffers "voluntarily reported patron records or behaviors to authorities in relation to terrorism" rather than require a court order, the study found.

A separate study of 344 public and academic libraries in California found that 16 libraries reported having informal contact with FBI agents since Sept. 11, 2001, and six complied with their requests for information.

That study, conducted for The Bee by the California Library Association, found that 14 libraries reported having "formal" contact with FBI agents during that time, and that 11 complied with the requests.

For the purposes of the survey, a "formal" contact was one involving a court order, said Karen Schneider, chairwoman of the Intellectual Freedom Committee of the California Library Association.

Schneider took issue with Ashcroft's assertion that the FBI has not asked libraries for information under Section 215, saying she found that "highly unlikely." But given the section prohibits librarians from discussing such visits, she said, it is impossible to know for sure what law enforcement is asking for in these visits or what legal authority they are citing.

"This is the whole Catch-22 of 215. You can't talk about it. How are we supposed to know they're happening?" she said.

"That's why Section 215 is bad. It doesn't matter if it's one or 10,000 inquiries, once you start down this slippery slope of gagging people and cloak-and-dagger secrecy, you remove such an important check in the checks and balances of intellectual freedom versus national security that there's bound to be abuse."

The survey, which kept the identities of libraries anonymous, also found that many are taking steps to maintain the privacy of records on who has checked out books or signed up to use computers.

Of those that responded, 78 percent said they shred paper documents such as computer sign-in sheets, while 73 percent delete computer files and logs.

Forty-one percent of the libraries polled said they had implemented new policies as a direct result of the Patriot Act, and most of those said they had altered policies related to patron confidentiality and retention of records to keep them out of the FBI's hands.

"They've really been in a hurry to implement any of the necessary procedures before the knock on the door comes," Schneider said. "It's a tremendously proactive response on the part of the profession. Nationwide, it's typical of what's going on."

The concern among librarians reflects a long-held view that such institutions should be considered inviolate places of learning. A basic premise of academic freedom, they say, is that people should not be afraid to seek knowledge of any subject, and the threat of government snooping violates that notion.

"Libraries have always made it safe for people to look for information in a private way," said Griffin, director of the Berkeley Public Library.

"There's a fundamental idea here that if you look at a site about terrorism or look at a site about how to make a bomb or you look at a site that's about any of these ideas, somehow that's bad in and of itself. People have to have the ability to look and to judge and to find out for themselves. Our best defense against terrorism is to have a well-informed public."

Federal officials seem baffled by the outrage and contend that any use of the provision would be for valid investigative purposes only, not wholesale sweeps.

"Contrary to the perception that the FBI in Anytown, America, is going into the libraries and saying, 'Here's a warrant, we want the names of everybody who checks this book on bomb-making and violent jihad out,' we're going to a federal judge and saying we have reason to believe there's a terrorist cell or this person is a terrorist and that they are using the public library as a base of operations," said Ashcroft spokesman Mark Corallo. "It's a very narrow category."

But that message is met with skepticism in many quarters, including bookstores, where owners say that unless customers pay cash for their purchases their reading habits may be available to federal agents. Neal Coonerty, who owns a bookshop in Santa Cruz, sent newsletters to 10,000 of his customers warning of that possibility.

"We don't believe that reading a murder mystery at the beach here means you're plotting a murder," Coonerty said. "And reading about Hitler doesn't mean you're a Nazi."

To some extent, bookstore patrons are more vulnerable to government probes than those who use libraries, Coonerty said, noting that the Internal Revenue Service requires store owners to save their paperwork for seven years, including cash register tape rolls.

"Unlike libraries, we can't destroy information after the books are sold," he said.

And paying cash isn't always a guarantee of anonymity.

At Coonerty's shop, members of the Frequent Buyers Club receive a 5 percent discount after buying 20 items from the store. Each member is assigned a number, which appears on the cash register receipt along with the names of the books that are purchased.

"That's a problem," Coonerty said, adding that about 10,000 customers belong to the club.

"We can't really change anything. We have to be able to track them. Between the IRS keeping our records for seven years, and our main marketing tool, which is our Frequent Buyers Club for our most important customers, we're sort of stuck."

Determining whether FBI agents have sought information from bookstores is difficult because of the provision that forbids the stores from telling anyone the information is being sought.

"We have advised booksellers that if they receive such an order, they can call us to request legal counsel," said Chris Finan, president of the American Booksellers Foundation for Free Expression. "We have told them they can't tell us what they're calling about."

So far, there are no indications that bookstores have been targeted, Finan said. But he added that there is no way to tell.

"We're unaware of any, which doesn't mean there haven't been any," he said.

*Sam Stanton and Emily Bazar are reporters for the *Sacramento Bee*. Bazar's work has also appeared in the *San Francisco Chronicle*, the *Los Angeles Daily News*, and the California HealthCare Foundation's Center for Health Reporting.

Stanton, Sam, and Emily Bazar. "Liberty in the Balance: Librarians Step Up." *Sacramento Bee*, September 22, 2003. http://www.calstate .edu/pa/clips2003/september/22sept/library.shtml.

# The Proven Tactics in the Fight Against Crime

*by John Ashcroft\**

Good afternoon. Thank you for that introduction, Skip.

It is a pleasure to be here at the National Restaurant Association. I thank all of you for coming to Washington.

The genius of our system of government is that in America, we believe that it is the people who grant the government its powers. We believe that it is the people's values that should be imposed on Washington—not Washington's values on the people.

Your willingness to visit this city is a valuable reminder of the patriotism and entrepreneurship that make this nation great. These are the values that should sustain our hearts and inform our actions in these perilous times.

Of course, Washington is often known as a town filled with debates where people lose sight of the issues most important to the citizens. Your visits and your voices remind this city of the values of the people—the values that are truly important.

Unfortunately, at this moment, Washington is involved in a debate where hysteria threatens to obscure the most important issues.

If you were to listen to some in Washington, you might believe the hysteria behind this claim: "Your local library has been surrounded by the FBI." Agents are working round-the-clock. Like the X-Files, they are dressed in raincoats, dark suits, and sporting sunglasses. They stop patrons and librarians and interrogate everyone like Joe Friday. In a dull monotone they ask every person exiting the library, "Why were you at the library? What were you reading? Did you see anything suspicious?"

According to these breathless reports and baseless hysteria, some have convinced the American Library Association that under the bipartisan Patriot Act, the FBI is not fighting terrorism. Instead, agents are checking how far you have gotten on the latest Tom Clancy novel.

Now you may have thought with all this hysteria and hyperbole, something had to be wrong. Do we at the Justice Department really care what you are reading? No.

The law enforcement community has no interest in your reading habits. Tracking reading habits would betray our high regard for the First Amendment. And even if someone in the government wanted to do so, it would represent an impossible workload and a waste of law enforcement resources.

The fact is that our laws are very particular and very demanding. There are strict legal requirements. A federal judge must first determine that there is an existing investigation of an international terrorist or spy, or a foreign intelligence investigation into a non-U.S. person, and that the business records being sought are relevant to that investigation. Without meeting these legal requirements, obtaining business records, including library records, is not even an option.

With only 11,000 FBI agents in the entire country, it is simply ridiculous to think we could or would track what citizens are reading. I am not in a position to know, but according to the American Library Association there are more than 117,400 libraries in the United States. The American Library Association tells me that Americans visit our nation's libraries more than one billion times a year—1,146,284,000, to be exact. While there, they check out nearly two billion books a year—1,713,967,000, to be precise.

The hysteria is ridiculous. Our job is not.

It is the solemn belief of the United States Department of Justice that the first and primary responsibility of government is: to preserve the lives and protect the liberty of the people.

No one believes in our First Amendment civil liberties more than this administration. It is what we are fighting for in this war against tyranny. On my watch, we seek a war for justice that reflects the noblest ideals and highest standards set by the United States Constitution. I would not support or invite any change that might restructure or endanger our individual liberties and personal freedoms.

It would be a tragedy if the hysteria surrounding certain aspects of our war against terror were to obscure the important evidence that the Department of Justice has protected the lives and liberties of the citizenry [...].

[...]

In every corner of the nation and at every level of government, the justice community has worked together, shared information, and struck at terrorist cells who would do us harm. Law enforcement has embraced the tools and spirit of the Patriot Act by communicating information, coordinating their efforts, and cooperating toward our integrated strategy of preventing terrorism. This has meant smarter, better-focused law enforcement—law enforcement that targets terrorists and secures our borders, letting hard-working immigrants and free trade prosper in a nation blessed by freedom.

In fact, the results of our anti-terrorism efforts are just as impressive and just as undeniable as our success in driving crime to a 30-year low.

All told, two-thirds of Al Qaeda's senior leadership have been captured or killed. And more than 3,000 suspected terrorists have been arrested in countries around the world. Many more have met a different fate.

Specifically:

- We have dismantled terrorist operations in New York, Michigan, Washington State, Oregon, and North Carolina;

- We have brought criminal charges against 262 individuals;

- 143 individuals have been convicted or pled guilty, including shoe-bomber Richard Reid, "American Taliban" John Walker Lindh, six members of the Buffalo cell, and two members of the Detroit cell;

- We have deported more than 515 individuals with links to the September 11th investigation; and

- We have stopped more than $200 million from funding terrorist groups.

This nation has never asked more of the men and women of law enforcement. And law enforcement has never achieved more than these past few years.

At every level of law enforcement, in every area of fighting crime, we have committed ourselves to a new strategy—a strategy of prevention. It is rooted in our Constitutional liberties, built on communication and cooperation and driven by the courage and integrity of the men and women of law enforcement. From the FBI in Washington to the local cop with his feet on the street, we owe our thanks for their hard work and respect for freedom and the law.

By attacking crime and terrorist operations at every point of vulnerability, we have communicated to the lawful and the lawless that in America we will fight to preserve lives and protect liberty.

[...]

*John Ashcroft served as the United States attorney general during the administration of Pres. George W. Bush. He is a former governor and senator from Missouri. In 2005, he founded The Ashcroft Group, LLC, a strategy firm specializing in lobbying.

Ashcroft, John. "The Proven Tactics in the Fight Against Crime." Prepared remarks before the National Restaurant Association, Washington, D.C., September 15, 2003. http://www.justice.gov/archive/ag/speeches/2003/091503nationalrestaurant.htm.

# Debate on Sanders Amendment

**Mr. WOLF.** Mr. Chairman, I yield myself such time as I may consume before I recognize the gentleman from North Carolina (Mr. Coble), to respond.

We just received a letter from the Justice Department, and I wanted to read it for the Members.

It said, "In anticipation of the U.S. House of Representatives' consideration of an amendment that would prevent the Justice Department from obtaining records from public libraries and book stores under section 215 of the USA PATRIOT Act, your staff has recently inquired about whether terrorists have ever utilized public library facilities to communicate with others about committing acts of terrorism. The short answer is 'yes.'"

The letter continued: "You should know that we have confirmed that, as recently as this past winter and spring, a member of a terrorist group closely affiliated with al Qaeda used Internet services provided by a public library. This terrorist used the library's computer to communicate with his confederates. Beyond this we are unable to comment."

**Mr. WOLF.** Mr. Chairman, I yield 2 minutes to the gentleman from North Carolina (Mr. Coble).

**Mr. COBLE.** Mr. Chairman, I thank the gentleman from Virginia for yielding me this time.

Mr. Chairman, reasonable men and women can disagree, and hopefully disagree agreeably, and this is a situation where this is going to happen. I think convincing arguments can be made on each side of the issue. And I do not want to sound like I am knee-jerking responding to this, but should terrorists be able to use taxpayer-funded public library facilities to plot a major attack without fear they will be investigated by the FBI?

I think that could come to play if this amendment is, in fact, enacted. As I understand my friend from Vermont, the amendment would exempt public libraries and book stores from section 215 of the USA PATRIOT Act, which permits the FBI, after obtaining a Federal court order, and I repeat, after obtaining a Federal court order, to obtain documents and other records relevant to international terrorism and espionage cases. Now, there has been no abuse in this matter, Mr. Chairman. On September 18 of last year, the number of times to date that the Justice Department had utilized section 215 of the USA PATRIOT Act relating to the production of business records was declassified, and at that time it was made known that the number of times section 215 had been used as of that date was zero. So, obviously, there is no abuse here.

Furthermore, section 215, Mr. Chairman, provides for a thorough congressional oversight. Every 6 months the Attorney General is required to inform the Congress on the number of times agents have sought a court order under section 215, as well as the number of times its requests were granted, modified, or denied. No abuse at all on this. And I just believe we should vote down the amendment.

**Mr. SANDERS.** Mr. Chairman, I yield myself 15 seconds before I yield to the gentleman from New York (Mr. Nadler) to tell my friends that it is not accurate that under this amendment that the FBI cannot go into libraries and book stores. They sure can. They can get subpoenas. They can go to the grand jury. They can do it in the conventional way. We have no objection to that. But they cannot have a carte blanche, no probable cause to check on the reading records of the American people.

Mr. Chairman, I yield 2 minutes to the gentleman from New York (Mr. Nadler).

**Mr. NADLER.** Mr. Chairman, we have to be very careful that because of this war on the Islamic terrorists we do not destroy our own civil liberties. The PATRIOT Act was passed in great haste, and parts of it do exactly that.

The gentleman from Virginia says this amendment should not be considered without hearings by the Committee on the Judiciary and given proper consideration, but the fact is there were no hearings before we passed the PATRIOT Act. The PATRIOT Act was warm to the touch. No one read it before it passed this House. No one knew what was in it. The bill that came out of committee was not the bill considered by the House. So that is where the original flaw lies.

We should now pass this amendment not to make libraries an exempt zone. As the sponsor, the gentleman from Vermont (Mr. Sanders), said, police will still be able to obtain records, so long as they can justify their actions based on probable cause. What is the difference if this amendment passes? The difference is between good police work and a fishing expedition.

Do we want the government rummaging through the records of average Americans without reason, or do we want to insist at the very least that searches be based on probable cause? That is the issue. That is the issue: probable cause.

The Supreme Court of the United States, the Rehnquist court, gave a rap in the teeth to the administration last week for claiming powers that no executive in an English-speaking society has claimed since before Magna Carta. We do not want tyranny. We do not want tyranny.

This amendment is designed to say you can read without being afraid the government will someday reveal what you are reading. We do not want the chilling effect on free speech. If there is a real reason, if the government suspects someone is looking up how to make atom bombs, go to a court and get a search warrant, show probable cause. That is the way it worked for 200 years. It worked against the Nazis in World War II, it worked in the Civil War, and it will work today. We need not surrender fundamental liberty, and we should not.

That is what this amendment is about, and that is why we should urge its adoption.

**Mr. WOLF.** Mr. Chairman, I yield 3 minutes to the gentleman from Connecticut (Mr. Shays).

**Mr. SHAYS.** Mr. Chairman, I thank the gentleman for yielding me this time.

I have 70 constituents who lost their rights on September 11; and to hear this debate, I am not sure we seem to care about that. Something told me on September 11 that we had received a wake-up call from hell, and that wake-up call from hell indicated we have to detect and prevent, because the old Cold War philosophy of contain and react and mutually assured destruction went out the window.

On an appropriations bill, we are trying to amend the PATRIOT Act because some librarians find it offensive that we may want to go in and find out who a terrorist talks with when they use a computer, and we are going to have another amendment that basically says we need to tell them first that we think they are a terrorist.

If we are going to detect and prevent, we have to break into these cells, and the only alternative left if we see this amendment pass is that we would then have to go before a grand jury and state our case, without probable cause, I might add, but state our case when we are talking about significant national security issues. We may be talking about a chemical weapon, a nuclear weapon. We may be talking about a biological agent. We may be talking about breaking into a cell to prevent that, and yet we are going to be told now we need to go before a grand jury to do the same things we can do in ordinary criminal cases.

I am amazed beyond comprehension at the lack of recognition that it is not a question of if; it is a question of when, where, and what magnitude we are going to have to face these kinds of attacks.

And I know what is going to happen when these attacks happen. There will be Members coming back to the floor saying how come the CIA did not know? How come our intelligence community did not know? Why did they fail us again? And we are going to tie their hands behind their backs anyway and say we have to let a terrorist know first before we break into a terrorist cell.

The gentleman from Vermont (Mr. Sanders) can throw his hands any way he wants, but the bottom line is we are at war with terrorists and we want to break into those cells and detect what is going on; and we sure as hell do not want to tell them we're coming.

Debate on the floor of the United States House of Representatives, July 8, 2004. Concerning Senator Sanders's proposed amendment to the USA PATRIOT Act. *Congressional Record,* 108th Cong., pp. H5349–5351.

# Speech on the USA PATRIOT Act to the University of Wisconsin Chapter of the Federalist Society

*by F. James Sensenbrenner, Jr.\**

Good afternoon. I appreciate the opportunity to address the University of Wisconsin Chapter of the Federalist Society to discuss the USA PATRIOT Act.

The attacks of September 11, 2001, tragically affirmed the urgency of updating our laws to address the clear and present danger presented by international terrorism. The 19 hijackers and other terrorists were too easily able to exploit the divisions between our law enforcement and intelligence communities. This limited the dissemination of vital and timely information and increased America's vulnerability to terrorist attack.

Following the 9/11 terrorist attacks that killed 3,000 innocent Americans, I drafted the PATRIOT Act. Congress worked with the Administration around the clock to craft this law as expeditiously as possible, while at the same time ensuring civil liberties protections for all American citizens.

The PATRIOT Act has helped keep America safe from another attack the last eight years. This historic legislation provides law enforcement and intelligence agencies additional tools that are needed to address the threat of terrorism and to find and prosecute terrorist criminals. It knocked down that wall that prohibited law enforcement and intelligence communities from effectively sharing information, and it enhanced the investigatory tools necessary to assess, detect, and prevent future attacks.

While we've been fortunate in not being attacked, terrorists have not given up since their successful attacks in 2001. Attacks continue throughout the world. London's subway system was attacked. Madrid bombings brought terror to the people in Spain. And just weeks ago our intelligence agencies foiled another plot that stretched from New York City to Denver.

After passing the PATRIOT Act in 2001, I pledged to use my position as Chairman of the House Judiciary Committee to rigorously examine the law's implementation. I included a sunset provision so Congress would have the opportunity to review the Act and make corrections as needed. In 2005, I again spearheaded the effort to reauthorize the PATRIOT Act. Recognizing the significance of the Act to America's counter-terrorism operations and the need for thorough oversight, in 2005 my committee held 12 hearings and heard from 35 witnesses when we completed the reauthorization.

The PATRIOT Act has three provisions set to expire at the end of this year, and the clock is ticking. In less than three months, the tools used to prevent another horrific attack on America will expire. FBI Director Mueller, in his recent testimony before the Senate Judiciary Committee, urged Congress to renew what he called "exceptional" intelligence-gathering tools.

In recent weeks, the Obama Administration finally made public its views on the three expiring provisions. I am dismayed as to why it took nine months to assess just three measures. But I commend the administration for recognizing the value of these important national security tools and for rightly urging Congress to reauthorize each of them. The administration has also promised to reject any changes to these or other PATRIOT Act provisions that would undermine their effectiveness.

[...]

Section 215 of the Act allows the FBI to apply to the FISA court to issue orders granting the government access to any tangible items in foreign intelligence, international terrorism, and clandestine intelligence cases. The USA PATRIOT Improvement and Reauthorization Act of 2005 significantly expanded the safeguards against potential abuse of Section 215 authority, including additional Congressional oversight, procedural protections, application requirements, and judicial review. FBI Director Mueller noted before the House Judiciary Committee that the business records provision "has been exceptionally useful for us over the period of time that it has been on the record books and we have used it over 230 times."

There has been plenty of interest and debate about the PATRIOT Act's civil liberty protections and constitutionality. Congress has a substantial record of bipartisan letters sent to the Justice Department, Inspector General reports, and hearing records that have accumulated thousands of pages.

The PATRIOT Act contained 16 provisions that were scheduled to be sunsetted. 13 of the 16 provisions were not controversial. At the request of Senator Dianne Feinstein of California, the Justice Department issued a report analyzing each of the sixteen provisions.

In addition to this report, the Attorney General submits semi-annual reports to the Permanent Select Committee on Intelligence of the House of Representatives and the

Select Committee on Intelligence of the Senate regarding the Department's use of the Foreign Intelligence Surveillance Act.

Furthermore, Section 1001 of the USA PATRIOT Act requires the Department's Office of Inspector General to submit to the House and Senate Judiciary Committees on a semi-annual basis a report detailing any abuses of civil rights and civil liberties by Department employees or officials. 15 reports have been submitted by the Office of the Inspector General, with the most recent one summarizing the OIG's Section 1001-related activities from January 1, 2009, through June 30, 2009. To date, the Office of the Inspector General has not documented any abuse of civil rights or civil liberties by the Department related to the use of any substantive provision of the USA PATRIOT Act.

[...]

Besides the NSLs, perhaps the one provision that has received the most attention in the PATRIOT Act is Section 215. This section allows the FISA court to order the production of business records and other items, in the context of a national security investigation, to obtain foreign intelligence information not concerning a U.S. person; or to protect against international terrorism or clandestine intelligence activities. Section 215 cannot be used to investigate ordinary crimes or domestic terrorism, and it is expressly provided that the FBI cannot conduct an investigation on a U.S. citizen solely on the basis of activities protected by the First Amendment.

Section 215 has gained notoriety as the so-called "library provision." In 2001, Section 215 of the USA PATRIOT ACT made several changes to the procedures under FISA for obtaining business records. Among these was an expansion of the scope of records that were subject to compulsory production.

Prior to enactment of the USA PATRIOT ACT, only records from four explicit categories of businesses could be obtained. Section 215 expanded business records to "any tangible things."

This expanded scope drew strong opposition from the library community, so much so that Section 215 came to be known as the "library provision" despite the fact that the original text of the provision did not mention libraries. Opposition from this group was based upon the alleged "chilling effect" such access could have on the exercise of First Amendment rights and purported intrusions into areas protected by the Fourth Amendment.

In response to these concerns, a library-specific amendment was made to the § 215 procedures by the USA PATRIOT Improvement and Reauthorization Act of 2005. Under this amendment, if the records sought were "library circulation records, library patron lists, book sales records, book customer lists, firearms sales records, tax return records, educational records, or medical records containing information that would identify a person," the application has to be approved by one of three high-ranking FBI officers.

[ ... ]

Most of the USA PATRIOT Act's sunsetted provisions have not been constitutionally challenged. Others initially challenged have seen those challenges withdrawn. The only two provisions that have been struck down—FISA provisions and NSLs—existed long before the PATRIOT Act passed in October 2001.

The PATRIOT Act sets expiration dates on certain provisions, but I believed in 2001, as I do today, that congressional oversight of the entire Act must be perpetual.

Let me conclude with the following point: for too long opponents of the PATRIOT Act have transformed it into a grossly distorted caricature that bears no relationship whatsoever to the legislation itself. The PATRIOT Act has been misused by some as a springboard to launch limitless allegations that are not only unsubstantiated but are false and irresponsible. The fact remains that the USA PATRIOT Act is vital to maintaining America's safety.

[...]

*F. James Sensenbrenner is a United States representative from Wisconsin. He was chair of the House Judiciary Committee in 2001 and helped write the PATRIOT Act.

Sensenbrenner, F. James. "Speech on the USA PATRIOT Act to the University of Wisconsin Chapter of the Federalist Society." Madison, WI, October 12, 2009. http://sensenbrenner.house.gov/news/documentsingle.aspx?DocumentID=149591.

# PART 3

# Gag Orders and Government Secrecy

At the same time that the 2001 PATRIOT Act was expanding government surveillance of Americans, it gave the government permission to keep its own activities secret. One way it did this was to expand the FBI's authority to issue National Security Letters (NSLs). Gregory T. Nojeim, director of the Project on Freedom, Security & Technology for the Center for Democracy & Technology, argues ("Statement of Gregory T. Nojeim") that, as a result of changes made by the PATRIOT Act, NSLs have become a threat to free speech because they can be used to secretly collect sensitive information about people engaged in First Amendment-protected activities, including protests against the government. The PATRIOT

Act authorizes the FBI to use NSLs to search the records of anyone who is "relevant to" a terrorism investigation, including those who are not suspected of a crime. Since 9/11, the agency has issued more than 300,000 NSLs.

NSLs became a free speech issue because they prohibit recipients from revealing that their records have been searched; these gag orders are permanent. In 2004, the American Civil Liberties Union (ACLU) challenged the constitutionality of the NSL gag orders because they are a "prior restraint" on speech. Prior restraints are a greater threat to free speech than other types of restrictions because they prohibit a person from speaking until a judge decides it is permissible. Because this can cause a prolonged ban, the courts usually overturn prior restraints as violations of the First Amendment. In the ACLU case, which was filed on behalf of a client who was identified as John Doe because he was forbidden to identify himself, David W. Szady, an assistant director of the FBI, submitted a written statement about the importance of secrecy in the fight against terrorism, ("Declaration in *John Doe*..."). In his ruling ("Opinion: *John Doe*"), however, U.S. District Court Judge Victor Marrero declared the gag order to be an unconstitutional prior restraint. Marrero was also deeply troubled by the potential use of NSLs to identify and punish people engaged in free speech on the Internet.

The following year, four Connecticut librarians joined the ACLU in challenging an NSL that had been issued to Library Connection, a consortium that provides electronic services, including Internet access, to a number of library systems. The FBI was seeking information about a patron who it claimed had used a library computer "to send information about a potential terrorist threat." The librarians asked the court to lift their gag orders so they could reveal the fact that they had received an NSL. When the government finally agreed to let them speak, George Christian, director of Library Connection, explained during a Senate hearing that the librarians had wanted to rebut Attorney General John Ashcroft's claim that the FBI was not using the PATRIOT Act to search library records ("Testimony by George Christian"). At the time, Congress was debating reauthorization of the PATRIOT Act, and the librarians hoped their experiences would help to make changes in the law. However, by the time the gag orders were removed, the reauthorization had been passed.

Civil libertarians have also objected to the fact that the FBI does not need a judge's approval to issue NSLs, arguing that this increases the likelihood that the agency will abuse its power. Congress ordered the inspector general of the Department of Justice to conduct audits to determine how the department was using the powers it was granted under the PATRIOT Act. The audits revealed evidence of widespread mismanagement by the FBI. The ACLU summarized the audits in a report, "Evidence of Abuse: The Inspector General Audits National Security Letters." In a "Statement Before the Senate Committee on the Judiciary" in March 2007, FBI Director Robert S. Mueller III did not disagree with the inspector general but insisted that the bureau had not broken the law intentionally and would do better in the future

The number of NSLs issued by the FBI has declined from a peak of 49,425 in 2006 to 15,229 in 2012. However, the legal challenges to their constitutionality continue. In March 2013, a second federal judge ruled that NSLs violate the First Amendment. The government is appealing her decision.

Here are questions to think about as you read this section:

- Does the government need secrecy?

- Why are gag orders a threat to free speech?

- Were the Connecticut librarians right to challenge their NSLs?

# Statement of Gregory T. Nojeim

*by Gregory T. Nojeim\**

[...]

## The Evolution of NSLs: Broad Scope + Low Standards + Secrecy + Indefinite Retention + Widespread Sharing = A Privacy Nightmare

It is helpful first to recall how we arrived at this point. National Security Letters, which started out quite modestly, have grown into something of a monstrosity. Cumulatively, a series of factors have combined to produce a "perfect storm" of intrusive and inadequately controlled power.

The intelligence investigations in which NSLs are issued are not only secretive and long running but also encompass purely legal, even political activity. The PATRIOT Act seriously weakened the standard for issuance of NSLs, loosened internal oversight, and allowed NSLs to be used to get sensitive records on innocent persons suspected of absolutely no involvement in terrorism or espionage. The Intelligence Authorization Act for FY 2004 dramatically expanded the scope of NSLs, so they can now be served on the US Postal Service, insurance companies, travel agents, jewelers, and car dealers, among others. Moreover, agencies other than the FBI have been authorized to issue NSLs, and the number of government officials who can authorize NSLs has been expanded.

In addition, the digital revolution has put in the hands of banks, credit card companies, telephone companies, Internet Service Providers, insurance companies, and travel agents a wealth of information, rich in what it reveals about our daily lives. Information that was previously stored on paper files or incompatible electronic formats is now far easier to transfer, store, manipulate and analyze.

These realities are compounded by the fact that the FBI keeps records for a very long time, even when it concludes that the person to whom the information pertains is innocent of any crime and is not of any continuing intelligence interest. Information is increasingly being shared across agency boundaries, but without audit trails or the ability to reel back erroneous or misleading information, or information that is about people who are of no continuing criminal or intelligence interests. Finally, the PATRIOT reauthorization act made many NSLs for the first time ever compulsory and placed criminal penalties on violation of the non-disclosure requirement (commonly known as a "gag"), changes that probably make it even less likely NSLs will be challenged.

Some of these developments are outside the government's control, driven by changes in technology and business. Some are desirable. Notably, information sharing is needed if we are to connect the dots to prevent terrorist attacks, although legislative and Presidential mandates recognize that information sharing carries threats to privacy. In other regards, the technological and legal changes outlined above may in fact hamper the effectiveness of the government, drowning it in irrelevant information.

Taken together, however, these changes have made National Security Letters a risky power that sits outside the normal privacy rules. Left over from the pre-digital era, they should be replaced with a system of expeditious prior judicial approval when used to seek sensitive personal information.

Undeniably, terrorism poses a serious, continuing threat to our nation. Undeniably, the FBI needs prompt access to some of the kinds of information currently acquired under NSLs. However, given the precipitous legislative weakening of the NSL standards, changes in technology outlined above, and the findings of the IG reports, it is time to conclude that NSLs are in need of a major overhaul.

Self-policing doesn't work. Investigative techniques involving government collection of sensitive information require checks and balances, and those checks and balances must involve all three branches of government. CDT has long recommended adoption of a system of prior judicial approval, based on a factual showing, for access to sensitive information (excluding subscriber identifying information), with a reasonable exception for emergency situations. Going to a judge makes a difference, in a way that is unachievable by merely internal reviews. In an era of cell phones, BlackBerries and ubiquitous Internet access, there is no reason why a system of judicial review and consistent, searching Congressional oversight cannot be designed to serve the government's legitimate needs. In an age where our lives are stored with banks, credit card companies and insurance companies, such a system is vitally needed to protect privacy.

## What Is a National Security Letter?

National Security Letters are simple form documents signed by officials of the FBI and other agencies, with no judicial approval, compelling disclosure of sensitive information held by banks, credit companies, telephone carriers and Internet Service Providers, among others. [ ... ]

[ ... ]

Recipients of NSLs are usually gagged from disclosing the fact or nature of a request.

## The PATRIOT Act Dramatically Weakened the Standard for NSLs

Before the PATRIOT Act, the FBI and other governmental agencies could issue NSLs only if there was a factual basis for believing that the records pertained to a suspected spy or possible terrorist (in statutory terms, an "agent of a foreign power"). The PATRIOT Act eliminated both prongs of that standard:

- The PATRIOT Act eliminated the requirement that agents provide any factual basis for seeking records. Whatever internal requirements the FBI or another agency may have, there is no statutory requirement that the government articulate the facts showing why it wants the records it seeks.

- The PATRIOT Act eliminated the requirement that the information being sought "pertain to" a foreign power or the agent of a foreign power. Instead, it is sufficient for the FBI to merely assert that the records are "relevant to" an investigation to protect against international terrorism or foreign espionage.

- The PATRIOT Act also expanded FBI issuing authority beyond FBI headquarter officials to include the heads of the FBI field offices (i.e., Special Agents in Charge).

Thus the PATRIOT Act eliminated any effective standard from the NSL authorities. Now, the main requirement is that the FBI must state for internal purposes that the records are "relevant to" or "sought for" foreign counter intelligence or terrorism purposes. Since foreign counterintelligence and terrorism investigations can investigate lawful, even political conduct, and since the FBI conducts wide-ranging investigations on an ongoing basis of many terrorist groups, the requirement that the agents state that the records are sought in connection with some investigation is not a meaningful limit. (Remarkably, the DOJ Inspector General found that FBI agents had issued NSLs without complying even with this minimal administrative requirement.) The requirement that issuance of an NSL for records about a U.S. person not be based solely on First Amendment activities affords very limited protection. It is generally easy for an agent to point to other circumstances that warrant the inquiry.

With these changes, field offices can issue NSLs without providing to anyone outside the Bureau any fact-based explanation as to why the records are sought, and the records sought can be about any person, even someone not suspected of being a terrorist or spy.

[...]

## The PATRIOT Reauthorization Act Further Expanded the NSL Power

[...]

The PATRIOT reauthorization act also made it clear that businesses that receive NSLs can challenge them, but this option is not a meaningful protection. Few businesses that receive NSLs have the incentive to challenge them: the cost of providing the records is far less than the cost of hiring a lawyer to challenge the request; the requests are secret, so customers never learn of them and companies cooperating with the government do not have to justify compliance; and the companies that comply have immunity, so even if a customer found out, there would be no statutory remedy against the company that disclosed the records. As we learn from the IG's reports, some companies actually get paid by the government to turn over records pursuant to NSLs.

[...]

## Intelligence Investigations Require More Control, Not Less

Proponents of NSLs frequently argue that they are just like subpoenas in criminal cases, which are issued without prior judicial review. However, intelligence investigations are more dangerous to liberty than criminal investigations—they are broader, they can encompass First Amendment activities, they are more secretive and they are less subject to after-the-fact scrutiny—and therefore intelligence powers require stronger compensating protections.

First, intelligence investigations are broader. They are not limited by the criminal code. They can investigate legal activity. In the case of foreign nationals in the United States, they can focus solely on First Amendment activities. Even in the case of U.S. persons, they can collect information about First

Amendment activities, so long as First Amendment activities are not the sole basis of the investigation.

Secondly, intelligence investigations are conducted in much greater secrecy than criminal cases, even perpetual secrecy. When a person receives a grand jury subpoena or an administrative subpoena in an administrative proceeding, normally he can publicly complain about it. In a criminal case, even the target of the investigation is often notified while the investigation is underway. Most searches in criminal cases are carried out with simultaneous notice to the target. In intelligence cases, in contrast, neither the target nor any of the individuals scrutinized because of their contacts with the target are ever told of the government's collection of information about them. The businesses that are normally the recipients of NSLs are effectively gagged from complaining and are perpetually blocked from notifying their customers that their records have been turned over to the government.

Third, in a criminal investigation almost everything the government does is ultimately exposed to scrutiny (or is locked up under the rule of grand jury secrecy). A prosecutor knows that, at the end of the criminal process, his actions will all come out in public. If he is overreaching, if he went on a fishing expedition, that will all be aired, and he will face public scrutiny and even ridicule. That's a powerful constraint. Similarly, an administrative agency like the SEC or the FTC must ultimately account in public for its actions, its successes and its failures. But most intelligence investigations never result in a trial or other public proceeding. The evidence is used clandestinely. Sometimes the desired result is the mere sense that the government is watching.

Since intelligence investigations are broader, more secretive and subject to less probing after-the-fact scrutiny, protections must be built in at the beginning.

[ ... ]

*Gregory T. Nojeim** is a senior counsel at the Center for Democracy & Technology, a nonprofit organization focused on promoting democratic values. He directs its Project on Freedom, Security & Technology and has worked to protect individual privacy from government intrusion.

Statement of Gregory T. Nojeim, Director Project on Freedom, Security & Technology Center for Democracy & Technology, before the Senate Judiciary Committee. April 23, 2008. National Security Letters, The Need for Greater Accountability and Oversight. 110th Congress. https://www.cdt.org/files/pdfs/20080421_nsl_testimony.pdf.

# Declaration in *John Doe;*
# *American Civil Liberties Union;*
# *and American Civil Liberties Union*
# *Foundation v. John Ashcroft*

*by David W. Szady**

David W. Szady, pursuant to 28 U.S.C. Section 1746, declares the following under penalty of perjury:

1. I am the Assistant Director of the Counterintelligence Division of the Federal Bureau of Investigation ("FBI"), United States Department of Justice. [...]

2. I have over 30 years of service with the FBI including 25 years experience in espionage and foreign counterintelligence investigations. During my career, I have served as Assistant Special Agent in Charge of the FBI's San Francisco Division with responsibility for foreign counterintelligence and terrorism programs, and as chief of the Central Intelligence Agency's ("CIA") Counterintelligence Counterespionage Group.

[...]

## The Nature of Foreign Intelligence and Counter-Terrorism Investigations and the Need for Secrecy in Conducting Such Investigations

[...]

6. The United States government is conducting extensive, world-wide investigations into threats, conspiracies, and attempts to perpetrate terrorist acts and foreign intelligence operations against the United States and its interests abroad. The FBI has been actively conducting its investigations in conjunction with other federal, state and local agencies. Approximately 2,500 FBI agents are engaged in an unprecedented world-wide effort to prevent terrorist attacks by apprehending those responsible for past attacks and by detecting, disrupting, and dismantling terrorist organizations.

[...]

8. Counterintelligence and counter-terrorism investigations are different in key respects from traditional criminal investigations. The primary objective of such investigations is not to gather evidence for prosecution of past crimes, but rather to disrupt and interdict clandestine intelligence activities and terrorist acts *before* they occur. Counterintelligence and counter-terrorism investigations are thus forward looking, and often long range. [...]

9. Accordingly, secrecy in conducting such foreign counterintelligence and counter-terrorism investigations is essential. If targets learn that they are the subjects of investigation, they will likely take action to avoid detection or to disrupt the Government's

intelligence gathering. This could include the target's abscondment, destruction of damaging evidence, creation of false evidence, or use of different methods of communications.

10. It is also essential that the foreign intelligence and terrorist organizations not learn the scope, focus, or progress of any particular investigation. Armed with such knowledge, these organizations could take action to avoid further detection or to subvert the Government's attempts to thwart any particular planned terrorist act or clandestine intelligence operations. [...]

11. As the FBI has determined through its past and ongoing counter-terrorism and counterintelligence investigations, terrorist and foreign intelligence organizations have the sophistication and capability to closely analyze publicly available information concerning the United States' intelligence gathering activities. Terrorist and foreign intelligence organizations can and do piece together publicly available information— sometimes seemingly innocuous details standing on their own—to determine the scope, focus, and progress of ongoing [...] investigations, and can thereafter use such information to circumvent and disrupt the investigations.

12. Although some general information about how the United States conducts its investigations in publicly available, it is essential that terrorist and foreign counterintelligence organizations not learn exactly how the Government uses its investigative tools. [...]

[...]

## Risks Associated with Disclosure of NSLs

[...]

18.  The broad non-disclosure provision in Section 2709(c) is critical to ensure the integrity and efficacy of [...] investigations. Disclosure of the FBI's issuance or use of a particular NSL could compromise [...] investigations in a variety of ways.

19.  Disclosure of a particular NSL seeking information about a person who is the target of a[n] [...] investigation could alert the target that he or she is being investigated by the FBI. The target could then take action to avoid further investigation or to disrupt the ongoing investigation. For example, the target could stop using the particular communication services related to the NSL, thereby impeding the FBI"s ability to monitor his or her activities and to identify other co-conspirators with whom the target is corresponding. [...]

20.  Disclosure of a particular NSL [...] could also allow terrorist and foreign intelligence organizations to know that a particular operative is under investigation. Armed with that information, these organizations could substitute another operative for the target, warn operatives who are in contact with the target that they may also be the target of investigation or use the target to disseminate false information to thwart the FBI's investigation.

21.  Even if an NSL seeks information about a person who is not the direct target of an FBI investigation, disclosure of the NSL could allow the person to warn others. [...]

[...]

## Need for Continuing Non-Disclosure of NSLs

29. Regardless of whether the subject of an NSL remains the target of an ongoing [ ... ] investigation, the critical need for non-disclosure of NSLs continues.

[ ... ]

31. Thus, for example, even if the subject of an NSL were arrested and prosecuted, that person may have been in communication with co-conspirators through the services described in the NSL. The FBI's NSL inquiry must remain confidential, to ensure that co-conspirators do not learn that the FBI is aware of the fact that they communicated with the person about who information was sought through the NSL.

32. In addition, an NSL might have been issued based on information provided by a confidential informant; disclosure of the NSL at any time could lead to identification of the confidential informant and retaliation against the informant and/or his family.

[ ... ]

*David W. Szady was the Federal Bureau of Investigation's assistant director for counterintelligence from 2001 to 2006.

Declaration of David W. Szady. *American Civil Liberties Union and American Civil Liberties Union Foundation v. Ashcroft,* June 20, 2004. http://www.aclu.org/files/nsl/legal/5b_DeclDavidWSzady.pdf.

# Opinion: *John Doe; American Civil Liberties Union; and American Civil Liberties Union Foundation v. John Ashcroft*

*by Victor Marrero**

[...]

Plaintiffs in this case challenge the constitutionality of 18 U.S.C. § 2709 ("§ 2709"). That statute authorizes the Federal Bureau of Investigation ("FBI") to compel communications firms, such as internet service providers ("ISPs") or telephone companies, to produce certain customer records whenever the FBI certifies that those records are "relevant to an authorized investigation to protect against international terrorism or clandestine intelligence activities." The FBI's demands under § 2709 are issued in the form of national security letters ("NSLs"), which constitute a unique form of administrative subpoena cloaked in secrecy and pertaining to national security issues. The statute bars all NSL recipients from ever disclosing that the FBI has issued an NSL.

The lead plaintiff, called "John Doe" ("Doe") for purposes of this litigation, is described in the complaint as an internet access firm that received an NSL. The other plaintiffs are the American Civil Liberties Union ("ACLU") and the American Civil Liberties Union Foundation, which is also acting as counsel to Doe (collectively with Doe, "Plaintiffs"). Plaintiffs contend that § 2709's broad subpoena power violates the First, Fourth and Fifth Amendments of the United States Constitution, and that the non-disclosure provision violates the First Amendment. They argue that § 2709 is unconstitutional on its face and as applied to the facts of this case. Plaintiffs' main complaints are that, first, § 2709 gives the FBI extraordinary and unchecked power to obtain private information without any form of judicial process, and, second, that § 2709's non-disclosure provision burdens speech categorically and perpetually, without any case-by-case judicial consideration of whether that speech burden is justified. The parties have cross-moved for summary judgment on all claims.

For the reasons explained below, the Court grants Plaintiffs' motion. The Court concludes that § 2709 violates the Fourth Amendment because, at least as currently applied, it effectively bars or substantially deters any judicial challenge to the propriety of an NSL request. In the Court's view, ready availability of judicial process to pursue such a challenge is necessary to vindicate important rights guaranteed by the Constitution or by statute. On separate grounds, the Court also concludes that the permanent ban on disclosure contained in § 2709(c), which the Court is unable to sever from the remainder of the statute, operates as an unconstitutional prior restraint on speech in violation of the First Amendment. [ ... ]

[ ... ]

In particular, the Court agrees with Plaintiffs that § 2709(c), the non-disclosure provision, is unconstitutional. In simplest terms, § 2709(c) fails to pass muster under the exacting First Amendment standards applicable here because it is so broad and open-ended. In its all-inclusive sweep, it prohibits the NSL recipient, or its officers, employees, or agents, from revealing the existence of an NSL inquiry the FBI pursued under § 2709 in every case, to any person, in perpetuity, with no vehicle for the ban to ever be lifted from the recipient or other persons affected, under any circumstances, either by the FBI itself, or pursuant to judicial process. Because the Court cannot sever § 2709(c) from § 2709(a) and (b), the Court grants the remedy Plaintiffs request enjoining the Government from using § 2709 in this or any other case as a means of gathering information from the sources specified in the statute. [ ... ]

## NSLs May Violate ISP Subscribers' Rights.

Plaintiffs have focused on the possibility that § 2709 could be used to infringe subscribers' First Amendment rights of anonymous speech and association. Though it is not necessary to precisely define the scope of ISP subscribers' First Amendment rights, the Court concludes that § 2709 may, in a given case, violate a subscriber's First Amendment privacy rights, as well as other legal rights, if judicial review is not readily available to an ISP that receives an NSL. This conclusion buttresses the Court's holding that, at least as applied, § 2709 does not permit sufficient judicial review to preserve individual subscribers' rights, where impairment of such rights may be implicated by a given NSL.

The Supreme Court has recognized the First Amendment right to anonymous speech at least since *Talley v. California,* which invalidated a California law requiring that handbills distributed to the public contain certain identifying information about the source of the handbills. The Court stated that the "identification requirement would tend to restrict freedom to distribute information and thereby freedom of expression."

The Supreme Court has also invalidated identification requirements pertaining to persons distributing campaign literature, persons circulating petitions for state ballot initiatives, and persons engaging in door-to-door religious advocacy.

In a related doctrine, the Supreme Court has held that "compelled disclosure of affiliation with groups engaged in advocacy" amounts to a "restraint on freedom of association" where disclosure could expose the members to "public hostility." Laws mandating such disclosures will be upheld only where the Government interest is compelling.

The Court concludes that such First Amendment rights may be infringed by application of § 2709 in a given case. For example, the FBI theoretically could issue to a political campaign's computer systems operator a § 2709 NSL compelling production of the names of all persons who have email addresses through the campaign's computer systems. The FBI theoretically could also issue an NSL under § 2709 to discern the identity of someone whose anonymous online web log, or "blog," is critical of the Government. Such inquiries might be beyond the permissible scope of the FBI's power under § 2709 because the targeted information might not be relevant to an authorized investigation to protect against international terrorism or clandestine intelligence activities, or because the inquiry might be conducted solely on the basis of activities protected by the First Amendment. These prospects only highlight the potential danger of the FBI's self-certification process and the absence of judicial oversight.

Other rights may also be violated by the disclosure contemplated by the statute; the statute's reference to "transactional records" creates ambiguity regarding the scope of the information required to be produced by the NSL recipient. If the recipient—who in the NSL is called upon to exercise judgment in determining the extent to which complying materials constitute transactional records rather than content—interprets the NSL broadly as requiring production of all e-mail header information, including subject lines, for example, some disclosures conceivably may reveal information protected by the subscriber's attorney-client privilege, e.g., a communication with an attorney where the subject line conveys privileged or possibly incriminating information. Indeed, the practical absence of judicial review may lead ISPs to disclose information that is protected from disclosure by the NSL statute itself, such as in a case where the NSL was initiated solely in retaliation for the subscriber's exercise of his First Amendment rights, as prohibited by § 2709(b)(1)-(b)(2). Only a court would be able to definitively construe the statutory and First Amendment rights at issue in the "First Amendment retaliation" provision of the statute, and to strike a proper balance among those interests. [ ... ]

Moreover, the Court notes that the implications of the Government's position are profound. Anonymous internet speakers could be unmasked merely by an administrative, civil, or trial subpoena, or by any state or local disclosure regulation directed at their ISP, and the Government would not have to provide any heightened justification for revealing the speaker. The same would be true for attempts to compile membership lists by seeking the computerized records of an organization which uses a third-party electronic communications provider. Considering, as is undisputed here, the importance of the internet as a forum for speech and association, the Court rejects the invitation to permit the rights of internet anonymity and association to be placed at such grave risk.

The Court reaches this conclusion by determining that NSLs issued pursuant to § 2709 may seek information about or indirectly obtained from subscribers that may be protected from disclosure by the First Amendment or other rights-protecting constitutional provisions or statutes. Echoing the Supreme Court's observation that "differences in the characteristics of new media justify differences in the First Amendment standards applied to them," the Court concludes that even though *Smith* and *Miller* might suggest that there is no First Amendment interest at stake in compelling the disclosure by telephone companies and banks of certain transactional information derived from customer records, in deciding this case the Court must take account of the unique features of internet communications that may warrant application of different rules. The Court is persuaded that, for First Amendment purposes, internet records of the type obtained via a § 2709 NSL could differ substantially from transactional bank or phone records.

The evidence on the record now before this Court demonstrates that the information available through a § 2709 NSL served upon an ISP could easily be used to disclose vast amounts of anonymous speech and associational activity. For instance, § 2709 imposes a duty to provide "electronic communication transactional records," a phrase which, though undefined in the statute, certainly encompasses a log of email addresses with whom a subscriber has corresponded and the web pages that a subscriber visits. Those transactional records can reveal, among other things, the anonymous message boards to which a person logs on or posts, the electronic newsletters to which he subscribes, and the advocacy websites he visits. Moreover, § 2709 imposes a duty on ISPs to provide the names and addresses of subscribers, thus enabling the Government to specifically identify someone who has written anonymously on the internet. As discussed above, given that an NSL recipient is directed by the FBI to turn over all information "which you consider to be an electronic communication transactional record," the § 2709 NSL could also reasonably be interpreted by an ISP to require, at minimum, disclosure of all e-mail header information, including subject lines.

In stark contrast to this potential to compile elaborate dossiers on internet users, the information obtainable by a pen register is far more limited. As the Supreme Court in *Smith* was careful to note:

[Pen registers] disclose only the telephone numbers that have been dialed—a means of establishing communication. Neither the purport of any communication between the caller and the recipient of the call, their identities, nor whether the call was even completed is disclosed by pen registers.

The Court doubts that the result in *Smith* would have been the same if a pen register operated as a key to the most intimate details and passions of a person's private life.

The more apt Supreme Court case for evaluating the assumption of risk argument at issue here is *Katz v. United States*, the seminal decision underlying both *Smith* and *Miller*. *Katz* held that the Fourth Amendment's privacy protections applied where the Government wiretapped a telephone call placed from a public phone booth. Especially noteworthy and pertinent to this case is the Supreme Court's remark that: "The Government's activities in electronically listening to and recording the petitioner's words violated the privacy upon which he justifiably relied while using the telephone booth and thus constituted a 'search and seizure' within the meaning of the Fourth Amendment." The Supreme Court also stated that a person entering a phone booth who "shuts the door behind him" is "surely entitled to assume that the words he utters into the mouthpiece will not be broadcast to the world," and held that, "[t]o read the Constitution more narrowly is to ignore the vital role that the public telephone has come to play in private communication."

Applying that reasoning to anonymous internet speech and associational activity is relatively straightforward. A person who signs onto an anonymous forum under a pseudonym, for example, is essentially "shut[ting] the door behind him," and is surely entitled to a reasonable expectation that his speech, whatever form the expression assumes, will not be accessible to the Government to be broadcast to the world absent appropriate legal process. To hold otherwise would ignore the role of the internet as a remarkably powerful forum for private communication and association. Even the Government concedes here that the internet is an "important vehicle for the free exchange of ideas and facilitates associations."

To be sure, the Court is keenly mindful of the Government's reminder that the internet may also serve as a vehicle for crime. The Court equally recognizes that circumstances exist in which the First Amendment rights of association and anonymity must yield to a more compelling Government interest in obtaining records from internet firms. To this end, the Court re-emphasizes that it does not here purport to set forth the scope of these First Amendment rights in general, or define them in this or any other case. The Court holds only that such fundamental rights are certainly implicated in some cases in which the Government may employ § 2709 broadly to gather information, thus requiring that the process incorporate the safeguards of some judicial review to ensure that if an infringement of those rights is asserted, they are adequately protected through fair process in an independent neutral tribunal. Because the necessary procedural protections are wholly absent here, the Court finds on this ground additional cause for invalidating § 2709 as applied.

*Victor Marrero is a judge in the United States District Court for the Southern District of New York.

*John Doe; American Civil Liberties Union; and American Civil Liberties Union Foundation v. John Ashcroft.* United States District Court, Southern District. New York, September 28, 2004, 334 F. Supp.2d, 471 (2004), 475–476, 506–511.

# Testimony of George Christian

*by George Christian\**

Thank you for this opportunity to share with you my experiences as a recipient of a national security letter. My name is George Christian, and I, along with three of my colleagues, are the only recipients of an NSL who can legally talk about the experience.

We won the right to do so in Federal District Court and have now become known as the "Connecticut John Doe's" or the "Connecticut Four." Ours is a story that we hope will provoke serious thought. Though our gag order was lifted, several hundred thousand other recipients of national security letters must carry the secret of their experiences to their graves.

My colleagues and I would, at first, not seem to be likely recipients of an NSL. I am the Executive Director of Library Connection, Inc., a consortium of 27 libraries in the Hartford, Connecticut area. At the time, along with myself, our Executive Committee included Barbara Bailey, Board president and Director of the Welles-Turner Memorial Library in Glastonbury, Peter Chase, vice-president of the Board and Director of the Plainville Public Library (who is now the current Board president), and Janet Nocek, secretary of the Board and Director of the Portland Public Library. Our primary function is to provide a common computer system that controls the catalog information, patron records, and circulation information of our libraries. Having this information in a common system greatly facilitates sharing our resources. Most patrons treat our member libraries as if they were branches of a common library. At the time we were served with a national security letter, in July 2005, we were also providing telecommunications services to half our member libraries.

[...]

[...] On July 8, 2005, an FBI agent phoned Ken Sutton, our systems and telecommunications manager, and informed him that Library Connection would be served with a national security letter, and asked to whom it should be addressed. Ken said it should be addressed to myself as the Executive Director.

While I had been aware of the cautions raised by the ALA, ACLU, and others, until Ken related this phone conversation to me, I had not really thought about the term "national security letter." Nor are all attorneys familiar with the term. This is not surprising, since every recipient of a NSL is prohibited by a perpetual gag order from mentioning receipt of the letter or anything associated with it.

In considering how we should respond, I had learned that the District Court in New York had found the entire NSL statute unconstitutional because of prima facie violations of the 1st, 4th and 5th amendments. So, by the time the letter arrived, on July 13, 2005, I had made up my mind to oppose this effort. One of the two FBI agents served the letter on me, and pointed out that the letter requested information we had about the use of a specific IP address that was registered to Library Connection, Inc. He also pointed out the letter's gag order prohibited Library Connection from disclosing to anyone that the FBI was attempting to obtain information from our library business records.

We could not fathom any "exigent" nature for the FBI request. I was struck that: 1) the letter was dated May 19, almost two months before the FBI served the letter on July 13th and 2) it was addressed to Ken Sutton, the person they had called to get the correct addressee. The requested information was for use of an IP address five months earlier, on February 15.

At the same time, I did not want to impede the investigation of a perilous situation that endangered my country or my fellow citizens. Because the letter was dated two months before it was delivered to me, it seemed reasonable to conclude that the FBI was not in a rush to get the information they wanted. I told the Agent that I had reason to believe that the use of NSLs was unconstitutional, and that I wanted to consult my attorney before complying with the request. The agent wrote a phone number on the back of his business card and said my attorney could call that number.

After the FBI agents left, I called Library Connection's attorney and asked what to do. The attorney informed me that the only way I could contest compliance with a national security letter was to go to court against the Attorney General of the United States.

I did not feel that I could take a step like that on my own. [...]

I therefore decided to ask the Executive Committee of the Board of Directors to make the decision on behalf of Library Connection. [...]

The next day, the Executive Committee met with our attorney. I informed them about the National Security Letter, and our attorney informed us that we were now all bound by its associated gag order. After learning that the NSL statute had been ruled unconstitutional in district court, the committee decided to resist complying with the request. The Executive Committee and I met with attorneys from the ACLU in late July of 2005. After discussing a variety of options, the Executive Committee decided to engage the National Office of the ACLU to seek an injunction relieving Library Connection from complying with the NSL and to seek a broader ruling that the use of NSLs is unconstitutional. The Committee also decided to seek relief from the gag rules associated with NSLs in order to 1) allow the Executive Committee's actions to be presented to the full Board, and 2) to allow the fact that an NSL was served on a library organization to become part of the national debate over renewal of the PATRIOT Act.

[…]

The national security letter asked for all of the "subscriber information" of "any person or entity related to" a specific IP address for a 45-minute period on February 15, 2005. We knew that the address was the address of a router at one of our libraries. Routers use address translation schemes to shield the true addresses of the computers behind them in order to make hacking into those computers more difficult. They do this by randomly assigning a different address to the computers behind them every time those computers are turned on. Since there was no way of tracing the path from the router to a specific personal computer, the FBI would have to find out who was using every computer in the library on that day. And since there was no way of determining who was using the computers in the library five months after the fact, we felt that "subscriber information of any entity related" to the IP address meant a request for the information we had on all the patrons of that library. That seemed like a rather sweeping request. Some would call it a fishing expedition.

Let me reemphasize: we did not want to aid terrorists or criminals. One of us, Janet Nocek, had actually lost a friend on one of the planes that crashed into the World Trade Center. All four of us were deeply affected by the September 11 attacks, and none of us wanted any further harm to come to our country or its citizens. But we did not feel we would be helping the country or making anyone safer by throwing out the Constitution either. All we wanted was some kind of judicial review of the FBI request.

I am not a lawyer; I manage a library organization. I understand from the attorneys that it is technically legal for the FBI to deploy NSLs without judicial review. However, as a law-abiding citizen and as a person committed to the principles of librarianship, it did not nor does not make sense to me that such intrusions into the privacy of our library patrons is reasonable, especially a wholesale request for information about many patrons, not necessarily a library patron that is the legally deemed to be specific target of an investigation. [...] [S]uch fishing expeditions should not be allowed in libraries, bookstores or other places of inquiry.

In August, the ACLU filed suit in Federal District Court in Bridgeport, Connecticut. Peter Chase and I prepared affidavits to be filed with the suit. Imagine our surprise to learn we would not be allowed to attend the hearing in person because of the risk that we would be identified as the plaintiffs. Instead we had to watch the proceedings via closed circuit TV from a locked room in the Hartford Federal Court Building.

In the hearing, Judge Hall asked to review the government's evidence for keeping us gagged. The government insisted on submitting secret evidence, which they would not provide to our attorneys or us. Like the judge in New York who had ruled on the issue, Judge Hall ruled that a perpetual gag amounted to prior restraint, and was therefore unconstitutional. She also ruled that her review of the evidence found no compelling national security reasons for keeping us gagged. Her ruling was immediately appealed by the Justice Department. While the case was under appeal, we remained gagged.

The gag order caused us troubling dilemmas personally as well as professionally. We had no desire to talk about the specifics of the national security letter we received but we wanted to tell our fellow librarians that NSLs posed a threat to patron privacy as well as what it was like to be under a federal gag order. We wanted to tell our patrons that we were trying to protect their confidentiality. We also wanted to tell Members of Congress, at a time when you all were debating the renewal and sunset provisions of the USA PATRIOT Act, that the national security letter provision was being used against libraries, and that librarians felt this was a huge threat to the privacy that they and their patrons trusted to exist at libraries.

Being gagged was also frustrating on other professional and personal levels. I felt compromised since I could not reveal the problem to the full board nor to our member libraries or my own staff that had seen the FBI arrive, announce themselves and hand me a letter. No one could bring up the topic at Library Connection Board meetings, nor at meetings of the full membership. I knew that all the board members and all the member library directors knew of the case, and I suspected the Executive Committee and I had their approval. However, I had no idea whether the approval was unanimous, or whether there was a significant dissenting opinion. I felt terrible I could not let anyone know that the struggle was not depleting our capital reserves and putting the corporation at risk. I could not even tell our auditors that the corporation was engaged in a major lawsuit—a direct violation of my fiduciary responsibilities. I pride myself on my integrity and openness. I worried if, knowing I was participating in this court case behind their backs, the members of the board and other library directors were starting to wonder what else I might be concealing.

[...]

At various times we had to go to extreme measures to keep from talking with the press or answering questions from colleagues and family. One of the John Doe's even had his son ask "Dad, is the FBI after you?" All he could say was that he was involved in a court case and it was extremely confidential.

[...]

After our court hearing, all of this became even more difficult, as the national and local papers were full of stories about a library consortium in Connecticut that had taken the Attorney General to court over receipt of an NSL and its associated gag order. The consortium was described as "John Doe," as our case was officially known as Doe v. Gonzales. There are only four library consortia in Connecticut, so speculation about the identity of John Doe was swarming all around us.

[...]

Within a few weeks, the *New York Times* discovered that Library Connection's identity as the plaintiff had been inadvertently disclosed on the court's web site. The *Times* published a story revealing Library Connection's name on September 21. [...] [T]he press soon discovered my name among the documents and a reference to one of the other plaintiffs as "chairman of the Intellectual Freedom Committee of the Connecticut Library Association." Only one person could fit that description, Peter Chase. Papers around the country picked up articles identifying Peter and me from the *New York Times* and AP wire services.

[...]

[...] We were soon deluged with phone calls from the press at work and at home. Initially this was a very delicate situation. Our attorneys had cautioned us that even a "no comment" was tantamount to admitting we were John Doe. Our attorneys felt it was therefore better just not to discuss the issue. Everyone who read the *New York Times,* the *Washington Post,* and many other papers throughout the country knew about the Library Connection, Inc. I even received letters and clippings from around the country. Yet still we could not share our experience with Congress while Congress was debating the renewal of the PATRIOT Act.

The 2nd Circuit Court of Appeals in New York heard our case in November 2005. At least this time we were allowed to be present at our own court case. However, we had to conceal our identities by entering and leaving the court building and the courtroom separately, not sitting together, and not establishing eye contact with each other or our attorneys.

In court the government argued that merely revealing ourselves as recipients of a national security letter would violate national security. Our attorneys filed more legal papers to try to lift the gag, and attached copies of the *New York Times* articles. The government claimed that all the press coverage revealing our names did not matter because 1) no one in Connecticut reads the *New York Times,* and 2) surveys prove that 58% of the public disbelieves what they read in newspapers. To add to the absurdity, the government insisted that the copies of the news stories our attorneys had submitted remain under seal in court papers.

[...]

It appeared that Congress would vote on the renewal of the PATRIOT Act before the Appellate Court would rule on our gag order. Our attorneys took the case all the way up to the Supreme Court in an emergency attempt to lift the gag. Though clearly troubled by the case, the Court refused to lift the gag at that point.

On March 9, 2006, President Bush signed into law the revised USA PATRIOT Act. A few weeks later the government decided that our silence was no longer needed to preserve national security. They told the Second Circuit that the FBI would lift the gag order, and then they tried to get Judge Hall's decision vacated as moot. The Second Circuit refused to erase Judge Hall's decision from the books, and expressed concern about the breadth of the NSL gag provision. Judge Cardamone of the Second Circuit wrote, "A ban on speech and a shroud of secrecy in perpetuity are antithetical to democratic concepts and do not fit comfortably with the fundamental rights guaranteed American citizens. Unending secrecy of actions taken by government officials may also serve as a cover for possible official misconduct and/or incompetence." The court referred the rest of our case back to district court. Justice Hall's original opinion that our perpetual gag order was unconstitutional now became part of case law.

A few weeks after that, the FBI said they no longer needed the information they had sought from us and thus abandoned the case completely. In doing so, they removed the PATRIOT Act from the danger of court review.

We held our first press conference on May 31, 2006 at the offices of the ACLU in New York City. Since then, we have tried to accept every invitation to library groups, colleges and civic organizations. We want people to know that the FBI is spying on thousands of completely innocent Americans. We feel an obligation to the tens of thousands of others who received National Security Letters and now will live under a gag order for the rest of their lives.

[...]

*George Christian is the executive director of Library Connection, Inc., a group of libraries in Connecticut. In 2005, he, along with three other librarians, received a National Security Letter requesting information about a patron's computer records. He testified about his experience before the Senate Judiciary Subcommittee on the Constitution.

Testimony of George Christian before the Senate Judiciary Committee. April 11, 2007. Responding to The Inspector General's Findings of Improper Use of National Security Letters by the FBI. 110th Congress. http://www.judiciary.senate.gov/hearings/testimony.cfm?id=e655f9 e2809e5476862f735da124b3b9&wit_id=e655f9e2809e5476862f735da 124b3b9-0-2.

# Evidence of Abuse:
# The Inspector General Audits
# National Security Letters

*by the American Civil Liberties Union\**

NSLs are secret demand letters issued without judicial review
to obtain sensitive personal information such as financial
records, credit reports, telephone and e-mail communications data and Internet searches. The FBI had authority to
issue NSLs through four separate statutes, but these authorities were significantly expanded by **section 505** of the Patriot
Act.[21] **Section 505** increased the number of officials who
could authorize NSLs and reduced the standard necessary
to obtain information with them, requiring only an internal certification that the records sought are "relevant" to an
authorized counterterrorism or counter-intelligence investigation. The Patriot Act reauthorization made the NSL provisions permanent.

The NSL statutes now allow the FBI and other executive
branch agencies to obtain records about people who are not
known—or even suspected—to have done anything wrong.
The NSL statutes also allow the government to prohibit NSL
recipients from disclosing that the government sought or
obtained information from them. While Congress modified
these "gag orders" in the Patriot Act reauthorization to allow
NSL recipients to consult a lawyer, under the current state of

the law NSLs are still not subject to any meaningful level of judicial review (ACLU challenges to the NSL gag orders are described below).[22]

The first two IG audits, covering NSLs and section 215 orders issued from 2003 through 2005, were released in March of 2007. They confirmed widespread FBI mismanagement, misuse and abuse of these Patriot Act authorities.[23] The NSL audit revealed that the FBI managed its use of NSLs so negligently that it literally did not know how many NSLs it had issued. As a result, the FBI seriously under-reported its use of NSLs in its previous reports to Congress. The IG also found that FBI agents repeatedly ignored or confused the requirements of the NSL authorizing statutes, and used NSLs to collect private information against individuals two or three times removed from the subjects of FBI investigations. Twenty-two percent of the audited files contained unreported legal violations.[24] Most troubling, FBI supervisors used hundreds of illegal "exigent letters" to obtain telephone records without NSLs by falsely claiming emergencies.[25]

On March 13, 2008, the IG released a second pair of audit reports covering 2006 and evaluating the reforms implemented by the DOJ and the FBI after the first audits were released in 2007.[26] Not surprisingly, the new reports identified many of the same problems discovered in the earlier audits. The 2008 NSL report shows that the FBI issued 49,425 NSLs in 2006 (a 4.7 percent increase over 2005), and confirms the FBI is increasingly using NSLs to gather information on U.S. persons (57 percent in 2006, up from 53 percent in 2005).[27]

The 2008 IG audit also revealed that high-ranking FBI officials, including an assistant director, a deputy assistant director, two acting deputy directors and a special agent in charge, improperly issued eleven "blanket NSLs" in 2006 seeking data on 3,860 telephone numbers.[28] None of these "blanket NSLs" complied with FBI policy and eight imposed unlawful non-disclosure requirements on recipients.[29] Moreover, the "blanket NSLs" were written to "cover information already acquired through exigent letters and other informal responses."[30] The IG expressed concern that such high-ranking officials would fail to comply with FBI policies requiring FBI lawyers to review all NSLs, but it seems clear enough that this step was intentionally avoided because the officials knew these NSL requests were illegal.[31] It would be difficult to call this conduct anything but intentional.

The ACLU successfully challenged the constitutionality of the original Patriot Act's gag provisions, which imposed a categorical and blanket non-disclosure order on every NSL recipient.[32] Upon reauthorization, the Patriot Act limited these gag orders to situations when a special agent in charge certifies that disclosure of the NSL request might result in danger to the national security, interference with an FBI investigation or danger to any person. Despite this attempted reform, the IG's 2008 audit showed that 97 percent of NSLs issued by the FBI in 2006 included gag orders, and that five percent of these NSLs contained "insufficient explanation to justify imposition of these obligations."[33] While a five percent violation rate may seem small compared to the widespread abuse of NSL authorities documented elsewhere, these audit findings demonstrate that the FBI continues to gag NSL recipients in an overly broad, and therefore unconstitutional manner. Moreover, the IG found that gags were improperly included in eight of the 11 "blanket NSLs" that senior FBI counterterrorism officials issued to cover hundreds of illegal FBI requests for telephone records through exigent letters.[34]

The FBI's gross mismanagement of its NSL authorities risks security as much as it risks the privacy of innocent persons. The IG reported that the FBI could not locate return information for at least 532 NSL requests issued from the field, and 70 NSL requests issued from FBI headquarters (28 percent of the NSLs sampled).[35] Since the law only allows the FBI to issue NSLs in terrorism and espionage investigations, it cannot be assumed that the loss of these records is inconsequential to our security. Intelligence information continuing to fall through the cracks at the FBI through sheer incompetence is truly a worrisome revelation.

### NOTES

21. The four NSL authorizing statutes include the Electronic Communications Privacy Act, 18 U.S.C. § 2709 (2000), the Right to Financial Privacy Act, 12 U.S.C. § 3401 (2000), the Fair Credit Reporting Act, 15 U.S.C. § 1681 et seq. (2000), and the National Security Act of 1947, 50 U.S.C. § 436(a)(1)(2000).

22. As amended, the NSL statute authorizes the Director of the FBI or his designee (including a Special Agent in Charge of a Bureau field office) to impose a gag order on any person or entity served with an NSL. *See* 18 U.S.C. § 2709(c). To impose such an order, the Director or his designee must "certify" that, absent the non-disclosure obligation, "there may result a danger to the national security of the United States, interference with a criminal, counterterrorism, or counterintelligence investigation, interference with diplomatic relations, or danger to the life or physical safety of any person." *Id.* at § 2709(c)(1). If the Director of the FBI or his designee so certifies, the recipient of the NSL is prohibited from "disclos[ing] to any person (other than those to whom such disclosure is necessary to comply with the request or an attorney to obtain legal advice or legal assistance with respect to the request) that the [FBI] has sought or obtained access to information or records under [the NSL statute]." *Id.* Gag orders imposed under the NSL

statute are imposed by the FBI unilaterally, without prior judicial review. While the statute requires a "certification" that the gag is necessary, the certification is not examined by anyone outside the executive branch. The gag provisions permit the recipient of an NSL to petition a court "for an order modifying or setting aside a nondisclosure requirement." *Id.* at § 3511(b)(1). However, in the case of a petition filed "within one year of the request for records," the reviewing court may modify or set aside the nondisclosure requirement only if it finds that there is "no reason to believe that disclosure may endanger the national security of the United States, interfere with a criminal, counterterrorism, or counterintelligence investigation, interfere with diplomatic relations, or endanger the life or physical safety of any person." *Id.* at § 3511(b)(2). Moreover, if a designated senior government official "certifies that disclosure may endanger the national security of the United States or interfere with diplomatic relations," the certification must be "treated as conclusive unless the court finds that the certification was made in bad faith." *Id.*

23. DEP'T OF JUSTICE, OFFICE OF INSPECTOR GENERAL, A REVIEW OF THE FEDERAL BUREAU OF INVESTIGATION'S USE OF NATIONAL SECURITY LETTERS (Mar. 2007), *available at* http://www.usdoj .gov/oig/special/s0703b/final.pdf [hereinafter 2007 NSL Report]; DEP'T OF JUSTICE, OFFICE OF INSPECTOR GENERAL, A REVIEW OF THE FEDERAL BUREAU OF INVESTIGATION'S USE OF SECTION 215 ORDERS FOR BUSINESS RECORDS (Mar. 2007), *available at* http://www.usdoj.gov/oig/special/s0703a/final.pdf [hereinafter 2007 Section 215 Report].

24. 2007 NSL Report, *supra* note 25, at 84.

25. *Id.* at 86-99.

26. DEP'T OF JUSTICE, OFFICE OF INSPECTOR GENERAL, A REVIEW OF THE FEDERAL BUREAU OF INVESTIGATION'S USE OF NATIONAL SECURITY LETTERS: ASSESSMENT OF CORRECTIVE ACTIONS AND EXAMINATION OF NSL USAGE IN 2006 (Mar. 2008), *available at* http://www.usdoj.gov/oig/special/s0803b/ final.pdf [hereinafter 2008 NSL Report]; DEP'T OF JUSTICE, OFFICE OF INSPECTOR GENERAL, A REVIEW OF THE FEDERAL

BUREAU OF INVESTIGATION'S USE OF SECTION 215 ORDERS FOR BUSINESS RECORDS IN 2006 (Mar. 2008), *available at* http://www.usdoj.gov/oig/special/s0803a/final.pdf [hereinafter 2008 Section 215 Report].

27. 2008 NSL Report, *supra* note 28, at 9.

28. 2008 NSL Report, *supra* note 26, at 127, 129 n.116.

29. 2008 NSL Report, *supra* note 26, at 127.

30. 2008 NSL Report, *supra* note 26, at 127.

31. 2008 NSL Report, *supra* note 26, at 130.

32. *See Doe v. Ashcroft*, 334 F. Supp. 2d 471 (S.D.N.Y 2004); *Doe v. Gonzales*, 500 F. Supp. 2d 379 (S.D.N.Y. 2007); *Doe v. Gonzales*, 386 F. Supp. 2d 66 (D. Conn. 2005); PIRA, Pub. L. No. 109-177, 120 Stat. 195 (2006); USA Patriot Act Additional Reauthorizing Amendments Act of 2006 (ARAA) Pub. L. No.109-178, 120 Stat. 278 (2006). The ACLU is still litigating the constitutionality of the gag order provisions in the USA PATRIOT Improvement and Reauthorization Act of 2005. *See* Press Release, American Civil Liberties Union, ACLU Asks Appeals Court to Affirm Striking Down Patriot Act 'National Security Letter' Provision (Mar. 14, 2008) (on file with author), *available at* http://www.aclu.org/safefree/nationalsecurityletters/34480prs20080314.html.

33. 2008 NSL Report, *supra* note 28, at 11, 124.

34. 2008 NSL Report, *supra* note 26, at 127.

35. 2008 NSL Report, *supra* note 26, at 81, 88.

*The **American Civil Liberties Union** is a national, nonprofit organization that aims to preserve individual rights in the United States. Its operations focus on lobbying, litigation, and education.

American Civil Liberties Union. *Reclaiming Patriotism: A Call to Reconsider the Patriot Act.* New York: ACLU, 2009, pp. 16–18. http://www.aclu.org/pdfs/safefree/patriot_report_20090310.pdf.

Used by permission of the American Civil Liberties Union.

# Statement Before the Senate Committee on the Judiciary

*by Robert S. Mueller, III\**

Good morning Mr. Chairman, Senator Specter, and members of the Committee. Thank you for opportunity to testify before you this morning.

Last week, the Committee heard testimony from Glenn Fine, the Inspector General of the Department of Justice, regarding a recent report issued by his office on the FBI's use of national security letters, or NSLs. The Inspector General and his staff conducted a thorough and fair review of this authority and the Congress is to be commended for requiring that this review be conducted. As you heard from the Inspector General, he did not find any deliberate or intentional misuse of the national security letter authorities, Attorney General Guidelines or FBI policy. Nevertheless, the review by the Office of Inspector General (OIG) identified several areas of inadequate auditing and oversight of these vital investigative tools, as well as processes that were inappropriate.

Although not intentionally, we fell short in our obligations to report to Congress on the frequency with which we use this tool and in the internal controls we put into place to make sure that it was used only in accordance with the letter of the law. I take responsibility for those shortcomings and for taking the steps to ensure that they do not happen again.

The OIG report made 10 recommendations designed to provide both the necessary controls over the issuance of NSLs and the creation and maintenance of accurate records. I fully support each recommendation and concur with the inspector general that, when implemented, these reforms will ensure full compliance with both the letter and the spirit of the authorities entrusted to the Bureau by the Congress and the American people.

National security letters generally permit us to obtain the same sort of documents from third-party businesses that prosecutors and agents obtain in criminal investigations with grand jury subpoenas. Unlike grand jury subpoenas, however, NSL authority comes through several distinct statutes and they have specific rules that accompany them.

NSLs have been instrumental in breaking up cells like the "Lackawanna Six" and the "Northern Virginia Jihad." Through the use of NSLs, the FBI has traced sources of terrorist funding, established telephone and e-mail linkages that resulted in further investigation and arrests, and arrested suspicious associates with deadly weapons and explosives.

## National Security Letter Authorities

The NSL authority used most frequently by the FBI is that provided by the Electronic Communications Privacy Act (ECPA). Through an ECPA NSL, the FBI can obtain subscriber information for telephones and electronic communications and can obtain toll billing information and electronic communication transaction records.

Significantly, the FBI cannot obtain the content of communications through an ECPA NSL.

[...]

The authority to issue an NSL lies at a senior level within the FBI. An NSL can be issued only by an official who ranks not lower than Special Agent in Charge or Deputy Assistant Director. All such officials are career government employees who are members of the Senior Executive Service.

Procedurally, an agent or analyst seeking an NSL must prepare a document (an electronic communication, or E.C.) in which the employee lays out the factual predicate for the request. The factual recitation must be sufficiently detailed so that the approving official can determine that the material sought is relevant to an investigation. Additionally, it needs to provide sufficient information concerning the underlying investigation so that reviewing officials can confirm that the investigation is adequately predicated and not based solely on the exercise of First Amendment rights.

Finally, the EC includes a "lead" to the Office of the General Counsel (OGC) for purposes of congressional reporting.

## The OIG Report

As directed by Congress, we endeavored to declassify as much information as possible concerning our use of NSLs in order to allow the maximum amount of public awareness of the extent of our use of the NSL tool consistent with national security concerns. To that end, for the first time the public has a sense of the frequency with which the FBI makes requests for data with national security letters. In the period covered by the report, the number of NSL requests has ranged from approximately 40,000 to 60,000 per year and we have requested information on less than 20,000 persons per year.

For a variety of reasons that will be discussed below, those numbers are not exact. Nevertheless, they, for the first time, allow the public to get some sense of the order of magnitude of these requests: There are a substantial number of requests, but we are not collecting information on hundreds of thousands of Americans.

There are three findings by the OIG that are particularly disturbing, and it is those three findings that I wish to address this morning: 1) inaccurate reporting to Congress of various data points we are obligated to report relative to NSLs; 2) the use of so-called exigent letters that circumvented the procedures required by ECPA; and 3) known violations (both previously self-reported by FBI and not previously reported) of law and policy with regard to usage of NSLs.

## Congressional Reporting

A finding of the report that particularly distresses me is the section that addresses the inaccuracies of the numbers we report to Congress. The process for tabulating NSLs simply did not keep up with the volume. Although we came to that realization prior to the OIG report and are working on a technological solution, that realization came later than it should have.

Approximately a year ago, we recognized that our technology was inadequate and began developing an automated system to improve our ability to collect this data. The system, in addition to improving data collection, will automatically prevent many of the errors in NSLs that we will discuss today. We are building an NSL system to function as a workflow tool that will automate much of the work that is associated with preparing NSLs and the associated paperwork.

The NSL system is designed to require the user to enter certain data before the workflow can proceed and requires specific reviews and approvals before the request for the NSL can proceed. Through this process, the FBI can automatically ensure that certain legal and administrative requirements are met and that required reporting data is accurately collected. [...]

[...]

As with the other shortcomings identified by the OIG, there was no finding of an intent to deceive Congress concerning our use of NSLs. In fact, as noted, we identified deficiencies in our system for generating data prior to the initiation of the OIG's review and flagged the issue for Congress almost one year ago. While we do not know the extent of the inaccuracies in past reporting, we are confident that the numbers will not change by an order of magnitude.

## Exigent Letters

[...]

The OIG rightfully objected to the FBI obtaining telephone records by providing a telephone carrier with a letter that states that a federal grand jury subpoena had been requested when that was untrue. It is unclear at this point why that happened. I have ordered a special inspection in order to better understand the full scope of internal control lapses.

We also concur with the OIG that it is inappropriate to obtain records on the basis of a purported emergency if, in fact, there is no emergency. We continue to believe, however, that providers had the right to rely on our representation that there was an emergency and that the "exigent letters"—had they been issued only when there was an exigent circumstance and had they correctly identified the legal process that would follow—would have been an appropriate tool to use.

[…]

## Intelligence Oversight Board Process

[…]

Of the 293 NSLs the OIG examined, 22 (7 percent) were judged to have potential unreported IOB violations associated with them. Moreover, of those 22 NSLs, 10—or almost 50 percent—were third-party errors—that is, the NSL recipient provided the FBI with information we did not seek. Only 12 of the NSLs examined—4 percent—had mistakes that the OIG rightfully attributes to the FBI.

Examining the 12 potential errors that were rightfully attributed to the FBI reveals a continuum of seriousness relative to the potential impact on individual rights. Four (or just over 1 percent of the sample) were serious violations.

Specifically, two of the violations involved obtaining full credit reports in counterintelligence investigations (which is not statutorily authorized), one involved issuing an NSL when authorization for the investigation to which it related had lapsed, and one involved issuing an NSL for information that was arguably content, and therefore not available pursuant to an NSL. (In the latter case, the ISP on which the NSL was served declined to produce the requested material so there was, in fact, no collection of information to which we were not entitled.)

The balance of the 12 potential violations identified by the OIG do not, in our view, rise to the same level of seriousness as those four. The remaining eight involve errors that are best characterized as arising from a lack of attention to detail, and did not result in the FBI seeking or obtaining any information to which it was not entitled.

Those eight potential violations involved errors such as using the wrong certification language in an NSL (although the appropriate certification is not materially different) and having the NSL and the EC seeking the NSL not entirely consistent. We do not excuse such lack of attention to detail, but we do not believe that such mistakes result in or cause a risk to civil liberties.

In short, approximately 1 percent of the NSLs examined by the OIG had significant errors that were attributable to FBI actions and that had not been, but should have been, reported as potential IOB violations. While a 1 percent error rate is not huge, it is unacceptable, and we have taken steps to reduce that error rate.

[...]

## Additional Corrective Steps

[...]

Mr. Chairman, the FBI is acutely aware that we cannot protect against threats at the expense of civil liberties. We are judged not just by our ability to defend the nation from terrorist attacks but also our commitment to defend the rights and freedoms we all enjoy. In light of the inspector general's findings, we are committed to demonstrating to this Committee, to the Congress, and to the American people that we will correct these deficiencies and utilize the critical tools Congress has provided us consistent with the privacy protections and civil liberties that we are sworn to uphold.

I appreciate the opportunity to appear before the Committee and look forward to answering your questions.

[...]

*Robert S. Mueller, III** was the director of the Federal Bureau of Investigation from 2001 to 2013.

Statement of Robert S. Mueller, III Before the Senate Committee on the Judiciary. March 27, 2007. Responding to The Inspector General's Findings of Improper Use of National Security Letters by the FBI. 110th Congress, 2007–2008. http://www.fbi.gov/news/testimony/the-fbis-use-of-national-security-letters-2.

## PART 4

# Are Whistleblowers Dangerous?

The government has a legitimate need for secrecy to conduct its investigations into terrorist threats. However, secrecy can be used to hide errors by government officials, failed policies, and other kinds of mismanagement. Whistleblowers are government employees who report wrongdoing that they believe may be hurting national security. Usually, these employees begin by following the chain of command, reporting problems to their supervisors. When their supervisors don't see the problem, then potential whistleblowers are forced to carry the complaint higher. Presidents George W. Bush and Barack Obama have praised whistleblowers who work within the system. But sometimes the whistleblowers can't find any government officials who agree with them; they then often contact a reporter who writes a story revealing government secrets. Official sympathy for the whistleblowers then vanishes. They have broken their oath not to reveal secret information and may have assisted the country's enemies. The FBI begins looking for the "leaker," and criminal prosecution may follow if the whistleblower is caught.

Freedom of speech is meaningless unless we have access to information. At a time when government secrecy has grown dramatically, whistleblowers are often the only ones willing to provide the facts that we need to debate the conduct of our government. Some believe that whistleblowers do more harm than good, however. Thomas M. Tamm was a government lawyer who revealed to the *New York Times* that the National Security Agency (NSA) was illegally spying on American citizens. His experience is told by Michael Isikoff in this section's first piece, "The Fed Who Blew the Whistle." At the time, some critics of the NSA program maintained that President Bush should be impeached for authorizing it. But others, including conservative national security expert Gabriel Schoenfeld ("Has the *New York Times* Violated the Espionage Act?"), have countered that it is Tamm and the *Times* who should be prosecuted for revealing to the terrorists that their communications were being monitored.

As a senator, Barack Obama criticized the NSA spying program, but, as we learn in "Prosecuting Whistleblowers," his administration has aggressively pursued whistleblowers who leak secrets to the press. Journalists, such as Margaret Sullivan, public editor of the *New York Times* ("The Danger of Suppressing the Leaks"), argue that Obama's policy will silence whistleblowers, making debating important government policies impossible.

One of the biggest leakers in American history is U.S. Army private Bradley Manning, who illegally released hundreds of thousands of classified Army reports and State Department cables to Wikileaks, a website that publishes secret documents and news leaks from anonymous sources. The Manning case raises the issue: When does leaking government documents cease to be an effort to reform government and become the exposure of legitimate government secrets? Even defenders of whistleblowers have criticized Wikileaks ("Wikileaks Fails 'Due Diligence' Review"). Secretary of State Hillary Rodham Clinton condemned the leaks in "Remarks to the Press on Release of Purportedly Confidential Documents by Wikileaks," asserting that they put people's lives in danger, threaten national security, and undermine U.S. efforts to work with other countries. But many civil libertarians, including Floyd Abrams, a lawyer who has litigated controversial free speech cases, and Yochai Benkler, a law professor at Harvard ("Death to Whistle-Blowers?") believe that the government's effort to punish Manning with life imprisonment will harm free speech.

In May 2013, the controversy over how to handle whistle-blowers erupted again when it was learned that the FBI had conducted surveillance of reporters in an effort to discover who had leaked government secrets to them. President Obama defended the leaks investigation but said he would support legislation that allows reporters to protect the identity of their sources. A federal "shield" bill was introduced in Congress in 2012 but failed to pass. It was reintroduced in 2013.

As you read the articles, consider these questions:

- Why do government employees violate their secrecy oaths?
- Should whistleblowers be punished?
- Should reporters be prosecuted for revealing secrets?

# The Fed Who Blew the Whistle

*by Michael Isikoff\**

Thomas M. Tamm was entrusted with some of the government's most important secrets. He had a Sensitive Compartmented Information security clearance, a level above Top Secret. Government agents had probed Tamm's background, his friends and associates, and determined him trustworthy.

It's easy to see why: he comes from a family of high-ranking FBI officials. During his childhood, he played under the desk of J. Edgar Hoover, and as an adult, he enjoyed a long and successful career as a prosecutor. Now gray-haired, 56 and fighting a paunch, Tamm prides himself on his personal rectitude. He has what his 23-year-old son, Terry, calls a "passion for justice." For that reason, there was one secret he says he felt duty-bound to reveal.

In the spring of 2004, Tamm had just finished a yearlong stint at a Justice Department unit handling wiretaps of suspected terrorists and spies—a unit so sensitive that employees are required to put their hands through a biometric scanner to check their fingerprints upon entering. While there, Tamm stumbled upon the existence of a highly classified National Security Agency program that seemed to be eavesdropping on U.S. citizens. The unit had special rules that appeared to be hiding the NSA activities from a panel of federal judges who are required to approve such surveillance. When Tamm started asking questions, his supervisors told him to drop the subject. He says one volunteered that "the program" (as it was commonly called within the office) was "probably illegal."

Tamm agonized over what to do. He tried to raise the issue with a former colleague working for the Senate Judiciary Committee. But the friend, wary of discussing what sounded like government secrets, shut down their conversation. For weeks, Tamm couldn't sleep. The idea of lawlessness at the Justice Department angered him. Finally, one day during his lunch hour, Tamm ducked into a subway station near the U.S. District Courthouse on Pennsylvania Avenue. He headed for a pair of adjoining pay phones partially concealed by large, illuminated Metro maps. Tamm had been eyeing the phone booths on his way to work in the morning. Now, as he slipped through the parade of midday subway riders, his heart was pounding, his body trembling. Tamm felt like a spy. After looking around to make sure nobody was watching, he picked up a phone and called The New York Times.

That one call began a series of events that would engulf Washington—and upend Tamm's life. Eighteen months after he first disclosed what he knew, the Times reported that President George W. Bush had secretly authorized the NSA to intercept phone calls and e-mails of individuals inside the United States without judicial warrants. The drama followed a quiet, separate rebellion within the highest ranks of the Justice Department concerning the same program. (James Comey, then the deputy attorney general, together with FBI head Robert Mueller and several other senior Justice officials, threatened to resign.) President Bush condemned the leak to the Times as a "shameful act." Federal agents launched a criminal investigation to determine the identity of the culprit.

The story of Tamm's phone call is an untold chapter in the history of the secret wars inside the Bush administration. The New York Times won a Pulitzer Prize for its story. The two reporters who worked on it each published books. Congress, after extensive debate, last summer passed a major new law to govern the way such surveillance is conducted. But Tamm—who was not the Times's only source, but played the key role in tipping off the paper—has not fared so well. The FBI has pursued him relentlessly for the past two and a half years. Agents have raided his house, hauled away personal possessions and grilled his wife, a teenage daughter and a grown son. More recently, they've been questioning Tamm's friends and associates about nearly every aspect of his life. Tamm has resisted pressure to plead to a felony for divulging classified information. But he is living under a pall, never sure if or when federal agents might arrest him.

Exhausted by the uncertainty clouding his life, Tamm now is telling his story publicly for the first time. "I thought this [secret program] was something the other branches of the government—and the public—ought to know about. So they could decide: do they want this massive spying program to be taking place?" Tamm told NEWSWEEK, in one of a series of recent interviews that he granted against the advice of his lawyers. "If somebody were to say, who am I to do that? I would say, 'I had taken an oath to uphold the Constitution.' It's stunning that somebody higher up the chain of command didn't speak up."

Tamm concedes he was also motivated in part by his anger at other Bush-administration policies at the Justice Department, including its aggressive pursuit of death-penalty cases and the legal justifications for "enhanced" interrogation techniques that many believe are tantamount to torture. But, he insists, he divulged no "sources and methods" that might compromise national security when he spoke to the Times. He told reporters Eric Lichtblau and James Risen nothing about the operational details of the NSA program because he didn't know them, he says. He had never been "read into," or briefed, on the details of the program. All he knew was that a domestic surveillance program existed, and it "didn't smell right."

[...]

Still, Tamm is haunted by the consequences of what he did—and what could yet happen to him. He is no longer employed at Justice and has been struggling to make a living practicing law. He does occasional work for a local public defender's office, handles a few wills and estates—and is more than $30,000 in debt. (To cover legal costs, he recently set up a defense fund.) He says he has suffered from depression. He also realizes he made what he calls "stupid" mistakes along the way, including sending out a seemingly innocuous but fateful e-mail from his Justice Department computer that may have first put the FBI on his scent. Soft-spoken and self-effacing, Tamm has an impish smile and a wry sense of humor. "I guess I'm not a very good criminal," he jokes.

At times during his interviews with NEWSWEEK, Tamm would stare into space for minutes, silently wrestling with how to answer questions. One of the most difficult concerned the personal ramifications of his choice. "I didn't think through what this could do to my family," he says.

Tamm's story is in part a cautionary tale about the perils that can face all whistleblowers, especially those involved in national-security programs. Some Americans will view him as a hero who (like Daniel Ellsberg and perhaps Mark Felt, the FBI official since identified as Deep Throat) risked his career and livelihood to expose wrongdoing at the highest levels of government. Others—including some of his former colleagues—will deride Tamm as a renegade who took the law into his own hands and violated solemn obligations to protect the nation's secrets. "You can't have runoffs deciding they're going to be the white knight and running to the press," says Frances Fragos Townsend, who once headed the unit where Tamm worked and later served as President Bush's chief counterterrorism adviser. Townsend made clear that she had no knowledge of Tamm's particular case, but added: "There are legal processes in place [for whistle-blowers' complaints]. This is one where I'm a hawk. It offends me, and I find it incredibly dangerous."

Tamm understands that some will see his conduct as "treasonous." But still, he says he has few regrets. If he hadn't made his phone call to the Times, he believes, it's possible the public would never have learned about the Bush administration's secret wiretapping program. "I don't really need anybody to feel sorry for me," he wrote in a recent e-mail to NEWSWEEK. "I chose what I did. I believed in what I did."

If the government were drawing up a profile of a national-security leaker, Tamm would seem one of the least likely suspects. He grew up in the shadow of J. Edgar Hoover's FBI. Tamm's uncle, Edward Tamm, was an important figure in the bureau's history. He was once a top aide to Hoover and regularly briefed President Franklin Roosevelt on domestic intelligence matters. He's credited in some bureau histories with inventing (in 1935) not only the bureau's name, but its official motto: Fidelity, Bravery, Integrity. Tamm's father, Quinn Tamm, was also a high-ranking bureau official. He too was an assistant FBI director under Hoover, and at one time he headed up the bureau's crime lab. Tamm's mother, Ora Belle Tamm, was a secretary at the FBI's identification division.

Tamm's brother also served for years as an FBI agent and later worked as an investigator for the 9/11 Commission. (He now works for a private consulting firm.) Tamm himself, after graduating from Brown University in 1974 and Georgetown Law three years later, chose a different path in law enforcement. He joined the state's attorney's office in Montgomery County, Md. (He was also, for a while, the chairman of the county chapter of the Young Republicans.) Tamm eventually became a senior trial attorney responsible for prosecuting murder, kidnapping and sexual-assault cases.

[...]

[Tamm joined the Justice Department in 1998. In] early 2003, he applied and was accepted for transfer to the Office of Intelligence Policy and Review (OIPR), probably the most sensitive unit within the Justice Department. It is the job of OIPR lawyers to request permission for national-security wiretaps. These requests are made at secret hearings of the Foreign Intelligence Surveillance Court, a body composed of 11 rotating federal judges.

Congress created the FISA court in 1978 because of well-publicized abuses by the intelligence community. It was designed to protect the civil liberties of Americans who might come under suspicion. The court's role was to review domestic national-security wiretaps to make sure there was "probable cause" that the targets were "agents of a foreign power"—either spies or operatives of a foreign terrorist organization. The law creating the court, called the Foreign Intelligence Surveillance Act, made it a federal crime—punishable by up to five years in prison—for any official to engage in such surveillance without following strict rules, including court approval.

But after arriving at OIPR, Tamm learned about an unusual arrangement by which some wiretap requests were handled under special procedures. These requests, which could be signed only by the attorney general, went directly to the chief judge and none other. It was unclear to Tamm what was being hidden from the other 10 judges on the court (as well as the deputy attorney general, who could sign all other FISA warrants). All that Tamm knew was that the "A.G.-only" wiretap requests involved intelligence gleaned from something that was obliquely referred to within OIPR as "the program."

The program was in fact a wide range of covert surveillance activities authorized by President Bush in the aftermath of 9/11. At that time, White House officials, led by Vice President Dick Cheney, had become convinced that FISA court procedures were too cumbersome and time-consuming to permit U.S. intelligence and law-enforcement agencies to quickly identify possible Qaeda terrorists inside the country. (Cheney's chief counsel, David Addington, referred to the FISA court in one meeting as that "obnoxious court," according to former assistant attorney general Jack Goldsmith.) Under a series of secret orders, Bush authorized the NSA for the first time to eavesdrop on phone calls and e-mails between the United States and a foreign country without any court review. The code name for the NSA collection activities—unknown to all but a tiny number of officials at the White House and in the U.S. intelligence community—was "Stellar Wind."

The NSA identified domestic targets based on leads that were often derived from the seizure of Qaeda computers and cell phones overseas. If, for example, a Qaeda cell phone seized in Pakistan had dialed a phone number in the United States, the NSA would target the U.S. phone number—which would then lead agents to look at other numbers in the United States and abroad called by the targeted phone. Other parts of the program were far more sweeping. The NSA, with the secret cooperation of U.S. telecommunications companies, had begun collecting vast amounts of information about the phone and e-mail records of American citizens. [...]

[...]

[...] Tamm was puzzled by the unusual procedures—which sidestepped the normal FISA process—for requesting wiretaps on cases that involved program intelligence. He began pushing his supervisors to explain what was going on. [...]

At one point, Tamm says, he approached Lisa Farabee, a senior counsel in OIPR who reviewed his work, and asked her directly, "Do you know what the program is?" According to Tamm, she replied: "Don't even go there," and then added, "I assume what they are doing is illegal." Tamm says his immediate thought was, "I'm a law-enforcement officer and I'm participating in something that is illegal?" [...]

[...]

Tamm [...] decided independently to get in touch with Sandra Wilkinson, a former colleague of his on the Capital Case Unit who had been detailed to work on the Senate Judiciary Committee. He met with Wilkinson for coffee in the Senate cafeteria, where he laid out his concerns about the program and the unusual procedures within OIPR. "Look, the government is doing something weird here," he recalls saying. "Can you talk to somebody on the intelligence committee and see if they know about this?"

Some weeks passed, and Tamm didn't hear back. So he e-mailed Wilkinson from his OIPR computer (not a smart move, he would later concede) and asked if they could get together again for coffee. This time, when they got together, Wilkinson was cool, Tamm says. What had she learned about the program? "I can't say," she replied and urged him to drop the subject. "Well, you know, then," he says he replied, "I think my only option is to go to the press." [ ... ]

The next few weeks were excruciating. Tamm says he consulted with an old law-school friend, Gene Karpinski, then the executive director of a public-interest lobbying group. He asked about reporters who might be willing to pursue a story that involved wrongdoing in a national-security program, but didn't tell him any details. [ ... ] Tamm says he initially considered contacting Seymour Hersh, the investigative reporter for The New Yorker, but didn't know where to reach him. He'd also noticed some strong stories by Eric Lichtblau, the New York Times reporter who covered the Justice Department—and with a few Google searches tracked down his phone number.

Tamm at this point had transferred out of OIPR at his own initiative, and moved into a new job at the U.S. Attorney's Office. He says he "hated" the desk work at OIPR and was eager to get back into the courtroom prosecuting cases. His new offices were just above Washington's Judiciary Square Metro stop. When he went to make the call to the Times, Tamm said, "My whole body was shaking." Tamm described himself to Lichtblau as a "former" Justice employee and called himself "Mark," his middle name. He said he had some information that was best discussed in person. He and Lichtblau

arranged to meet for coffee at Olsson's, a now shuttered bookstore near the Justice Department. After Tamm hung up the
phone, he was struck by the consequences of what he had
just done. "Oh, my God," he thought. "I can't talk to anybody
about this." An even more terrifying question ran through his
mind. He thought back to his days at the capital-case squad
and wondered if disclosing information about a classified program could earn him the death penalty.

[...]

Tamm grew frustrated when the story did not immediately
appear. He was hoping, he says, that Lichtblau and his partner
Risen (with whom he also met) would figure out on their own
what the program was really all about and break it before the
2004 election. He was, by this time, "pissed off" at the Bush
administration, he says. He contributed $300 to the Demo-
cratic National Committee in September 2004, according to
campaign finance records.

It wasn't until more than a year later that the paper's executive editor, Bill Keller, rejecting a personal appeal and warning by President Bush, gave the story a green light. (Bush
had warned "there'll be blood on your hands" if another
attack were to occur.) BUSH LETS U.S. SPY ON CALLERS
WITHOUT COURTS, read the headline in the paper's Dec.
16, 2005, edition. The story—which the Times said relied on
"nearly a dozen current and former officials"—had immediate repercussions. Democrats, including the then Sen. Barack
Obama, denounced the Bush administration for violating the
FISA law and demanded hearings. James Robertson, one of
the judges on the FISA court, resigned. And on Dec. 30, the
Justice Department announced that it was launching a criminal investigation to determine who had leaked to the Times.

Not long afterward, Tamm says, he started getting phone calls at his office from Jason Lawless, the hard-charging FBI agent in charge of the case. The calls at first seemed routine. Lawless was simply calling everybody who had worked at OIPR to find out what they knew. But Tamm ducked the calls; he knew that the surest way to get in trouble in such situations was to lie to an FBI agent. Still, he grew increasingly nervous. The calls continued. Finally, one day, Lawless got him on the phone. "This will just take a few minutes," Lawless said, according to Tamm's account. But Tamm told the agent that he didn't want to be interviewed—and he later hired a lawyer. [ ... ]

In the months that followed, Tamm learned he was in even more trouble. He suspected the FBI had accessed his former computer at OIPR and recovered the e-mail he had sent to Wilkinson. The agents tracked her down and questioned her about her conversations with Tamm. By this time, Tamm was in the depths of depression. He says he had trouble concentrating on his work at the U.S. Attorney's Office and ignored some e-mails from one of his supervisors. He was accused of botching a drug case. By mutual agreement, he resigned in late 2006. He was out of a job and squarely in the sights of the FBI. Nevertheless, he began blogging about the Justice Department for liberal Web sites.

Early on the morning of Aug. 1, 2007, 18 FBI agents— some of them wearing black flak jackets and carrying guns— showed up unannounced at Tamm's redbrick colonial home in Potomac, Md., with a search warrant. While his wife, wearing her pajamas, watched in horror, the agents marched into the house, seized Tamm's desktop computer, his children's laptops, his private papers, some of his books (including one about Deep Throat) and his family Christmas-card list. Terry

Tamm, the lawyer's college-age son, was asleep at the time and awoke to find FBI agents entering his bedroom. He was escorted downstairs, where, he says, the agents arranged him, his younger sister and his mother around the kitchen table and questioned them about their father. (Thomas Tamm had left earlier that morning to drive his younger son to summer school and to see a doctor about a shoulder problem.) "They asked me questions like 'Are there any secret rooms or compartments in the house'?" recalls Terry. "Or did we have a safe? They asked us if any New York Times reporters had been to the house. We had no idea why any of this was happening." Tamm says he had never told his wife and family about what he had done.

After the raid, Justice Department prosecutors encouraged Tamm to plead guilty to a felony for disclosing classified information—an offer he refused. More recently, Agent Lawless, a former prosecutor from Tennessee, has been methodically tracking down Tamm's friends and former colleagues. The agent and a partner have asked questions about Tamm's associates and political meetings he might have attended, apparently looking for clues about his motivations for going to the press, according to three of those interviewed.

In the meantime, Tamm lives in a perpetual state of limbo, uncertain whether he's going to be arrested at any moment. He could be charged with violating two laws, one concerning the disclosure of information harmful to "the national defense," the other involving "communications intelligence." Both carry penalties of up to 10 years in prison. "This has been devastating to him," says Jeffrey Taylor, an old law-school friend of Tamm's. "It's just been hanging over his head for such a long time . . . Sometimes Tom will just zone out. It's like he goes off in a special place. He's sort of consumed with this because he doesn't know where it's going."

[...]

Paul Kemp, one of Tamm's lawyers, says he was recently told by the Justice Department prosecutor in charge of Tamm's case that there will be no decision about whether to prosecute until next year—after the Obama administration takes office. The case could present a dilemma for the new leadership at Justice. During the presidential campaign, Obama condemned the warrantless-wiretapping program. So did Eric Holder, Obama's choice to become attorney general. In a tough speech last June, Holder said that Bush had acted "in direct defiance of federal law" by authorizing the NSA program.

Tamm's lawyers say his case should be judged in that light. "When I looked at this, I was convinced that the action he took was based on his view of a higher responsibility," says Asa Hutchinson, the former U.S. attorney in Little Rock and under secretary of the Department of Homeland Security who is assisting in Tamm's defense. "It reflected a lawyer's responsibility to protect the rule of law." Hutchinson also challenged the idea—argued forcefully by other Bush administration officials at the time—that The New York Times story undermined the war on terror by tipping off Qaeda terrorists to surveillance. "Anybody who looks at the overall result of what happened wouldn't conclude there was any harm to the United States," he says. After reviewing all the circumstances, Hutchinson says he hopes the Justice Department would use its "discretion" and drop the investigation. In judging Tamm's actions—his decision to reveal what little he knew about a secret domestic spying program that still isn't completely

known—it can be hard to decipher right from wrong. Sometimes the thinnest of lines separates the criminal from the
hero.

*__Michael Isikoff__ is an investigative journalist for NBC News and for-
merly for *Newsweek*. He reports on national issues such as the war on
terrorism, prisoner abuse, and presidential politics.

Isikoff, Michael. "The Fed Who Blew the Whistle." *Newsweek*, Dec. 12,
2008. http://www.thedailybeast.com/newsweek/2008/12/12/the-fed
-who-blew-the-whistle.html.

# Has the *New York Times* Violated the Espionage Act?

*by Gabriel Schoenfeld\**

"Bush Lets U.S. Spy on Callers Without Courts." Thus ran the headline of a front-page news story whose repercussions have roiled American politics ever since its publication last December 16 in the *New York Times.* The article, signed by James Risen and Eric Lichtblau, was adapted from Risen's then-forthcoming book, *State of War.*[1]

In it, the *Times* reported that shortly after September 11, 2001, President Bush had "authorized the National Security Agency [NSA] to eavesdrop on Americans and others inside the United States... without the court-approved warrants ordinarily required for domestic spying."

Not since Richard Nixon's misuse of the CIA and the IRS in Watergate, perhaps not since Abraham Lincoln suspended the writ of habeas corpus, have civil libertarians so hugely cried alarm at a supposed law-breaking action of government. People for the American Way, the Left-liberal interest group, has called the NSA wiretapping "arguably the most egregious undermining of our civil liberties in a generation." The American Civil Liberties Union has blasted Bush for "violat[ing] our Constitution and our fundamental freedoms."

Leading Democratic politicians, denouncing the Bush administration in the most extreme terms, have spoken darkly of a constitutional crisis. Former Vice President Al Gore has accused the Bush White House of "breaking the law repeatedly and insistently" and has called for a special counsel to investigate. Senator Barbara Boxer of California has solicited letters from four legal scholars inquiring whether the NSA program amounts to high crimes and misdemeanors, the constitutional standard for removal from office. John Conyers of Michigan, the ranking Democrat on the House Judiciary Committee, has demanded the creation of a select panel to investigate "those offenses which appear to rise to the level of impeachment."

The President, for his part, has not only stood firm, insisting on both the legality and the absolute necessity of his actions, but has condemned the disclosure of the NSA surveillance program as a "shameful act." In doing so, he has implicitly raised a question that the *Times* and the President's foes have conspicuously sought to ignore—namely, what is, and what should be, the relationship of news-gathering media to government secrets in the life-and-death area of national security. Under the protections provided by the First Amendment of the Constitution, do journalists have the right to publish whatever they can ferret out? Such is certainly today's working assumption, and it underlies today's practice. But is it based on an informed reading of the Constitution and the relevant statutes? If the President is right, does the December 16 story in the *Times* constitute not just a shameful act, but a crime?

## II

Ever since 9/11, U.S. intelligence and law-enforcement authorities have bent every effort to prevent our being taken once again by surprise. An essential component of that effort, the interception of al-Qaeda electronic communications around the world, has been conducted by the NSA, the government arm responsible for signals intelligence. The particular NSA program now under dispute, which the *Times* itself has characterized as the U.S. government's "most closely guarded secret," was set in motion by executive order of the President shortly after the attacks of September 11. Just as the *Times* has reported, it was designed to track and listen in on a large volume of calls and e-mails without applying for warrants to the Foreign Intelligence Security Act (FISA) courts, whose procedures the administration deemed too cumbersome and slow to be effective in the age of cell phones, calling cards, and other rapidly evolving forms of terrorist telecommunication.

Beyond this, all is controversy. According to the critics, many of whom base themselves on a much-cited study by the officially nonpartisan Congressional Research Service, Congress has never granted the President the authority to bypass the 1978 FISA Act and conduct such surveillance. In doing so, they charge, the Bush administration has flagrantly overstepped the law, being guilty, in the words of the *New Republic*, of a "bald abuse of executive power."

Defenders answer in kind. On more than twelve occasions, as the administration itself has pointed out, leaders of Congress from both parties have been given regularly scheduled, classified briefings about the NSA program. In addition, the program has been subject to internal executive-branch review every 45 days, and cannot continue without explicit presidential reauthorization (which as of January had been granted more than 30 times). Calling it a "domestic surveillance program" is, moreover, a misnomer: the communications being swept up are international in nature, confined to those calls or e-mails one terminus of which is abroad and at one terminus of which is believed to be an al-Qaeda operative.

Defenders further maintain that, contrary to the Congressional Research Service, the law itself is on the President's side.[2] In addition to the broad wartime powers granted to the executive in the Constitution, Congress, immediately after September 11, empowered the President "to take action to deter and prevent acts of international terrorism against the United States." It then supplemented this by authorizing the President to "use all necessary and appropriate force against those nations, organizations, or persons he determines planned, authorized, committed, or aided the terrorist attacks." The NSA surveillance program is said to fall under these specified powers.[3]

The debate over the legality of what the President did remains unresolved, and is a matter about which legal minds will no doubt continue to disagree, largely along partisan lines. What about the legality of what the *Times* did?

[...]

## VI

If prosecuted, or threatened with prosecution, under Section 798, today's *New York Times* would undoubtedly seek to exploit the statute's only significant loophole. This revolves around the issue of whether the information being disclosed was improperly classified as secret. In all of the extensive debate about the NSA program, no one has yet convincingly made such a charge.

The *Times* would also undoubtedly seek to create an additional loophole. It might assert that [...] the disclosure at issue is of an *illegal* governmental activity, in this case warrantless wiretapping, and that in publishing the NSA story the paper was fulfilling a central aspect of its public-service mission by providing a channel for whistleblowers in government to right a wrong. In this, it would assert, it was every bit as much within its rights as when newspapers disclosed the illegal "secret" participation of the CIA in Watergate.

But this argument, too, is unlikely to gain much traction in court. As we have already seen, congressional leaders of both parties have been regularly briefed about the program. Whether or not legal objections to the NSA surveillance ever arose in those briefings, the mere fact that Congress has been kept informed shows that, whatever legitimate objections there might be to the program, this is not a case, like Watergate, of the executive branch running amok. Mere allegations of illegality do not, in our system of democratic rule, create any sort of terra firma—let alone a presumption that one is, in turn, entitled to break the law.

As for whistleblowers unhappy with one or another government program, they have other avenues at their disposal than splashing secrets across the front page of the *New York Times*. The Intelligence Community Whistleblower Protection Act of 1998 shields employees from retribution if they wish to set out evidence of wrongdoing. When classified information is at stake, the complaints must be leveled in camera, to authorized officials, like the inspectors general of the agencies in question, or to members of congressional intelligence committees, or both. Neither the *New York Times* nor any other newspaper or television station is listed as an authorized channel for airing such complaints.

Current and former officials who choose to bypass the provisions of the Whistleblower Protection Act and to reveal classified information directly to the press are unequivocally lawbreakers. This is not in dispute. What Section 798 of the Espionage Act makes plain is that the same can be said about the press itself when, eager to obtain classified information however it can, and willing to promise anonymity to leakers, it proceeds to publish the government's communications-intelligence secrets for all the world to read.

## VII

If the *Times* were indeed to run afoul of a law once endorsed by the American Society of Newspaper Editors, it would point to a striking role reversal in the area of national security and the press.

Back in 1942, the *Chicago Tribune* was owned and operated by Colonel Robert R. McCormick. In the 1930's, as Hitler plunged Europe into crisis, his paper, pursuing the isolationist line of the America First movement, tirelessly editorialized against Franklin Roosevelt's "reckless" efforts to entangle the U.S. in a European war. Once war came, the *Tribune* no less tirelessly criticized Roosevelt's conduct of it, lambasting the administration for incompetence and much else.

In its campaign against the Roosevelt administration, one of the *Tribune*'s major themes was the evils of censorship; the paper's editorial page regularly defended its publication of secrets as in line with its duty to keep the American people well informed. On the very day before Pearl Harbor, it published an account of classified U.S. plans for fighting in Europe that came close to eliciting an indictment.[9]

The subsequent disclosure of our success in breaking the Japanese codes was thus by no means a singular or accidental mishap but an integral element in an ideological war that called for pressing against the limits.

During World War II, when the *Chicago Tribune* was recklessly endangering the nation by publishing the most closely guarded cryptographic secrets, the *New York Times* was by contrast a model of wartime rectitude. It is inconceivable that in, say, June 1944, our leading newspaper would have carried a (hypothetical) dispatch beginning: "A vast Allied invasion force is poised to cross the English Channel and launch an invasion of Europe, with the beaches of Normandy being the point at which it will land."

In recent years, however, under very different circumstances, the *Times* has indeed reversed roles, embracing a quasi-isolationist stance. If it has not inveighed directly against the war on terrorism, its editorial page has opposed almost every measure taken by the Bush administration in waging that war, from the Patriot Act to military tribunals for terrorist suspects to the CIA renditions of al-Qaeda operatives to the effort to depose Saddam Hussein. "Mr. Bush and his attorney general," says the *Times*, have "put in place a strategy for a domestic anti-terror war that [has] all the hallmarks of the administration's normal method of doing business: a Nixonian obsession with secrecy, disrespect for civil liberties, and inept management." Of the renditions, the paper has argued that they "make the United States the partner of some of the world's most repressive regimes"; constitute "outsourcing torture"; and can be defended only on the basis of "the sort of thinking that led to the horrible abuses at prisons in Iraq." The *Times*'s opposition to the Patriot Act has been even more heated: the bill is "unconstitutionally vague"; "a tempting bit of election-year politics"; "a rushed checklist of increased police powers, many of dubious value"; replete with provisions that "trample on civil liberties"; and plain old "bad law."

In pursuing its reflexive hostility toward the Bush administration, the *Times,* like the Chicago *Tribune* before it, has become an unceasing opponent of secrecy laws, editorializing against them consistently and publishing government secrets at its own discretion. [ . . . ]

[ . . . ]

"Unauthorized disclosures can be extraordinarily harmful to the United States national-security interests and . . . far too many such disclosures occur," said President Clinton on one occasion, adding that they "damage our intelligence relationships abroad, compromise intelligence gathering, jeopardize lives, and increase the threat of terrorism." To be sure, even as he uttered these words, Clinton was in the process of vetoing a bill that tightened laws against leaking secrets. But, his habitual triangulating aside, he was right and remains right. In recent years a string of such devastating leaks has occurred, of which the NSA disclosure is at the top of the list.

By means of that disclosure, the *New York Times* has tipped off al Qaeda, our declared mortal enemy, that we have been listening to every one of its communications that we have been able to locate, and have succeeded in doing so even as its operatives switch from line to line or location to location. Of course, the *Times* disputes that its publication has caused any damage to national security. In a statement on the paper's website, Bill Keller asserts complacently that "we satisfied ourselves that we could write about this program . . . in a way that would not expose any intelligence-gathering methods or capabilities that are not already on the public record." In his book,

James Risen goes even further, ridiculing the notion that the NSA wiretapping "is critical to the global war on terrorism." Government officials, he writes, "have not explained why any terrorist would be so naïve as to assume that his electronic communication was impossible to intercept."

But there are numerous examples of terrorists assuming precisely that. Prior to September 11, Osama bin Laden regularly communicated with top aides using satellite telephones whose signals were being soaked up by NSA collection systems. After a critical leak in 1998, these conversations immediately ceased, closing a crucial window into the activities of al Qaeda in the period running up to September 11.

Even after September 11, according to Risen and Eric Lichtblau in their December story, terrorists continued to blab on open lines. Thus, they wrote, NSA eavesdropping helped uncover a 2003 plot by Iyman Faris, a terrorist operative, who was apprehended and sentenced to 20 years in prison for providing material support and resources to al Qaeda and conspiring to supply it with information about possible U.S. targets. Another plot to blow up British pubs and subways stations using fertilizer bombs was also exposed in 2004, "in part through the [NSA] program." This is the same James Risen who blithely assures us that terrorists are too smart to talk on the telephone.

For its part, the *New York Times* editorial page remains serenely confident that the problem is not our national security but the overreaching of our own government. Condescending to notice that the "nation's safety is obviously a most serious issue," the paper wants us to focus instead on how "that very fact has caused this administration and many others to use it as a catch-all for any matter it wants to keep secret." If these are not the precise words used by Colonel McCormick's *Tribune* as it gave away secrets that could have cost untold numbers of American lives, the self-justifying spirit is exactly the same.

We do not know, in our battle with al Qaeda, whether we have reached a turning point. [...] Ongoing al-Qaeda strikes in the Middle East, Asia, and Europe suggest that the organization, though wounded, is still a coordinated and potent force. On January 19, after having disappeared from view for more than a year, Osama bin Laden surfaced to deliver one of his periodic threats to the American people, assuring us in an audio recording that further attacks on our homeland are "only a matter of time. They [operations] are in the planning stages, and you will see them in the heart of your land as soon as the planning is complete." Bin Laden may be bluffing; but woe betide the government that proceeds on any such assumption.

The 9/11 Commission, in seeking to explain how we fell victim to a surprise assault, pointed to the gap between our foreign and domestic intelligence-collection systems, a gap that over time had grown into a critical vulnerability. Closing that gap, in the wake of September 11, meant intercepting al-Qaeda communications all over the globe. This was the purpose of the NSA program—a program "essential to U.S. national security," in the words of Jane Harman, the ranking Democratic member of the House Intelligence Committee—the disclosure of which has now "damaged critical intelligence capabilities."

One might go further. What the *New York Times* has done is nothing less than to compromise the centerpiece of our defensive efforts in the war on terrorism. If information about the NSA program had been quietly conveyed to an al-Qaeda operative on a microdot, or on paper with invisible ink, there can be no doubt that the episode would have been treated by the government as a cut-and-dried case of espionage. Publishing it for the world to read, the *Times* has accomplished the same end while at the same time congratulating itself for bravely defending the First Amendment and thereby protecting us— from, presumably, ourselves. The fact that it chose to drop this revelation into print on the very day that renewal of the Patriot Act was being debated in the Senate—the bill's reauthorization beyond a few weeks is still not assured—speaks for itself.

The Justice Department has already initiated a criminal investigation into the leak of the NSA program, focusing on which government employees may have broken the law. But the government is contending with hundreds of national-security leaks, and progress is uncertain at best. The real question that an intrepid prosecutor in the Justice Department should be asking is whether, in the aftermath of September 11, we as a nation can afford to permit the reporters and editors of a great newspaper to become the unelected authority that determines for all of us what is a legitimate secret and what is not. Like the Constitution itself, the First Amendment's protections of freedom of the press are not a suicide pact. The laws governing what the *Times* has done are perfectly clear; will they be enforced?

**NOTES**

1. *State of War: The Secret History of the CIA and the Bush Administration.* Free Press, 240 pp., $26.00.

2. The non-partisan status of the Congressional Research Service has been called into question in this instance by the fact that the study's author, Alfred Cumming, donated $1,250 to John Kerry's presidential campaign, as was reported by the *Washington Times*.

3. What the U.S. government was doing, furthermore, differed little if at all from what it had done in the past in similar emergencies. "For as long as electronic communications have existed," as Attorney General Alberto Gonzalez has pointed out, "the United States has conducted surveillance of [enemy] communications during wartime—all without judicial warrant."

[...]

9. If the Japanese were not paying close attention to American newspapers, the Germans were. Within days of Pearl Harbor, Hitler declared war on the United States, indirectly citing as a *casus belli* the American war plans revealed in the *Tribune*.

*Gabriel Schoenfeld is a senior fellow at the Hudson Institute and the author of *Necessary Secrets: National Security, the Media, and the Rule of Law*. He was the senior editor of *Commentary* from 1994 to 2008.

Schoenfeld, Gabriel. "Has the *New York Times* Violated the Espionage Act?" *Commentary*, March 2006. http://www.commentarymagazine.com/article/has-the-%e2%80%9cnew-york-times%e2%80%9d-violated-the-espionage-act/.

# Prosecuting Whistleblowers

*by Mike German and Jay Stanley**

During his campaign, candidate Obama praised whistleblow-ers and committed to making sure they receive adequate pro-tection. The Obama-Biden plan published by the Office of the President-Elect included a whistleblower protection platform in its agenda:

> Often the best source of information about waste, fraud, and abuse in government is an existing government employee com-mitted to public integrity and willing to speak out. Such acts of courage and patriotism, which can sometimes save lives and often save taxpayer dollars, should be encouraged rather than stifled. We need to empower federal employees as watchdogs of wrongdoing and partners in performance.

Rather than empowering whistleblowers, however, the administration has been prosecuting them—and doing so with more vigor and legal creativity than any previous admin-istration.

- In a case the Washington Post called "overkill," the Obama DOJ charged former National Security Agency official Thomas Drake with allegedly mishandling classified infor-mation, using an aggressive application of the 1917 Espio-nage Act even though there was clearly no intent to harm the United States or aid its enemies. Drake had been report-ing agency waste, mismanagement and abuse to his supe-riors, to the inspector general and to Congress, and was suspected of, but not charged with, leaking information to the press. During this period the Baltimore Sun published several articles about NSA waste, mismanagement and abuse of Americans' privacy. On the eve of trial, and after a five-year ordeal for Drake, the government dropped all felony charges in exchange for Drake pleading guilty to a misdemeanor charge of "exceeding authorized use of a computer."

- FBI linguist Shamai Leibowitz received 20 months in prison after pleading guilty to charges of leaking classified information to an unnamed blogger. Though what he divulged remains unknown even to the sentencing judge, Leibowitz stated that, "[t]his was a one-time mistake that happened to me when I worked at the FBI and saw things that I considered a violation of the law."

- The Obama DOJ charged former CIA officer Jeffrey Sterling with leaking classified information about failures in the CIA's Iranian operations to a reporter, widely believed to be James Risen of the New York Times. Sterling's previous racial discrimination lawsuit against the CIA was dismissed after a Bush administration invocation of the state secrets privilege. The Sterling prosecution is disturbing on two additional counts. First, because the FBI reportedly collected Risen's credit reports, telephone and travel records, and issued a subpoena to compel him to testify about the sources for his reporting, threatening First Amendment press freedoms. Second, in addition to Espionage Act violations, Sterling is charged with "unauthorized conveyance of government property" and "mail fraud" for providing government information to a reporter. Such charges, if this case is successful, could later be used against someone who leaks even unclassified government information to a reporter.

- The Obama DOJ charged Bradley Manning, a 22-year-old Army intelligence analyst, with "aiding the enemy" for allegedly providing a large cache of classified information to WikiLeaks, a website devoted to revealing government secrets. Manning was reportedly motivated by a desire to expose secret government activities to public scrutiny. And while the data cache was so large the leaker was unlikely to have known all its contents, the materials did reveal significant evidence of U.S. and other government abuse and corruption. Indeed, U.S. diplomatic cables leaked to WikiLeaks are credited with instigating the democratic revolt in Tunisia, which became a catalyst for the "Arab Spring" movements across the Middle East and North Africa. And despite government claims of severe damage done to national security, the government has yet to identify any specific person harmed because of the leaks, and Defense Secretary William Gates reported that no sensitive intelligence sources or methods had been revealed. Gates also called the later leak of diplomatic cables "embarrassing" and "awkward," but said the consequences for U.S. foreign policy were "fairly modest." Yet the government subjected Manning to uncharacteristically harsh and clearly retaliatory conditions of pre-trial confinement that a State Department spokesman called "ridiculous and counterproductive and stupid."

- The Obama DOJ charged State Department contractor Stephen Kim with leaking rather innocuous information about North Korea's expected reaction to new economic sanctions to Fox News.

The fact is, government officials leak classified information all the time—to influence policy, take credit or deflect blame—yet few are investigated, much less prosecuted. That leaks exposing internal wrongdoing or failures of government policy are aggressively investigated and prosecuted while other potentially more damaging leaks are not only adds to the perception that these prosecutions are simply another form of whistleblower retaliation. For example, in September 2009, Bob Woodward of the Washington Post obtained a leaked copy of a confidential military assessment of the war in Afghanistan that included General Stanley McChrystal's opinion that more troops were necessary to avoid mission failure. The purpose of this leak was undoubtedly to manipulate the policy debate by putting public pressure on President Obama to comply with the commanding general's preferred strategy. Amid the mountains of innocuous and illegitimately classified documents the government produces each year, this leak involved one of the small categories of documents that are appropriately kept secret: a war planning document. Yet, the Pentagon showed little interest in discovering who was responsible for leaking the war plans—even as prosecutors relentlessly hounded critics of the national security policies for revealing much less harmful information. The failure to investigate or prosecute the vast majority of officials who leak classified information demonstrates the arbitrary and discriminatory fashion in which the Justice Department is now prosecuting whistleblowers.

*__Mike German__ is the senior policy counsel for the ACLU Washington Legislative Office and a former FBI agent.

__Jay Stanley__ is the senior policy analyst for the ACLU Speech, Privacy and Technology Project and focuses on technology-related privacy and liberty issues.

German, Mike, and Jay Stanley. *Drastic Measures Required: Congress Needs to Overhaul U.S. Secrecy Laws and Increase Oversight of the Secret Security Establishment.* New York: ACLU, 2011, pp. 10–13. http://www .aclu.org/files/assets/secrecyreport_20110727.pdf. Footnotes omitted.

# The Danger of Suppressing the Leaks

*by Margaret Sullivan**

IMAGINE if American citizens never learned about the abuse of prisoners at Abu Ghraib. Imagine not knowing about the brutal treatment of terror suspects at United States government "black sites." Or about the drone program that is expanding under President Obama, or the Bush administration's warrantless wiretapping of Americans.

This is a world without leaks.

And a world without leaks—the secret government information slipped to the press—may be the direction we're headed in. Since 9/11, leakers and whistle-blowers have become an increasingly endangered species. Some, like the former C.I.A. official John Kiriakou, have gone to jail. Another, Pfc. Bradley Manning, is charged with "aiding the enemy" for the masses of classified information he gave to Julian Assange's WikiLeaks. He could face life in prison.

The government has its reasons for cracking down. Obama administration officials have consistently cited national security concerns and expressed their intention to keep prosecuting leakers.

"The government has legitimate secrets that should remain secrets," Michael V. Hayden, the former C.I.A. director, said in a telephone interview.

Journalists tend to view the situation differently, and not just because they want, in the oft-heard phrase, "to sell newspapers." They see leaks—which have many motivations, not all altruistic—as vital to news gathering.

Declan Walsh, a reporter who wrote many WikiLeaks-based stories for The Guardian before coming to The Times, calls leaks "the unfiltered lifeblood of investigative journalism." He wrote in an e-mail from his post in Pakistan: "They may come from difficult, even compromised sources, be ridden with impurities and require careful handling to produce an accurate story. None of that reduces their importance to journalism."

Readers whom I hear from on this topic tend to express one of two opposite viewpoints: 1) The Times should relentlessly find out and print whatever it can about clandestine government activities, and 2) The Times has no business determining what is in the best interest of national security, or pursuing classified information that is passed along illegally.

Whatever one's view, one fact is clear: Leakers are being prosecuted and punished like never before. Consider that the federal Espionage Act, passed in 1917, was used only three times in its first 92 years to prosecute government officials for press leaks. But the Obama administration, in the president's first term alone, used it six times to go after leakers. Now some of them have gone to jail.

The crackdown sends a loud message. Scott Shane, who covers national security for The Times, says that message is being heard—and heeded.

"There's definitely a chilling effect," he told me. "Government officials who might otherwise discuss sensitive topics will refer to these cases in rebuffing a request for background information."

And that, says Michael Leiter, is as it should be. Mr. Leiter, the former director of the United States National Counterterrorism Center, says the prosecutions are "intended to have a deterrent effect. We've come too far toward willy-nilly leaking of sensitive information."

Many observers, though, see a useful middle ground. "This is often looked at as a battle of good versus evil, and both sides see it that way," Mr. Hayden said. "But that's not the case." He believes that for a national security effort to succeed, it must not only be "operationally effective, technologically possible and lawful," it must also be "politically sustainable."

The latter requires public support, he said, "which is only shaped by informed debate." You can't have debate without knowledge, and given the growing penchant for overclassification, that's where the press steps in.

Mr. Shane looks back on a Pentagon Papers affidavit written in 1971 by Max Frankel, then The Times's Washington bureau chief and later its executive editor, which described Washington reality: "The government hides what it can, pleading necessity as long as it can, and the press pries out what it can, pleading a need and a right to know. When the government loses a secret or two, it simply adjusts to a new reality. When the press loses a quest or two, it simply reports (or misreports) as best it can."

David McCraw, the lawyer for The Times's newsroom, said, "The system works because of restraint on both sides." Dean Baquet, the managing editor, agreed: "We've proven that we can be responsible with information. In fact, sometimes we even overdo it."

But the ramped-up prosecutions threaten this fragile eco-system that has served the public pretty well.

Private Manning's extreme treatment, in particular, worries Mr. Walsh and others because of the example it sets. (That case is in a class by itself, of course, with the wholesale transfer of some 700,000 documents. The Times reported many articles from the material, as did others.)

Many observers are quick to note a double standard for leak prosecutions: tightly controlled leaks from the highest levels ruffle no feathers.

Chris Hedges, an author, columnist and former Times reporter, thinks powerful institutions like The Times ought to push back harder—showing solidarity, including "legal common cause" with Mr. Manning and Mr. Assange, providing more detailed coverage of leak prosecutions, and crusading in editorials. "Beyond what's right, even enlightened self-interest should dictate it," he told me.

To its credit, The Times repeatedly has gone to court to seek material related to the drone program and other issues, has covered Mr. Kiriakou's case heavily, and consistently has written editorials defending press rights.

"Obviously, everybody in the industry could do more," Mr. McCraw said of legal efforts. "Resources are limited, but we're picking the best possible shots."

The Times needs to keep pressing on all these fronts, and with more zeal in print than it has so far. If news organizations don't champion press interests, who will?

In the meantime, the chilling effect continues apace. That is troubling for journalists, but even worse for citizens, who should not be in the dark about what their government is doing.

*__Margaret Sullivan__ is the public editor of the *New York Times*. She serves as the director of the American Society of News Editors, where she previously led the First Amendment committee.

Sullivan, Margaret, "The Danger of Suppressing the Leaks." *New York Times*, March 9, 2013. http://www.nytimes.com/2013/03/10/public -editor/the-danger-of-suppressing-the-leaks.html?_r=0.

# WikiLeaks Fails "Due Diligence" Review

*by Steven Aftergood\**

In the past week, both the Washington Post and the New York Times have referred to WikiLeaks.org, the web site that publishes confidential records, as a "whistleblower" site. This conforms to WikiLeaks' own instructions to journalists that "WikiLeaks should be described, depending on context, as the 'open government group', 'anti-corruption group,' 'transparency group' or 'whistleblower's site.'"

But calling WikiLeaks a whistleblower site does not accurately reflect the character of the project. It also does not explain why others who are engaged in open government, anti-corruption and whistleblower protection activities are wary of WikiLeaks or disdainful of it. [ ... ]

From one perspective, WikiLeaks is a creative response to a real problem afflicting the U.S. and many other countries, namely the over-control of government information to the detriment of public policy. WikiLeaks has published a considerable number of valuable official records that had been kept unnecessarily secret and were otherwise unavailable, including some that I had attempted and failed to obtain myself. Its most spectacular disclosure was the formerly classified videotape showing an attack by a U.S. Army helicopter crew in Baghdad in 2007 which led to the deaths of several non-combatants. Before mostly going dormant late last year, it also published numerous documents that have no particular policy significance or that were already placed in the public domain by others (including a few that were taken from the FAS web site).

WikiLeaks says that it is dedicated to fighting censorship, so a casual observer might assume that it is more or less a conventional liberal enterprise committed to enlightened democratic policies. But on closer inspection that is not quite the case. In fact, WikiLeaks must be counted among the enemies of open society because it does not respect the rule of law nor does it honor the rights of individuals.

Last year, for example, WikiLeaks published the "secret ritual" of a college women's sorority called Alpha Sigma Tau. Now Alpha Sigma Tau (like several other sororities "exposed" by WikiLeaks) is not known to have engaged in any form of misconduct, and WikiLeaks does not allege that it has. Rather, WikiLeaks chose to publish the group's confidential ritual just because it could. This is not whistleblowing and it is not journalism. It is a kind of information vandalism.

In fact, WikiLeaks routinely tramples on the privacy of non-governmental, non-corporate groups for no valid public policy reason. It has published private rites of Masons, Mormons and other groups that cultivate confidential relations among their members. Most or all of these groups are defenseless against WikiLeaks' intrusions. The only weapon they have is public contempt for WikiLeaks' ruthless violation of their freedom of association, and even that has mostly been swept away in a wave of uncritical and even adulatory reporting about the brave "open government," "whistleblower" site.

On occasion, WikiLeaks has engaged in overtly unethical behavior. Last year, without permission, it published the full text of the highly regarded 2009 book about corruption in Kenya called "It's Our Turn to Eat" by investigative reporter Michela Wrong (as first reported by Chris McGreal in The Guardian on April 9). By posting a pirated version of the book and making it freely available, WikiLeaks almost certainly disrupted sales of the book and made it harder for Ms. Wrong and other anti-corruption reporters to perform their important work and to get it published. Repeated protests and pleas from the author were required before WikiLeaks (to its credit) finally took the book offline.

"Soon enough," observed Raffi Khatchadourian in a long profile of WikiLeaks' Julian Assange in The New Yorker (June 7), "Assange must confront the paradox of his creation: the thing that he seems to detest most—power without accountability—is encoded in the site's DNA, and will only become more pronounced as WikiLeaks evolves into a real institution."

Much could be forgiven to WikiLeaks if it were true that its activities were succeeding in transforming government information policy in favor of increased openness and accountability—as opposed to merely generating reams of publicity for itself. WikiLeaks supporter Glenn Greenwald of Salon.com wrote that when it comes to combating government secrecy, "nobody is doing that as effectively as WikiLeaks." But he neglected to spell out exactly what effect WikiLeaks has had. Which U.S. government programs have been cancelled as a result of WikiLeaks' activities? Which government policies have been revised? How has public discourse shifted? (And, by the way, who has been injured by its work?)

A less sympathetic observer might conclude that WikiLeaks has squandered much of the impact that it might have had.

A telling comparison can be made between WikiLeaks' publication of the Iraq Apache helicopter attack video last April and The New Yorker's publication of the Abu Ghraib abuse photographs in an article by Seymour Hersh in May 2004. Both disclosures involved extremely graphic and disturbing images. Both involved unreleased or classified government records. And both generated a public sensation. But there the similarity ends. The Abu Ghraib photos prompted lawsuits, congressional hearings, courts martial, prison sentences, declassification initiatives, and at least indirectly a revision of U.S. policy on torture and interrogation. By contrast, the WikiLeaks video tendentiously packaged under the title "Collateral Murder" produced none of that—no investigation (other than a leak investigation), no congressional hearings, no lawsuits, no tightening of the rules of engagement. Just a mild scolding from the Secretary of Defense, and an avalanche of publicity for WikiLeaks.

Of course, it's hard for anyone to produce a specific desired outcome from the national security bureaucracy, and maybe WikiLeaks can't be faulted for failing to have done so. But with the whole world's attention at its command for a few days last April, it could have done more to place the focus on the victims of the incident that it had documented, perhaps even establishing a charitable fund to assist their families. But that's not what it chose to do. Instead, the focus remained firmly fixed on WikiLeaks itself and its own ambitious fundraising efforts.

[…]

*Steven Aftergood is the director of the Federation of American Scientists' Project on Government Secrecy. He is a critic of United States secrecy policy and writes about relevant developments in his blog, Secrecy News.

Aftergood, Steven. "WikiLeaks Fails 'Due Diligence' Review." *Secrecy News,* June 28, 2010. http://www.fas.org/blog/secrecy/2010/06/wikileaks_review.html.

Used by permission of Secrecy News from the Federation of American Scientists. Published on June 28, 2010.

# Remarks to the Press on Release of Purportedly Confidential Documents by Wikileaks

*by Hillary Rodham Clinton\**

SECRETARY CLINTON: Well, good afternoon. Do we have enough room in here? I want to take a moment to discuss the recent news reports of classified documents that were illegally provided from United States Government computers. [...]

The United States strongly condemns the illegal disclosure of classified information. It puts people's lives in danger, threatens our national security, and undermines our efforts to work with other countries to solve shared problems. This Administration is advancing a robust foreign policy that is focused on advancing America's national interests and leading the world in solving the most complex challenges of our time, from fixing the global economy, to thwarting international terrorism, to stopping the spread of catastrophic weapons, to advancing human rights and universal values. In every country and in every region of the world, we are working with partners to pursue these aims.

So let's be clear: this disclosure is not just an attack on America's foreign policy interests. It is an attack on the international community—the alliances and partnerships, the conversations and negotiations, that safeguard global security and advance economic prosperity.

[...]

I will not comment on or confirm what are alleged to be stolen State Department cables. But I can say that the United States deeply regrets the disclosure of any information that was intended to be confidential, including private discussions between counterparts or our diplomats' personal assessments and observations. I want to make clear that our official foreign policy is not set through these messages, but here in Washington. Our policy is a matter of public record, as reflected in our statements and our actions around the world.

I would also add that to the American people and to our friends and partners, I want you to know that we are taking aggressive steps to hold responsible those who stole this information. I have directed that specific actions be taken at the State Department, in addition to new security safeguards at the Department of Defense and elsewhere to protect State Department information so that this kind of breach cannot and does not ever happen again.

Relations between governments aren't the only concern created by the publication of this material. U.S. diplomats meet with local human rights workers, journalists, religious leaders, and others outside of governments who offer their own candid insights. These conversations also depend on trust and confidence. For example, if an anti-corruption activist shares information about official misconduct, or a social worker passes along documentation of sexual violence, revealing that person's identity could have serious repercussions: imprisonment, torture, even death.

So whatever are the motives in disseminating these documents, it is clear that releasing them poses real risks to real people, and often to the very people who have dedicated their own lives to protecting others.

Now, I am aware that some may mistakenly applaud those responsible, so I want to set the record straight: There is nothing laudable about endangering innocent people, and there is nothing brave about sabotaging the peaceful relations between nations on which our common security depends.

There have been examples in history in which official conduct has been made public in the name of exposing wrongdoings or misdeeds. This is not one of those cases. In contrast, what is being put on display in this cache of documents is the fact that American diplomats are doing the work we expect them to do. They are helping identify and prevent conflicts before they start. They are working hard every day to solve serious practical problems—to secure dangerous materials, to fight international crime, to assist human rights defenders, to restore our alliances, to ensure global economic stability. This is the role that America plays in the world. This is the role our diplomats play in serving America. And it should make every one of us proud.

The work of our diplomats doesn't just benefit Americans, but also billions of others around the globe. In addition to endangering particular individuals, disclosures like these tear at the fabric of the proper function of responsible government.

People of good faith understand the need for sensitive diplomatic communications, both to protect the national interest and the global common interest. Every country, including the United States, must be able to have candid conversations about the people and nations with whom they deal. And every country, including the United States, must be able to have honest, private dialogue with other countries about issues of common concern. I know that diplomats around the world share this view—but this is not unique to diplomacy. In almost every profession—whether it's law or journalism, finance or medicine or academia or running a small business—people rely on confidential communications to do their jobs. We count on the space of trust that confidentiality provides. When someone breaches that trust, we are all worse off for it. And so despite some of the rhetoric we've heard these past few days, confidential communications do not run counter to the public interest. They are fundamental to our ability to serve the public interest.

In America, we welcome genuine debates about pressing questions of public policy. We have elections about them. That is one of the greatest strengths of our democracy. It is part of who we are and it is a priority for this Administration. But stealing confidential documents and then releasing them without regard for the consequences does not serve the public good, and it is not the way to engage in a healthy debate.

[...]

Thank you, and I'd be glad to take a few questions.

*Hillary Rodham Clinton served as the United States secretary of state from 2009 to 2013 under Pres. Barack Obama.

Clinton, Hillary Rodham. "Remarks to the Press on Release of Purportedly Confidential Documents by Wikileaks." November 29, 2010. http://www.state.gov/secretary/rm/2010/11/152078.htm.

# Death to Whistle-Blowers?

*by Floyd Abrams and Yochai Benkler\**

LAST month Pfc. Bradley Manning pleaded guilty to several offenses related to leaking hundreds of thousands of documents to WikiLeaks in 2010, a plea that could land him in jail for 20 years. But Private Manning still faces trial on the most serious charges, including the potential capital offense of "aiding the enemy"—though the prosecution is not seeking the death penalty in this case, "only" a life sentence.

If successful, the prosecution will establish a chilling precedent: national security leaks may subject the leakers to a capital prosecution or at least life imprisonment. Anyone who holds freedom of the press dear should shudder at the threat that the prosecution's theory presents to journalists, their sources and the public that relies on them.

You don't have to think that WikiLeaks is the future of media, or Private Manning a paragon of heroic whistle-blowing, to understand the threat. Indeed, the two of us deeply disagree with each other about how to assess Private Manning's conduct and WikiLeaks's behavior.

Mr. Abrams, who represented The New York Times in the Pentagon Papers case, has argued that both Daniel Ellsberg, who provided the documents to the newspaper, and The Times acted with far more restraint and responsibility than Private Manning and WikiLeaks have, and that both have repeatedly behaved with a devil-may-care obliviousness to genuine national security interests.

Mr. Benkler, a law professor, has argued that Private Manning and Mr. Ellsberg (himself a Manning supporter) played a similar public role, that WikiLeaks behaved reasonably under the circumstances and that the revelations, including American forces' complicity in abuses by Iraqi allies, understatement of civilian casualties and abuses by contractors deserve recognition, not criticism.

We write together because we believe our disagreements are characteristic of many who think about the WikiLeaks/Manning affair; public feelings range from respect to deep discomfort. When it decided the Pentagon Papers case, in 1971, the Supreme Court was well aware that, as Justice Potter Stewart put it, "It is elementary that the successful conduct of international diplomacy and the maintenance of an effective national defense require both confidentiality and secrecy."

Despite this clear understanding of the risks involved in leaks and disclosure, the court's decision was encapsulated in Justice Hugo L. Black's simple statement: "The guarding of military and diplomatic secrets at the expense of informed representative government provides no real security for our Republic."

And what could be more destructive to an informed citizenry than the threat of the death penalty or life imprisonment without parole for whistle-blowers?

Under the prosecution's theory, because Private Manning knew the materials would be published and that Al Qaeda could read them once published, he indirectly communicated with the enemy. But in this theory, whether publication is by

WikiLeaks or The Times is entirely beside the point. Defendants are guilty of "aiding the enemy" for leaking to a publishing medium simply because that publication can be read by anyone with an Internet connection.

In a January hearing the judge, Col. Denise Lind, asked prosecutors directly whether they would have brought the same charges had Private Manning leaked the materials to The New York Times instead of WikiLeaks. The prosecutors' answer was unambiguously yes.

That yes was not courtroom bluster, but a necessary concession regarding what their theory means. And nothing in that theory would limit its application to the release of hundreds of thousands of documents. It could apply as effectively to a single abuse-revealing document.

So yes, we continue to disagree about what to make of Private Manning and WikiLeaks. But we agree that WikiLeaks is part of what the Fourth Estate is becoming, that the leaks included important disclosures and that their publication is protected by the First Amendment no less than the publication of the Pentagon Papers was.

Private Manning's guilty plea gives the prosecution an opportunity to rethink its strategy. The extreme charges remaining in this case create a severe threat to future whistle-blowers, even when their revelations are crystal-clear instances of whistle-blowing. We cannot allow our concerns about terrorism to turn us into a country where communicating with the press can be prosecuted as a capital offense.

***Floyd Abrams** is an American attorney, expert in constitutional law, and author of *Friend of the Court: On the Front Lines with the First Amendment*.

**Yochai Benkler** is a law professor at Harvard Law School and codirector of the Berkman Center for Internet & Society at Harvard.

Abrams, Floyd, and Yochai Benkler. "Death to Whistle-Blowers?" *New York Times,* March 13, 2013. http://www.nytimes.com/2013/03/14/opinion/the-impact-of-the-bradley-manning-case.html?_r=1&.

# PART 5
# Government Surveillance

One of the most important goals of post-Watergate reforms was ending efforts by federal, state, and local law enforcement officials to disrupt the exercise of free speech by individuals and groups critical of the government. The FBI's counterintelligence program (COINTELPRO) played a major role in the demise of the Communist Party in the 1940s and 1950s and cast suspicion on anyone espousing even liberal ideas. The FBI also secretly worked to undermine the civil rights and antiwar movements in the 1960s. To prevent future abuses, Pres. Gerald Ford banned the CIA from spying on groups in the United States, and his attorney general, Edward H. Levi, created guidelines to prevent the FBI from conducting surveillance in the absence of evidence of criminal conduct.

After 9/11, Attorney General John Ashcroft and others argued that the restrictions imposed on police in the 1970s were a barrier to preventing terrorist attacks. In 2002, Ashcroft loosened the Levi guidelines, maintaining in "Remarks of the Attorney General: Attorney General Guidelines" that the new guidelines did little more than permit agents to attend public meetings and search the Internet. But the American Civil Liberties Union ("Interested Persons Memo: Analysis of Changes to Attorney General's Guidelines") charged that relaxation of the restrictions had swept away the protections that were in place since the 1970s and would lead to spying on political groups engaged in peaceful protest. This prediction proved to be correct. In 2010, the Justice Department's inspector general confirmed that the FBI had conducted surveillance of several groups, including antiwar activists, without evidence that they were engaged in illegal acts, as reported by the *Washington Times* in "Internal Report Raps FBI's Probes of Advocacy Groups." The FBI also cited the threat of terrorism as the pretext for investigating the Occupy Wall Street movement ("F.B.I. Counterterrorism Agents Monitored Occupy Movement").

Restrictions on spying by local police were also loosened after 9/11. In August 2011, reporters from The Associated Press (AP) revealed the New York Police Department's extensive surveillance program targeting the city's Muslims ("With CIA Help, NYPD Moves Covertly in Muslim Areas"). Critics of the program, including members of the Muslim American Civil Liberties Coalition ("Mapping Muslims"), believe that such monitoring is making Muslims afraid to discuss politics and even tell jokes. Defenders, such as Mitchell D. Silber ("Who Will Defend the Defenders?"), former director of intelligence analysis for the New York Police Department, argue that the AP investigation has misrepresented a program that has helped keep the city safe.

In February 2013, lawyers filed a lawsuit challenging the constitutionality of the New York Police Department's program for conducting surveillance of and in the Muslim community. But the Boston Marathon bombing in April 2013 was cited by New York mayor Michael Bloomberg and other government officials as evidence that police surveillance remains critically important for apprehending terrorists. Pictures taken at the scene revealed the identity of the bombers, and calls were heard for expanding the use of police cameras on city streets.

Think about these questions as you read this section:

- Is government surveillance necessary?

- Does government surveillance threaten free speech?

- Should the NYPD surveillance program continue?

# Remarks of the Attorney General: Attorney General Guidelines

*by John Ashcroft\**

In its 94-year history, the Federal Bureau of Investigation has been many things—the defender of the nation from organized crime, the guardian of our security from international espionage, and the tireless protector of civil rights and civil liberties for all Americans.

On September 11, a stunned nation turned once again to the brave men and women of the FBI, and they, once again, answered the call. I spent the hours, days, and most of the first weeks after the attack in the FBI's Strategic Information and Operations Center with Director Mueller. Even today, eight months later, it is difficult to convey the professionalism, dedication and quiet resolve I witnessed in those first, 24-hour days. I saw men and women work themselves beyond fatigue to prevent new terrorist attacks. I witnessed individuals put aside their personal lives, personal agendas and personal safety to answer our nation's call.

From the first moments we spent together, launching the largest investigation in history, we understood that the mission of American justice and law enforcement had changed. That day, in those early hours, the prevention of terrorist acts became the central goal of the law enforcement and national security mission of the FBI. And from that time forward, we in the leadership of the FBI and the Department of Justice began a concerted effort to free the field agents—the brave men and women on the front lines—from the bureaucratic, organizational, and operational restrictions and structures that hindered them from doing their jobs effectively.

As we have heard recently, FBI men and women in the field are frustrated because many of our own internal restrictions have hampered our ability to fight terrorism. The current investigative guidelines have contributed to that frustration. In many instances, the guidelines bar FBI field agents from taking the initiative to detect and prevent future terrorist acts unless the FBI learns of possible criminal activity from external sources.

Under the current guidelines, FBI investigators cannot surf the web the way you or I can. Nor can they simply walk into a public event or a public place to observe ongoing activities. They have no clear authority to use commercial data services that any business in America can use. These restrictions are a competitive advantage for terrorists who skillfully utilize sophisticated techniques and modern computer systems to compile information for targeting and attacking innocent Americans.

That is why the Attorney General's guidelines and procedures relating to criminal investigations and national security were high on the list of action items for reform. Beginning in the 1970s, guidelines have been developed to inform agents of the circumstances under which investigations may be opened, the permissible scope of these investigations, the techniques that may be used, and the objectives that should be pursued. These guidelines provide limitations and guidance over and above all requirements and safeguards imposed by the

Constitution and beyond the legal framework established by federal statutes enacted by Congress. Promulgated for different purposes and revised at various times, the guidelines currently cover FBI investigations, undercover operations, the use of confidential informants, and consensual monitoring of verbal communications.

The guidelines defining the general rules for FBI investigations, for example, were first issued over 20 years ago. They derive from a period in which Soviet communism was the greatest threat to the United States, in which the Internet did not exist, and in which concerns over terrorist threats to the homeland related mainly to domestic hate groups.

Shortly after September 11, I took two steps to free FBI field agents to prevent additional terrorist attacks. First, I authorized the FBI to waive the guidelines, with headquarters approval, in extraordinary cases to prevent and investigate terrorism. That authority has been used, but I am disappointed that it was not used more widely. This experience over the past few months reinforces my belief that greater authority to investigate more vigorously needs to be given directly to FBI field agents.

Second, I directed a top-to-bottom review of the guidelines to ensure that they provide front-line field agents with the legal authority they need to protect the American people from future terrorist attacks. That comprehensive review showed that the guidelines mistakenly combined timeless objectives—the enforcement of the law and respect for civil rights and liberties—with outdated means.

Today, I am announcing comprehensive revisions to the Department's investigative guidelines. As revised, the guidelines reflect four overriding principles.

First, the war against terrorism is the central mission and highest priority of the FBI. This principle is stated explicitly in the revised guidelines, and it is facilitated and reinforced through many specific reforms. The guidelines emphasize that the FBI must not be deprived of using all lawful authorized methods in investigations, consistent with the Constitution and statutory authority, to pursue and prevent terrorist actions.

Second, terrorism prevention is the key objective under the revised guidelines. Our philosophy today is not to wait and sift through the rubble following a terrorist attack. Rather, the FBI must intervene early and investigate aggressively where information exists suggesting the possibility of terrorism, so as to prevent acts of terrorism. The new guidelines advance this strategy of prevention by strengthening investigative authority at the early stage of preliminary inquiries. Also, even absent specific investigative predicates, FBI agents under the new guidelines are empowered to scour public sources for information on future terrorist threats.

Third, unnecessary procedural red tape must not interfere with the effective detection, investigation, and prevention of terrorist activities. To this end, the revised guidelines allow Special Agents in Charge of FBI field offices to approve and renew terrorism enterprise investigations, rather than having to seek and wait for approval from headquarters. I believe this responds to a number of concerns we have heard from our field agents. The guidelines expand the scope of those investigations to the full range of terrorist activities under the USA Patriot Act. These major changes will free field agents to counter potential terrorist threats swiftly and vigorously without waiting for headquarters to act.

Fourth, the FBI must draw proactively on all lawful sources of information to identify terrorist threats and activities. It cannot meet its paramount responsibility to prevent acts of terrorism if FBI agents are required, as they were in the past, to blind themselves to information that everyone else is free to see. Under the revised guidelines, the FBI can identify and track foreign terrorists by combining its investigative results with information obtained from other lawful sources, such as foreign intelligence and commercial data services. To detect and prevent terrorist activities, the FBI under the revised guidelines will also be able to enter and observe public places and forums just as any member of the public might.

Let me pause here for a moment. What I am saying is this: FBI field agents have been inhibited from attending public events, open to any other citizen—not because they are barred by the U.S. Constitution, or barred any federal law enacted by Congress, but because of the lack of clear authority under administrative guidelines issued decades ago. Today, I am clarifying that, for the specific purpose of detecting or preventing terrorist activities, FBI field agents may enter public places and attend events open to other citizens, unless they are barred from attending by the Constitution or federal law.

Our new guideline reads, "For the purpose of detecting or preventing terrorist activities, the FBI is authorized to visit any place and attend any event that is open to the public, on the same terms and conditions as members of the public generally."

I believe in the principle of community policing, in which an active, visible law enforcement presence is linked to communities and neighborhoods. Local police can enter public places and attend public events in their communities, and they detect and prevent crime by doing so. To protect our communities from terrorism, the FBI must be free to do the same.

The revised guidelines will take effect immediately and will be incorporated into the training of FBI agents. These guidelines will also be a resource to inform the American public and demonstrate that we seek to protect life and liberty from terrorism and other criminal violence with a scrupulous respect for civil rights and personal freedoms.

[ ... ]

*John Ashcroft served as the United States attorney general from 2001 to 2005.

Ashcroft, John. "Remarks of Attorney General John Ashcroft: Attorney General Guidelines." May 30, 2002. http://www.justice.gov/archive/ag/speeches/2002/53002agpreparedremarks.htm.

# Interested Persons Memo: Analysis of Changes to Attorney General Guidelines

*by American Civil Liberties Union\**

[...]

On May 30, 2002, Attorney General Ashcroft released new Guidelines on General Crimes, Racketeering Enterprise and Terrorism Enterprise Investigations. Sweeping away protections that have been in place since the 1970s, the new Guidelines allow the government to spy on domestic groups even when there is no suspicion of wrongdoing. Furthermore, the investigations the new Guidelines authorize can continue longer, with intrusive techniques and with less oversight, even when they produce no evidence of crime.

[...]

## Guideline Changes

The Domestic Guidelines were adopted to put the FBI out of the business of spying on Americans when there was no evidence that they were involved in criminal activity. The Ashcroft Guidelines put the FBI back in that business. The Ashcroft Guidelines represent a generalized lifting of restrictions on FBI spying activity that have worked well for many years. Under the old Domestic Guidelines, the FBI already had the operational freedom and authority to gather the information needed to do its job. The problem was its inability to analyze the information it already had. Now, the FBI will add to that mountain of information even more useless facts.

Additionally, the Attorney General has not demonstrated any need for relaxing the domestic guidelines.

The Domestic Guidelines were adopted to deal with three problems arising from abusive FBI investigations:

- Surveillance of dissenters from government policy because they dissent, not because they may be involved in criminal activity;

- Inadequate supervision of agents who engaged in objectionable investigative techniques; and

- The use of unlawful or otherwise objectionable investigative techniques to disrupt the efforts of those who dissented.

By severing the tie between investigative activity and crime and by lessening the accountability of agents in the field to superiors who could reign in or prevent unlawful conduct, the Attorney General has undermined two of the fundamental purposes for adopting the Guidelines in the first place.

### INCREASED SPYING ON DOMESTIC RELIGIOUS AND POLITICAL ORGANIZATIONS

That Ashcroft Guidelines state: "For the purpose of detecting or preventing terrorist activities, the FBI is authorized to visit any place and attend any event that is open to the public, on the same terms and conditions as members of the public generally. No information obtained from such visits shall be retained unless it relates to potential criminal or terrorist activity."[19] This was the same basis upon which the FBI sent agents into churches and other organizations during the civil rights movement, and then attempted to block the movement, suppress dissent, and protect the administration.

The old Domestic Guidelines required that FBI activity be predicated upon at least a modicum of suspicion that crime was afoot. After all, during the 1950s and 1960s the FBI routinely infiltrated political and religious groups to spy on their activities. The original Domestic Guidelines were designed to prevent these widespread fishing expeditions. [...]

The Ashcroft Guidelines permit FBI agents to attend every single public meeting or demonstration, from political conventions and demonstrations, to churches. So long as there is a claimed anti-terrorism purpose, nothing in the Ashcroft Guidelines imposes any judicial control, FBI Headquarters control, or even local Special Agent in Command control over this activity. While Attorney General Ashcroft is fond of saying agents may only conduct such surveillance for the purposes of ferreting out terrorism, the Ashcroft Guidelines permit the agent, once there, to collect information about *any* crime [...].

Proponents of this change—permitting the FBI to spy when there is no evidence of a crime—claim it is necessary because the requirement of evidence tied the hands of the FBI when suspects entered mosques or temples, or other houses of worship. In fact, the old guidelines did not prohibit FBI agents from entering houses of worship; it merely required that the agent be following a lead, or conducting an investigation or preliminary inquiry.[23]

Although the new guidelines say that information obtained from such surveillance must relate to potential criminal or terrorist activity, it is unclear how broad or attenuated that relation must be. The natural tendency is to gather as much information as possible, fitting together bits and pieces of information, many meaningless by themselves, to determine whether a pattern of criminal activity exists.[24] Therefore, the tendency will be to collect more information, rather than less, in the hopes some of this "innocuous" information will be helpful when it comes time to "connect the dots."

The danger of this provision is that the FBI will now be attending religious functions and political rallies to take note of who attends, what they say, and what they do. The administration will have its own taxpayer-financed intelligence arm to inform it of political moves and strategies its opponents may be hatching. Furthermore, the FBI will be wasting money and resources gathering information in situations in which there is no suspicion of any criminal conduct. And, most importantly, this will chill First Amendment activity from worship to free speech.

## INTERNET SPYING ON POLITICAL ACTIVITY WITH INSUFFICIENT OVERSIGHT

As noted above, the old Domestic Guidelines required that FBI activity be accomplished pursuant to a preliminary inquiry or investigation. The Ashcroft Guidelines allow the FBI to carry out and retain information resulting from general topical research.[25] This includes conducting online searches and accessing online sites and forums as part of such research. Once again, the FBI can use this information to suppress dissent and help cripple political enemies.

The Ashcroft Guidelines define "general topical research" as "research concerning subject areas that are relevant for the purpose of facilitating or supporting the discharge of investigative responsibilities."[26] "It does not include online searches for information by individuals' names or other individual identifiers, except where such searches are incidental to topical research, such as searching to locate writings on the topic by searching under the names of authors who write on the topic, or searching by the name of a party to a case in conducting legal research."[27]

First of all, the FBI has never been prohibited from reading the newspaper or surfing the Internet. For decades, and under the old Domestic Guidelines, it opened preliminary inquiries and investigations based on what agents have read in the newspaper about potential criminal activity.

Second, there is great concern over the types of topics the FBI will be researching. The FBI talks about searching for "anthrax" or "smallpox," neither of which would have been prohibited under the old guidelines, particularly after the initial anthrax scare. Neither of these topics inherently implicates privacy or civil liberties issues. However, it is a whole different matter to search for "Islam," "Pro-life," or "gun rights," and use the results to form the basis for suspicion. And, this new surveillance authority is not limited to searching for information on terrorism.

[. . .]

## USE OF COMMERCIAL DATA MINING TO SNOOP ON AMERICANS' BUYING HABITS

Commercial data mining has become a big business. Any time you write check, use a credit card, buy something on credit, make department store purchases, surf the Web, use an e-z pass to buy gasoline or pay a toll, you leave a record. Commercial companies take this information and build profiles, such as who reads Gun Week magazine, or who buys books online about terrorism. Those profiles are then used to send to catalogs, credit cards, spam, and much other information you may not wish to receive.

Under the Ashcroft Guidelines, once again, the FBI will be able to engage in a fishing expedition using these resources. With no evidence that any crime is even contemplated, the FBI can purchase detailed profiles compiled by the data miners. And, once it obtains this information it is entitled to retain possession of it indefinitely.[28] Thus, the FBI may purchase information about you that is incorrect. However, even if you are able to correct the data the data mining company gathered about you, the FBI will still have possession of incorrect data.

There is no provision in either the Ashcroft Guidelines or the law similar to that in the Fair Credit Reporting Act, which would allow an individual access to the information and the ability to correct it. The disadvantage of a data mining company having incorrect information about a person is that the person may receive more spam, credit cards, or unwanted catalogs. The disadvantage of the FBI having incorrect information about a person is that the person may be arrested. In fact, since September 11, the FBI has arrested people based on innocent activity.

[ … ]

## PERMITTING LENGTHY PRELIMINARY INQUIRIES AND INVESTIGATIONS EVEN WHERE NO EVIDENCE IS FOUND

The Ashcroft Guidelines will extend the authorized duration of preliminary inquiries from 90 days to 180 days. They also allow the Special Agent in Charge of field offices to authorize two ninety-day extensions. Thus, preliminary inquiries can now last for up to one year without any meaningful oversight by FBI Headquarters.

Remember, there are few constraints on the FBI in conducting preliminary inquiries. Under the new guidelines, the FBI is empowered to troll for information on the Internet, use commercial data mining services, and attend any public meetings, even when there is no suspicion of crime. This information however, may be used in order to form such a suspicion. Once that occurs, the FBI may use all lawful investigative techniques during the inquiry, with the exception of mail openings and nonconsensual electronic surveillance.[29] This includes physical or photographic surveillance, interviews of potential witnesses, examination of all public records, examination of federal, state, and local government records, interviews of the potential subject, interviews of the complainants, previously established informants, and other sources of information. Thus, with no reasonable indication an individual is involved [in] criminal activity, the FBI may use . . . highly intrusive techniques to conduct its preliminary inquiry for up to one year.

Under the old Domestic Guidelines, Racketeering and Domestic Security/Terrorism investigations could last for six months.[30] These are wide-ranging investigations that are less precise than investigations directed at more conventional types of crime. These investigations are of an entire enterprise rather than individual participants in a single criminal act, and seek to determine the scope of the enterprise as well as the relationship of the members. Thus, these investigations are disruptive to a wider range of people and businesses than a conventional criminal investigation. After six months, the FBI had to show that it found some evidence of crime in order to extend the investigation. Under the Ashcroft Guidelines, the FBI will be able to continue an investigation for up to one year, with the full panoply of its investigative powers, even though it found nothing to justify keeping the investigation open.[31]

Both of these changes are open invitations for fishing expeditions. Agents will be allowed to spy on citizens and noncitizens, and gather political intelligence for up to one year with no oversight from FBI Headquarters.

[...]


## Conclusion

By severing the tie between initial FBI surveillance and evidence of crime, the Ashcroft Guidelines fundamentally alter the role of the FBI in our society, and ignore the lessons of its past abuses. Now, the FBI is authorized to attend every public meeting and every demonstration, and to track the Internet activities of groups and individuals in chat rooms and on web sites, even though it lacks even a scintilla of evidence that a crime has been, is being, or may be committed. Similar activity prompted the Congressional action that resulted in adoption of the original Attorney General Guidelines a quarter century ago.

America is changing as a result of the 9/11 attacks, but many of the changes in the Ashcroft Guidelines are unnecessary. In fact, the Ashcroft Guidelines likely have nothing to do with heading off another attack from al Qaeda because its activities are investigated under an entirely different set of investigative guidelines, the Foreign Intelligence Guidelines. Instead, it appears that the FBI is using America's fear of terrorism to dramatically increase its power in areas that have little to do with terrorism. Despite its inability to manage and analyze the information it already gathers, it now wants to gather more information free from the constraints previously imposed. This not only makes the FBI less effective in preventing terrorism, but it chills Americans' freedom to associate and speak without the fear that their associations and speech will end up in an FBI database.

## NOTES

19. Ashcroft Domestic Guidelines, VI A 2.

[...]

23. *Washington Post*, 5/30/02 "Under guidelines have been in place for several decades, the FBI has not been permitted to send investigators into religious settings unless the agents can establish their following a lead, or conducting an investigation or preliminary inquiry. As a practical matter, the Justice Department officials said, "agents mistakenly think *they have to stop at the church door.*" [Emphasis added.]

24. Ashcroft Domestic Guidelines, III (discussing criminal intelligence investigations, noting these investigations are "broader and less discriminate than usual, involving 'the interrelation of various sources and types of information.'") The same rules apply for domestic terrorism investigations. Thus, a wide net is necessarily cast to gather this information.

25. Ashcroft Domestic Guidelines, VI B 1.

26. Id.

27. Id.

28. Ashcroft Domestic Guidelines, VI B. The Old Domestic Guidelines were silent on the retention of the data, but required some indication of criminal activity before the search was authorized.

29. Ashcroft Domestic Guidelines, II B (5). Note that this is also a change from the Old Domestic Guidelines. Under the Old Domestic Guidelines, preliminary inquiries were prohibited from using

mail covers, mail opening, and nonconsensual electronic surveillance. Old Domestic Guidelines II B (5). The Ashcroft Guidelines now only prohibit mail opening and nonconsensual electronic surveillance. Ashcroft Domestic Guidelines, II B (5). Thus, with no warrant or even a "reasonable indication" of criminal activity, the FBI may check a person's mail to determine who they are sending mail to, and who they receive mail from.

30. Old Domestic Guidelines, III B 4 b.

31. Ashcroft Domestic Guidelines, III B 4 b.


*The **American Civil Liberties Union** is a national, nonprofit organization that aims to preserve individual rights in the United States. Its operations focus on lobbying, litigation, and education.


American Civil Liberties Union. "Interested Persons Memo: Analysis of Changes to Attorney General Guidelines." June 6, 2002. http://www.aclu.org/national-security/interested-persons-memo-analysis-changes-attorney-general-guidelines.

Used by permission of the American Civil Liberties Union.

# Internal Report Raps FBI's Probes of Advocacy Groups

*by Jerry Seper\**

The FBI investigated several advocacy groups on "factually weak" information, extended those inquiries "without adequate basis," improperly retained information on some groups, and wrongly listed others under terrorism classifications, according to a report.

The Justice Department's office of inspector general, in a 191-page report released Monday, said the misclassification resulted in some activists—including members of Greenpeace US—being placed on government terrorist watch lists.

The report also states that because of inaccurate information given to FBI Director Robert S. Mueller III about the circumstances of the FBI's surveillance of an anti-war rally in Pittsburgh in 2002, the director unintentionally provided inaccurate testimony to Congress.

Inspector General Glenn A. Fine said Mr. Mueller wrongly testified that certain people of interest in international terrorism matters were expected at the rally sponsored by the Thomas Merton Center, a Pittsburgh-based peace activist group, when that was not the case.

The inquiry focused on FBI activities between 2001 and 2006 and also involved the People for the Ethical Treatment of Animals (PETA); Greenpeace USA; the Catholic Worker, a pacifist organization; and Glenn Milner, a Quaker peace activist. The investigation began in response to congressional concerns that the FBI had improperly targeted domestic groups for investigation based on their exercise of First Amendment rights.

"The [inspector general's] review did not indicate that the FBI targeted any of the groups for investigation on the basis of their First Amendment activities," the report said. "However, the [office] concluded that the factual basis for opening some of the investigations of individuals affiliated with the groups was factually weak."

"The FBI also classified some investigations relating to nonviolent civil disobedience under its 'Acts of Terrorism' classification, which resulted in the watchlisting of subjects during the pendency of the investigation," it said.

Some of the activists, as a result of the FBI investigations, were placed on the Violent Gang and Terrorist Organization File watch list.

In a response, FBI Deputy Director Timothy Murphy noted that the bureau had not targeted any groups for investigation on the basis of their First Amendment activities, but instead on concerns about potential criminal acts. He also said the FBI regretted that incorrect information had been given to Congress.

The report is not the first time Mr. Fine's office has questioned FBI surveillance and investigative tactics. In March 2007, he said the bureau failed to create "sufficient controls and oversight" in its domestic hunt for terrorists, leading to "widespread and serious" misuse of its authority to gather telephone and travel records, e-mails and financial documents.

A year later, the inspector general's office said that, despite assurances from Mr. Mueller that the FBI had enacted reforms to prevent more abuses, senior FBI counterterrorism officials improperly issued blanket national security letters for 3,860 telephone numbers to cover up the fact that the agency already improperly obtained the information.

The inspector general office's newest report said the Merton Center incident "raised the most troubling issues in this review."

According to the report, a probationary FBI agent in Pittsburgh was sent in November 2002 to an anti-war event sponsored by the Merton Center because it was "a slow day." The report said the agent was told to look for international terrorists, although no information suggested that terrorists might be present.

The report said the agent was unable to identify any terrorism subjects, but photographed a woman of Middle Eastern descent to have something to show his supervisor.

Four years later, the agent's report was released publicly in response to a Freedom of Information Act request. That prompted the FBI to say the agent had attended the event "for the sole purpose of determining the validity of information he received from another source establishing a link between an ongoing investigation and the [Merton Center]."

The inspector general's report said Mr. Mueller told Congress in May 2006 that the surveillance was an "outgrowth of an FBI investigation" and the agent was "attempting to identify an individual who happened to be, we believed, in attendance at the rally." The FBI declined to provide additional information, saying the investigation "is still ongoing."

The report concluded that the FBI was not targeting the Merton Center or its members for investigation because of its anti-war advocacy, but because the agent had been sent to the event "pursuant to an ill-conceived make-work assignment given to a probationary agent on a slow workday."

The report also noted that a Feb. 23, 2003, FBI memo "created the inaccurate impression that the Merton Center was the subject of an international terrorism investigation." In fact, the report said, the FBI's Pittsburgh office did not open an investigation of the Merton Center and the memo was neither approved nor disseminated outside the Pittsburgh office.

Others targeted by the FBI included:

- PETA in Norfolk, Va., in which the inspector general's report said the FBI's decision to continue the matter as a full investigation contributed to the case remaining open for six years. The report said the length of the investigation was inconsistent with FBI policy requiring that an investigation with potential impact on First Amendment activity "not be permitted to extend beyond the point at which its underlying justification no longer exists."

- Greenpeace, in which the inspector general's office said the FBI conducted a full investigation of the group's planned protests against Exxon Mobil and Kimberly-Clark, but "articulated little or no basis for suspecting a violation of any federal criminal statute, as opposed to a state or local crime, such as trespassing." The report said that, because the three-year probe was classified as a terrorism case, the subjects were placed on a federal watch list and information was collected on their travel and protest activities.

- The Catholic Worker, in which the report said it found two FBI documents in a domestic terrorism file that contained information about nonviolent civil disobedience by Catholic Worker members that involved the peaceful trespass on a military facility. The report questioned the FBI's targeting of lawful civil disobedience and described its classification of the inquiry as a terrorism case as "inappropriate, because the acts in question did not include the use of violence or force."

- Glenn Milner, a Seattle Quaker and peace activist who was placed "under watch" by the FBI for what the inspector general's office called protest activities carried out at the 2003 Seafair festival in Seattle. The report said investigators found no evidence that the FBI investigated the Quakers as a group, or any individuals identified in FBI documents as Quakers, for their protest activities.

*Jerry Seper is the investigative editor for the *Washington Times*.

Seper, Jerry. "Internal Report Raps FBI's Probes of Advocacy Groups." *Washington Times,* September 20, 2010. http://www.washingtontimes.com/news/2010/sep/20/internal-report-raps-fbis-probes-advocacy-groups/print/.

# F.B.I. Counterterrorism Agents Monitored Occupy Movement, Records Show

*by Michael S. Schmidt and Colin Moynihan**

WASHINGTON—The Federal Bureau of Investigation used counterterrorism agents to investigate the Occupy Wall Street movement, including its communications and planning, according to newly disclosed agency records.

The F.B.I. records show that as early as September 2011, an agent from a counterterrorism task force in New York notified officials of two landmarks in Lower Manhattan—Federal Hall and the Museum of American Finance—"that their building was identified as a point of interest for the Occupy Wall Street."

That was around the time that Occupy Wall Street activists set up a camp in Zuccotti Park in Lower Manhattan, spawning a protest movement across the United States that focused the nation's attention on issues of income inequality.

In the following months, F.B.I. personnel around the country were routinely involved in exchanging information about the movement with businesses, local law-enforcement agencies and universities.

An October 2011 memo from the bureau's Jacksonville, Fla., field office was titled Domain Program Management Domestic Terrorist.

The memo said agents discussed "past and upcoming meetings" of the movement, and its spread. It said agents should contact Occupy Wall Street activists to ascertain whether people who attended their events had "violent tendencies."

The memo said that because of high rates of unemployment, "the movement was spreading throughout Florida and there were several Facebook pages dedicated to specific chapters based on geographical areas."

The F.B.I. was concerned that the movement would provide "an outlet for a lone offender exploiting the movement for reasons associated with general government dissatisfaction."

Since the Sept. 11, 2001, attacks, the F.B.I. has come under criticism for deploying counterterrorism agents to conduct surveillance and gather intelligence on organizations active in environmental, animal-cruelty and poverty issues.

The disclosure of the F.B.I. records comes a little more than a year after the police ousted protesters from Zuccotti Park in November 2011. Law-enforcement agencies undertook similar actions around the country against Occupy Wall Street groups. Occupy Wall Street has lost much of its visibility since then, but questions remain about how local and federal law-enforcement officials monitored and treated the protesters.

The records were obtained by the Partnership for Civil Justice Fund, a civil-rights organization in Washington, through a Freedom of Information request to the F.B.I. Many parts of the documents were redacted by the bureau.

The records provide one of the first glimpses into how deeply involved federal law-enforcement authorities were in monitoring the activities of the movement, which is sometimes described in extreme terms.

For example, according to a memo written by the F.B.I.'s New York field office in August 2011, bureau personnel met with officials from the New York Stock Exchange to discuss "the planned Anarchist protest titled 'Occupy Wall Street,' scheduled for September 17, 2011."

"The protest appears on Anarchist Web sites and social network pages on the Internet," the memo said.

It added: "Numerous incidents have occurred in the past which show attempts by Anarchist groups to disrupt, influence, and or shut down normal business operations of financial districts."

A spokesman for the F.B.I. in Washington cautioned against "drawing conclusions from redacted" documents.

"The F.B.I. recognizes the rights of individuals and groups to engage in constitutionally protected activity," said the spokesman, Paul Bresson. "While the F.B.I. is obligated to thoroughly investigate any serious allegations involving threats of violence, we do not open investigations based solely on First Amendment activity. In fact, the Department of Justice and the F.B.I.'s own internal guidelines on domestic operations strictly forbid that."

But Mara Verheyden-Hilliard, executive director of the Partnership for Civil Justice Fund, said the documents demonstrated that the F.B.I. had acted improperly by gathering information on Americans involved in lawful activities.

"The collection of information on people's free-speech actions is being entered into unregulated databases, a vast storehouse of information widely disseminated to a range of law-enforcement and, apparently, private entities," she said.

"This is precisely the threat—people do not know when or how it may be used and in what manner."

The records show little evidence that the members of the movement planned to commit violence. But they do describe a discussion on the Internet "regarding the Occupy Wall Street movement about when it is okay to shoot a police officer" and a law-enforcement meeting held in Des Moines because "there may potentially be an attempt to stop the Iowa Caucuses by people involved in Occupy Iowa."

There are no references within the documents to agency personnel covertly infiltrating Occupy branches.

The documents indicate, however, that the F.B.I. obtained information from police departments and other law-enforcement agencies that appear to have been gathered by someone observing the protesters as they planned activities.

The documents do not detail recent activities by the F.B.I. involving Occupy Wall Street.

But one activist, Billy Livsey, 48, said two F.B.I. agents visited him in Brooklyn over the summer to question him about planned protests at the Republican National Convention in Tampa, Fla., and about plans to celebrate the first anniversary of Occupy Wall Street in September.

The agents, Mr. Livsey said, told him they knew he was among a group of people involved in the Occupy Wall Street "direct action" group that distributed information about the movement's activities.

He said he felt unnerved by the visit.

"It was surprising and troubling to me," Mr. Livsey said.

*Michael S. Schmidt and Colin Moynihan are reporters for the *New York Times*.

Schmidt, Michael S., and Colin Moynihan. "F.B.I. Counterterrorism Agents Monitored Occupy Movement, Records Show." *New York Times*, December 24, 2012. http://www.nytimes.com/2012/12/25/nyregion/occupy-movement-was-investigated-by-fbi-counterterrorism-agents-records-show.html?_r=0.

# With CIA Help, NYPD Moves Covertly in Muslim Areas

*by Matt Apuzzo and Adam Goldman\**

In New Brunswick, N.J., a building superintendent opened the door to apartment No. 1076 one balmy Tuesday and discovered an alarming scene: terrorist literature strewn about the table and computer and surveillance equipment set up in the next room.

The panicked superintendent dialed 911, sending police and the FBI rushing to the building near Rutgers University on the afternoon of June 2, 2009. What they found in that first-floor apartment, however, was not a terrorist hideout but a command center set up by a secret team of New York Police Department intelligence officers.

From that apartment, about an hour outside the department's jurisdiction, the NYPD had been staging undercover operations and conducting surveillance throughout New Jersey. Neither the FBI nor the local police had any idea.

Since the terrorist attacks of Sept. 11, 2001, the NYPD has become one of the country's most aggressive domestic intelligence agencies. A months-long investigation by The Associated Press has revealed that the NYPD operates far outside its borders and targets ethnic communities in ways that would run afoul of civil liberties rules if practiced by the federal government. And it does so with unprecedented help from the

CIA in a partnership that has blurred the bright line between foreign and domestic spying.

Neither the city council, which finances the department, nor the federal government, which contributes hundreds of millions of dollars each year, is told exactly what's going on.

The department has dispatched teams of undercover officers, known as "rakers," into minority neighborhoods as part of a human mapping program, according to officials directly involved in the program. They've monitored daily life in bookstores, bars, cafes and nightclubs. Police have also used informants, known as "mosque crawlers," to monitor sermons, even when there's no evidence of wrongdoing. NYPD officials have scrutinized imams and gathered intelligence on cab drivers and food cart vendors, jobs often done by Muslims.

[...]

The NYPD denied that it trolls ethnic neighborhoods and said it only follows leads. In a city that has repeatedly been targeted by terrorists, police make no apologies for pushing the envelope. NYPD intelligence operations have disrupted terrorist plots and put several would-be killers in prison.

"The New York Police Department is doing everything it can to make sure there's not another 9/11 here and that more innocent New Yorkers are not killed by terrorists," NYPD spokesman Paul Browne said. "And we have nothing to apologize for in that regard."

But officials said they've also been careful to keep information about some programs out of court, where a judge might take a different view. The NYPD considers even basic details, such as the intelligence division's organization chart, to be too sensitive to reveal in court.

One of the enduring questions of the past decade is whether being safe requires giving up some liberty and privacy. The focus of that debate has primarily been federal programs like wiretapping and indefinite detention. The question has received less attention in New York, where residents do not know for sure what, if anything, they have given up.

[…]

With his newfound authority, [David] Cohen [chief of the NYPD intelligence division] created a secret squad that would soon infiltrate Muslim neighborhoods, according to several current and former officials directly involved in the program.

The NYPD carved up the city into more than a dozen zones and assigned undercover officers to monitor them, looking for potential trouble.

At the CIA, one of the biggest obstacles has always been that U.S. intelligence officials are overwhelmingly white, their mannerisms clearly American. The NYPD didn't have that problem, thanks to its diverse pool of officers.

Using census data, the department matched undercover officers to ethnic communities and instructed them to blend in, the officials said. Pakistani-American officers infiltrated Pakistani neighborhoods, Palestinians focused on Palestinian neighborhoods. They hung out in hookah bars and cafes, quietly observing the community around them.

The unit, which has been undisclosed until now, became known inside the department as the Demographic Unit, former police officials said.

"It's not a question of profiling. It's a question of going where the problem could arise," said Mordecai Dzikansky, a retired NYPD intelligence officer who said he was aware of the Demographic Unit. "And thank God we have the capability. We have the language capability and the ethnic officers. That's our hidden weapon."

The officers did not work out of headquarters, officials said. Instead, they passed their intelligence to police handlers who knew their identities.

Cohen said he wanted the squad to "rake the coals, looking for hot spots," former officials recalled. The undercover officers soon became known inside the department as rakers.

A hot spot might be a beauty supply store selling chemicals used for making bombs. Or it might be a hawala, a broker that transfers money around the world with little documentation. Undercover officers might visit an Internet cafe and look at the browsing history on a computer, a former police official involved in the program said. If it revealed visits to radical websites, the cafe might be deemed a hot spot.

Ethnic bookstores, too, were on the list. If a raker noticed a customer looking at radical literature, he might chat up the store owner and see what he could learn. The bookstore, or even the customer, might get further scrutiny. If a restaurant patron applauds a news report about the death of U.S. troops, the patron or the restaurant could be labeled a hot spot.

The goal was to "map the city's human terrain," one law enforcement official said. The program was modeled in part on how Israeli authorities operate in the West Bank, a former police official said.

Mapping crimes has been a successful police strategy nationwide. But mapping robberies and shootings is one thing. Mapping ethnic neighborhoods is different, something that at least brushes against what the federal government considers racial profiling.

Browne, the NYPD spokesman, said the Demographic Unit does not exist. He said the department has a Zone Assessment Unit that looks for locations that could attract terrorists. But he said undercover officers only followed leads, disputing the account of several current and former police and federal officials. They do not just hang out in neighborhoods, he said.

"We will go into a location, whether it's a mosque or a bookstore, if the lead warrants it, and at least establish whether there's something that requires more attention," Browne said.

That conflicts with testimony from an undercover officer in the 2006 trial of Shahawar Matin Siraj, who was convicted of planning an attack on New York's subway system. The officer said he was instructed to live in Brooklyn and act as a "walking camera" for police.

"I was told to act like a civilian—hang out in the neighborhood, gather information," the Bangladeshi officer testified, under a false name, in what offered the first narrow glimpse at the NYPD's infiltration of ethnic neighborhoods.

Officials said such operations just made sense. Islamic terrorists had attacked the city on 9/11, so police needed people inside the city's Muslim neighborhoods. Officials say it does not conflict with a 2004 city law prohibiting the NYPD from using religion or ethnicity "as the determinative factor for initiating law enforcement action."

"It's not profiling," Cutter said. "It's like, after a shooting, do you go 20 blocks away and interview guys or do you go to the neighborhood where it happened?"

In 2007, the Los Angeles Police Department was criticized for even considering a similar program. The police announced plans to map Islamic neighborhoods to look for pockets of radicalization among the region's roughly 500,000 Muslims. Criticism was swift, and chief William Bratton scrapped the plan.

"A lot of these people came from countries where the police were the terrorists," Bratton said at a news conference, according to the Los Angeles Daily News. "We don't do that here. We do not want to spread fear."

In New York, current and former officials said, the lesson of that controversy was that such programs should be kept secret.

Some in the department, including lawyers, have privately expressed concerns about the raking program and how police use the information, current and former officials said. Part of the concern was that it might appear that police were building dossiers on innocent people, officials said. Another concern was that, if a case went to court, the department could be forced to reveal details about the program, putting the entire operation in jeopardy.

That's why, former officials said, police regularly shredded documents discussing rakers.

When Cohen made his case in court that he needed broader authority to investigate terrorism, he had promised to abide by the FBI's investigative guidelines. But the FBI is prohibited from using undercover agents unless there's specific evidence of criminal activity, meaning a federal raking program like the one officials described to the AP would violate FBI guidelines.

The NYPD declined to make Cohen available for comment. In an earlier interview with the AP on a variety of topics,

Police Commissioner Kelly said the intelligence unit does not infringe on civil rights.

"We're doing what we believe we have to do to protect the city," he said. "We have many, many lawyers in our employ. We see ourselves as very conscious and aware of civil liberties. And we know there's always going to be some tension between the police department and so-called civil liberties groups because of the nature of what we do."

The department clashed with civil rights groups most publicly after Cohen's undercover officers infiltrated anti-war groups before the 2004 Republican National Convention in New York. A lawsuit over that program continues today.

During the convention, when protesters were arrested, police asked a list of questions which, according to court documents, included: "What are your political affiliations?" "Do you do any kind of political work?" and "Do you hate George W. Bush?"

"At the end of the day, it's pure and simple a rogue domestic surveillance operation," said Christopher Dunn, a New York Civil Liberties Union lawyer involved in the convention lawsuit.

Undercover agents like the rakers were valuable, but what Cohen and [Larry] Sanchez [a CIA officer who was temporarily assigned to the NYPD] wanted most were informants.

The NYPD dedicated an entire squad, the Terrorist Interdiction Unit, to developing and handling informants. Current and former officials said Sanchez was instrumental in teaching them how to develop sources.

For years, detectives used informants known as mosque crawlers to monitor weekly sermons and report what was said, several current and former officials directly involved in the informant program said. If FBI agents were to do that, they would be in violation of the Privacy Act, which prohibits the federal government from collecting intelligence on purely First Amendment activities.

The FBI has generated its own share of controversy for putting informants inside mosques, but unlike the program described to the AP, the FBI requires evidence of a crime before an informant can be used inside a mosque.

Valerie Caproni, the FBI's general counsel, would not discuss the NYPD's programs but said FBI informants can't troll mosques looking for leads. Such operations are reviewed for civil liberties concerns, she said.

"If you're sending an informant into a mosque when there is no evidence of wrongdoing, that's a very high-risk thing to do," Caproni said. "You're running right up against core constitutional rights. You're talking about freedom of religion."

That's why senior FBI officials in New York ordered their own agents not to accept any reports from the NYPD's mosque crawlers, two retired agents said.

It's unclear whether the police department still uses mosque crawlers. Officials said that, as Muslims figured out what was going on, the mosque crawlers became cafe crawlers, fanning out into the city's ethnic hangouts.

"Someone has a great imagination," Browne, the NYPD spokesman, said. "There is no such thing as mosque crawlers."

Following the foiled subway plot, however, the key informant in the case, Osama Eldawoody, said he attended hundreds of prayer services and collected information even on people who showed no signs of radicalization.

NYPD detectives have recruited shopkeepers and nosy neighbors to become "seeded" informants who keep police up to date on the latest happenings in ethnic neighborhoods, one official directly involved in the informant program said.

The department also has a roster of "directed" informants it can tap for assignments. For instance, if a raker identifies a bookstore as a hot spot, police might assign an informant to gather information, long before there's concrete evidence of anything criminal.

To identify possible informants, the department created what became known as the "debriefing program." When someone is arrested who might be useful to the intelligence unit—whether because he said something suspicious or because he is simply a young Middle Eastern man—he is singled out for extra questioning. Intelligence officials don't care about the underlying charges; they want to know more about his community and, ideally, they want to put him to work.

Police are in prisons, too, promising better living conditions and help or money on the outside for Muslim prisoners who will work with them.

Early in the intelligence division's transformation, police asked the taxi commission to run a report on all the city's Pakistani cab drivers, looking for those who got licenses fraudulently and might be susceptible to pressure to cooperate, according to former officials who were involved in or briefed on the effort.

That strategy has been rejected in other cities.

Boston police once asked neighboring Cambridge for a list of Somali cab drivers, Cambridge Police Chief Robert Haas said. Haas refused, saying that without a specific reason, the search was inappropriate.

"It really has a chilling effect in terms of the relationship between the local police department and those cultural groups, if they think that's going to take place," Haas said.

[ ... ]

The NYPD has faced little scrutiny over the past decade as it has taken on broad new intelligence missions, targeted ethnic neighborhoods and partnered with the CIA in extraordinary ways.

The department's primary watchdog, the New York City Council, has not held hearings on the intelligence division's operations and former NYPD officials said council members typically do not ask for details.

"Ray Kelly briefs me privately on certain subjects that should not be discussed in public," said City Councilman Peter Vallone. "We've discussed in person how they investigate certain groups they suspect have terrorist sympathizers or have terrorist suspects."

The city comptroller's office has audited several NYPD components since 9/11 but not the intelligence unit, which had a $62 million budget last year.

The federal government, too, has done little to scrutinize the nation's largest police force, despite the massive federal aid. Homeland Security officials review NYPD grants but not its underlying programs.

On Capitol Hill, where FBI tactics have frequently been criticized for their effect on civil liberties, the NYPD faces no such opposition.

In 2007, Sanchez testified before the Senate Homeland Security Committee and was asked how the NYPD spots signs of radicalization. He said the key was viewing innocuous activity, including behavior that might be protected by the First Amendment, as a potential precursor to terrorism.

That triggered no questions from the committee, which Sanchez said had been "briefed in the past on how we do business."

The Justice Department has the authority to investigate civil rights violations. It issued detailed rules in 2003 against racial profiling, including prohibiting agencies from considering race when making traffic stops or assigning patrols.

But those rules apply only to the federal government and contain a murky exemption for terrorism investigations. The Justice Department has not investigated a police department for civil rights violations during a national security investigation.

"One of the hallmarks of the intelligence division over the last 10 years is that, not only has it gotten extremely aggressive and sophisticated, but it's operating completely on its own," said Dunn, the civil liberties lawyer. "There are no checks. There is no oversight."

[...]

As Sanchez testified on Capitol Hill: "We've been given the public tolerance and the luxury to be very aggressive on this topic."

*Matt Apuzzo and Adam Goldman are Pulitzer Prize–winning investigative reporters for the Associated Press based in Washington, D.C.

Apuzzo, Matt, and Adam Goldman. "With CIA Help, NYPD Moves Covertly in Muslim Areas." Associated Press. August 23, 2011. http://www.ap.org/Content/AP-In-The-News/2011/With-CIA-help-NYPD-moves-covertly-in-Muslim-areas.

# Mapping Muslims

*by Muslim American Civil Liberties Coalition†*

## Stifling Speech and Association

*Free speech isn't a privilege that Muslims have.*—Ahsan
Samad, 26, Brooklyn.

The NYPD premises its surveillance of American Muslims not on suspicious activity, but on their speech and expres-
sive activities. Law enforcement officers focus on markers of
expression when choosing whom to monitor and what locations to mark as "hot spots." The NYPD considers a spectrum of political and religious speech to be "of concern." Such
speech includes mainstream Arabic-language news channels,
religious texts and discussions of political figures. NYPD's
Assistant Chief Thomas Galati also testified that merely speaking in certain languages, particularly Urdu and Arabic, could
trigger surveillance.[30] Ironically, the NYPD also found that
discussions about anti-Muslim bias by American Muslims to
be "of value."

American Muslim interviewees stress that the ever-present
surveillance chills—or completely silences—their speech
whether they are engaging in political debate, commenting
on current events, encouraging community mobilization or

joking around with friends. Political organizing, civic engagement and activism are among the first casualties of police surveillance. Based on our research and interviews, it is clear that the surveillance program has, in fact, quelled political activism, quieted community spaces and strained interpersonal relationships.

This curtailment of free speech not only implicates individual liberties but also reaches civic debate and the development of an informed electorate. Knowledge of surveillance leads not only to self-censorship on many religious and political topics, but also to an inability to discuss even the surveillance itself, thereby deterring a pivotal constitutional right—the discussion of problematic government policies. The Supreme Court has repeatedly held that speech concerning public affairs is the essence of self-government.[31] Though Americans, Muslim and non-Muslim alike, rally and organize against expansive surveillance, many American Muslim organizations and individuals hesitate to participate in protests, to lobby, and to speak out.

> *Even if we know we have rights, we know that they don't apply equally to everyone.*—AMIRA*, 22, SUNDAY SCHOOL TEACHER.

## 1. SELF-CENSORSHIP OF POLITICAL SPEECH & ACTIVISM

> *We're Arabs, we talk about politics all the time... Politics is all we do! Every coffee shop, it's either Al Jazeera or a soccer game on TV. This new idea that we must be suspicious of those who speak about politics-something's wrong.*—LINDA SARSOUR, COMMUNITY ORGANIZER.

Both keepers of community spaces and those who visit those spaces feel pressured to censor the discussions going on within their walls. Business owners, mosque leaders and community members alike actively censor conversations, event programming, and internet usage in hopes that avoiding certain political content will keep them and their respective religious and social spaces off the NYPD's radar.

Business owners are concerned that charged political discussion could garner increased law enforcement attention, or keep other, more wary customers away. Thus, some business owners have consciously taken steps to avoid political discussion by muting, or completely banning, popular news channels. When approached by CLEAR and AALDEF, many individuals or owners of businesses that were listed in the NYPD reports were unwilling to comment on the surveillance altogether, for fear of unwanted attention.

> I don't allow Al-Jazeera on in our hookah bar. Particularly when things flare up in the Middle East. We can't control what people start saying in response to the news, and we never know who else is in the bar listening.—HAMZA, OWNER OF BUSINESS MAPPED BY THE DEMOGRAPHICS UNIT.

Ironically, a leaked Demographics Unit document notes that the owner of a particular restaurant did not allow the screening of the Al Jazeera channel out of fear of attracting law enforcement attention.[32]

The stifling of expression is not limited to topics relating to Islamic nations, Arab politics and domestic surveillance policies. Even current events unrelated to Islam or Muslims but generally related to any type of protest or racially charged controversy made some members of the community uncomfortable.

> Even regular discussions, like Trayvon Martin, [people] say don't bring that up, let's just talk about Hajj [pilgrimage]. They

*wonder why this guy wants to talk about politics, it's seen as suspicious.*—Sheikh Mustapha\*, Imam, Brooklyn.

Surveillance has also deterred mobilization related to law enforcement accountability and reform because people fear that speaking out against surveillance would only lead to greater surveillance:

> *I don't talk about the NYPD on Facebook. We'll put articles up, but we will never comment on them, put our own words. Maximum we'll say "it's sad that this is happening." But we will never show our anger, that we're really, really angry. Some people aren't afraid, but I am.*—Amira\*, 22, Sunday school teacher.

As one activist in the Shi'a community described:

> *Many of the Shi'a organizations who were approached by activists to speak up or speak out were hesitant to do so…A lot of it seems to be fear, they don't want to be targeted for additional surveillance.*—Ali Naquvi, community organizer.

This concern was particularly evident among immigrant parents, who, out of concern for their more outspoken American Muslim children's safety, urged them to stay away from protesting the NYPD's policies, or even from being outspoken on political issues affecting Muslims in America.

> *I come from a family of activists. My parents, when I first told them the Associated Press story is about to break, my dad told me don't do anything about it. That was the first time my dad ever told me anything like that. This was the first time in my own family where safety trumped what was the right thing to do.*
> —Ali Naquvi, community organizer.

> *At [the] Youth Center, a girl said that the idea of being arrested isn't something that's far fetched, that's unbelievable; it's*

*something very real, very possible for her. She thought it was really important to lay low because it would break her mom's heart if she got arrested .... "Laying low" means not being politically active, literally going on with their everyday lives. A lot of people feel like being at these protests is counterproductive, that it would draw more attention, more of being spied on.*
—Sireen*, 23, student at Hunter College.

*My mother always tells us to be careful about Facebook, and tells us to be careful about rallies, or questions whether it's a good idea for us to go. Sometimes you just want to go out there, you want to join organizations or certain causes, but you stop yourself. When your speech is limited, you can't really do much: you can't write on the internet, you can't talk on the phone because they're tapped, you can't speak in public. When your speech is constrained you get lazy and you just go with the flow and try to survive and live a normal life, and not do much in society.*
—Amira*, 22, Sunday school teacher.

An American Muslim organizer we spoke with commented on the nature of organizing in a climate of fear:

*Almost every rally and public forum I've attended in the last year begins with some type of disclaimer or call-out of informants and undercovers who might be in attendance and recording the conversation. Most speakers don't even know if such a disclaimer protects them in any way, but I feel it to be a necessary announcement so that the audience participants are conscious of the environment in which we are organizing.*—Cyrus McGoldrick, community organizer.

Thus, NYPD surveillance of Muslim neighborhoods, activities, speech and religious practice has not only chilled and altered Muslims' political and religious expression, but has also stifled opposition to the surveillance itself, creating a space void of dissent, agitation and much needed calls for accountability.

## 2. A QUALITATIVE SHIFT: CLARIFICATIONS, MISTRANSLATIONS AND HUMOR

Alongside self-censorship interviewees feel the need to repeatedly emphasize their peaceful position or clarify their use of terminology when going about their day-to-day lives or discussing current events. When interviewees mention foreign policy or controversial individuals, they explain their position in detail. When they do discuss news of surveillance, they opt for cursory references shrouded in humor. The primacy of security concerns means that organizations and individuals spend their energies finding careful wording and caveats, rather than on the primary topic of conversation. At an organizational, religious, and communal level, this results in missed opportunities for richer conversations, for organizing, for developing institutions and agendas, and for participation in the public exchange of ideas.

> *The reality of surveillance is now always on our minds, when we organize, when we speak, when we meet, when we plan. Meetings for political organizing I leave until we can meet in person, and even when we do have in-person meetings, we are all very conscious of what we say and how, taking time to clarify or make a joke out of phrasing that could be interpreted as somehow contentious.* —CYRUS MCGOLDRICK, COMMUNITY ORGANIZER.

> *I think twice before every time I put something on Facebook. I have to make sure it doesn't give the wrong idea to law enforcement. I would never say 'jihad' on Facebook, or 'Osama Bin Laden.' If I want to say something about the uprisings*

*overseas, I try to be as detailed and precise as I can be, I won't talk about any of the violence going on there, will never say I don't like this person or that person.*—AMIRA\*, 22, SUNDAY SCHOOL TEACHER.

Those we interviewed also expressed concern with how terms and expressions they use in their native languages might be literally translated and misinterpreted by law enforcement. A prominent Queens business owner explained how a common Arabic phrase to denote excitement could be mistranslated into English to convey that the one is so excited that he will "explode." The business owner explained that such phrases, commonly used to denote emotion, are seldom used anymore.[33]

Similarly in Arabic, the term sarookh is used to humorously describe someone who is extremely good-looking. The literal translation is "missile." One interviewee, a young college student, commented on the use of this phrase: "you have to watch out how you joke around now."[34]

Walking on eggshells in their own safe spaces, individuals are also scared to directly address political comments that make them uncomfortable. Many interviewees noted that a common way to avoid such confrontations was by resorting to humor.

*The silencing is done through a joke. For example, if someone is talking about politics or surveillance, people joke "oh I'm going to go home now!"*—AMIRA\*, 23, SUNDAY SCHOOL TEACHER.

Everyday humor, allegory and metaphors are not only key parts of linguistic heritage but also function to relay emotion, inspire political mobilization and pass down stories within communities. By putting speech under the magnifying glass, surveillance impairs not only political speech in the American Muslim community but also the transmission of language and culture.

[ … ]

## In Focus: Campus Life

*"If they were[n't] already monitoring me, now that I'm in the MSA at Queens College, I'm definitely monitored."*
— SAMEERA\*, 19, CUNY STUDENT.

Muslim Student Associations (MSA) on campuses across New York City exhibit many of the same trends as other nodes of Muslim community life such as mosques or community centers, but also provide a unique lens on the impact that surveillance has on younger people within the targeted communities. The documents obtained by the Associated Press revealed that through online and in-person monitoring of Muslims students, the NYPD had for years crept into academic spaces. [ … ]

[ … ]

[ … ] [T]the NYPD Intelligence Division identified 31 MSAs in New York. It focused on at least seven that it listed as "of concern:" Baruch College, Hunter College, La Guardia Community College, City College, Brooklyn College, St. John's University, Queens College—all but one of which were public universities that are part of the City University of New York system.

Among the reasons listed for targeting these particular MSAs were their choice of speakers, organizing "militant paintball trips," or simply that students were "politically active" or trying to revive an MSA that had gone dormant.[68] Cyber-monitoring of students on their Yahoo groups, e-mail listservs, and blogs was done "as a daily routine."[69] [ ... ]

[ ... ]

## 3. CHILLED ACADEMIC EXPRESSION

*I think Muslim students are getting an inferior education because of this, and that's not fair.*—JEANNE THEOHARIS, PROFESSOR, BROOKLYN COLLEGE.

Police monitoring of Muslims' political opinions has devastating effects on classroom dynamics and stunts students' personal and academic growth. Open discussion, intellectual exchanges and even political and theoretical experimentation, role-playing and posturing are crucial aspects of an educational environment. Several of the students we interviewed described self-censoring classroom comments not only because of a fear of law enforcement scrutiny, but also because of concern that other classmates or professors would misinterpret their views, given the ambient discourse on young, overtly political Muslims.

*I personally ask [Council on American-Islamic Relations Civil Rights Manager] Cyrus about papers I write, and whether I say this or that. Even if I know that I shouldn't be worried about it, it's hard to not worry about it. Anything that has to do with criticizing the Iraq war, Hamas, I've been thinking about writing about the [National Defense Authorization Act]—I wonder whether I should even do it. Cyrus said write about it, but then if the teachers were ever asked, they'll have to produce that document. And you don't know what's going to be cut and pasted from that.*—FAREEDA\*, 21, BROOKLYN COLLEGE STUDENT.

Professor Theoharis, at Brooklyn College, recounts some of the concerns she hears about from students:

*I've certainly had lots of students coming to me about tough issues like speaking in class or in public. They have concerns about what their professors and other students think about them.*—JEANNE THEOHARIS, PROFESSOR, BROOKLYN COLLEGE.

Professor Bellamy, at Hunter College, noted the tense atmosphere whenever certain topics are raised in class:

*Israel/Palestine and Muslim youth culture are the two topics where you feel the air goes out of the room. Students get anxious. The conversation is uncomfortable, the atmosphere changes in the room.*—CARLA BELLAMY, PROFESSOR, BARUCH COLLEGE.

Jawad Rasul, one of the students on a whitewater rafting trip that was infiltrated by an NYPD undercover, reflected on his and his peers' experience:

*Colleges are a place where these discussions are supposed to happen so people can learn from each other. We're losing out.*—JAWAD RASUL, 25, CUNY STUDENT.

The stifling of class discussion is an overall loss, not just for Muslim students, but also to their peers and teachers, who are no longer exposed to a diverse set of views. As Jeanne Theoharis, a professor who works closely with many Muslim students, explained:

*College is a place where you try ideas out. It's the first time you get to choose your classes, think for yourself. Part of that process has to be about trying out ideas, and kind of seeing how ideas work. If you don't have a comfortable place in class and with other students to say or try ideas out, say what might be considered "radical" things, to draw parallels comfortably, and to get inside of ideas, you've lost one of the most important aspects of colleges. That's devastating. [...]*—JEANNE THEOHARIS, PROFESSOR, BROOKLYN COLLEGE.

With a general understanding that dealing with "politics" is controversial, Muslim students find themselves steering away from those majors, classes, or extracurricular activities. Two students, both active members of their MSAs, reported switching their majors from political science to more conventional majors after becoming concerned about law enforcement scrutiny of "political" young Muslim males.[82] In largely immigrant communities where social and familial pressures are to direct oneself towards professional degrees—business administration, accounting, engineering or medical schools—a secondary concentration or extracurricular activities have always been a way for students to explore their passions or their interests in other directions. Professor Theoharis observed a retreat from those majors at least at Brooklyn College.

> *You get this climate, and the parents feel even more emboldened to say "just be an engineer, just go to med school. Why do you have to do all this other stuff?"*—JEANNE THEOHARIS, PROFESSOR, BROOKLYN COLLEGE.

While the longer-term impacts of NYPD surveillance are yet to be fully understood, the prominence of surveillance for Muslim students on campuses raises serious concerns, as a generation of American Muslim youth adjust how they go about their studies, partake in extracurricular activities, choose their professions, and develop their social roles and relationships. The isolationism that comes with being a member of a "spied on" community means that Muslim students are getting a fundamentally different, and less rewarding college experience compared to their non-Muslim peers.

## NOTES

30. Handschu v. Special Servs. Div., No. 71CIV.2203, Galati Dep. 85-86 (June 28, 2012), available at http://www.nyclu.org/files/releases/Handschu_Galati_6.28.12.pdf.; Adam Martin, NYPD Spying Led to Lunches, Not Leads, The Atlantic Wire (August 21, 2012), available at http://www.theatlanticwire.com/national/2012/08/nypd-spying-led-lunches-not-terrorleads/56008/.

31. See, e.g., Garrison v. Louisiana, 379 U.S. 64, 74-75 (1964).

32. N.Y. Police Dep't, Egyptian Locations of Interest Report (July 7, 2006), available at http://hosted.ap.org/specials/.

33. Interview with Hamza, owner of a business mapped by the Demographics Unit.

34. Interview with Ayman*, 20, Brooklyn College.

[...]

68. N.Y. Police Dep't, Strategic Posture 2006, on file with authors.

69. N.Y. Police Dep't, Weekly MSA Report (2006), available at http://hosted.ap.org/specials/interactives/documents/nypd-msa-report.pdf.

[...]

82. Interviews with Sari,* 19, Brooklyn College, Ayman,* 20, Brooklyn College, Ismail,* 22, Brooklyn College, and Tarek,* 19, Brooklyn College.


†The **Muslim American Civil Liberties Coalition** is an alliance of organizations and individuals that acts as an advocate for the Muslim community, especially in New York. The coalition has joined with other community activists and civil rights groups to call for greater government accountability and transparency.


Muslim American Civil Liberties Coalition. "Stifling Speech and Association" and "In Focus—Campus Life," Sections 2 and 5 in *Mapping Muslims: NYPD Spying and Its Impact on American Muslims.* New York: Creating Law Enforcement Accountability & Responsibility

(CLEAR) Project, n.d. http://www.law.cuny.edu/academics/clinics/immigration/clear/Mapping-Muslims.pdf.

Reprinted with the permission of the Creating Law Enforcement Accountability & Responsibility (CLEAR) Project and the Asian American Legal Defense and Education Fund (AALDEF).

# Who Will Defend the Defenders?

*by Mitchell D. Silber\**

In April, the Pulitzer Prize for investigative reporting was awarded to the Associated Press for a series of articles it published about the New York Police Department's "clandestine spying program that monitored daily life in Muslim communities." The AP's assertions were so extensive that they filled more than 50 separate pieces, the first published in August of last year. Its reporters alleged that since the attacks of September 11, the New York City Police Department's Intelligence Division had placed entire Muslim communities under scrutiny with "no evidence of wrongdoing." The department, they wrote, had infiltrated mosques and Muslim student groups with no legal basis to do so. It had operated far outside its geographical jurisdiction and had cast too wide a net when monitoring and analyzing American Muslims.

[ ... ]

The articles were quickly and widely disseminated and elicited expressions of deep outrage among Muslim Americans and civil-liberties activists. They created fissures between the police and the communities it sought to protect, undermined confidence in the NYPD, and attracted national attention— which, according to the AP's Pulitzer citation, "result[ed] in congressional calls for a federal investigation and a debate over the proper role of domestic intelligence-gathering." As well they should have. A free citizenry relies on a free press to uncover civil-liberties abuses.

But any serious discussion about the alleged methods and practices of the NYPD Intelligence Division should have begun with one question: Was the AP's investigation accurate?

The answer is no.

The articles misrepresent the scope, purpose, and rationale behind many of the NYPD Intelligence Division's programs. They confuse events and policies in ways that are misleading and cast the tale they are telling in the worst possible light. I know all this to be true, because I worked directly for the deputy commissioner of the Intelligence Division for the last seven years, first as a special assistant and then, for the last four years, until May 2012, as his director of intelligence analysis, overseeing all the city's terrorism investigations.

[ ... ]

## The Demographics Unit

*The AP Claim: The NYPD has engaged in a "human-mapping" program without citing any evidence of wrongdoing. This program has placed entire Muslim communities under scrutiny.*

For some, the very act of gathering intelligence is an illegitimate use of police power. But to find and stop terrorists, the Police Department uses many of the same methods that are used to arrest drug dealers, human traffickers, and gang leaders. Detectives develop detailed information about the nature of the crime and the people involved. While tips from the public are useful, the police cannot rely on them exclusively to detect terrorism conspiracies.

In 2003, with that in mind, the Intelligence Division created the Demographics Unit. [...]

A September 22, 2011, AP article paints a frightening portrait of the Demographics Unit and the work it did: "The New York Police Department put American citizens under surveillance and scrutinized where they ate, prayed, and worked, not because of charges of wrongdoing but because of their ethnicity, according to interviews and documents obtained by the *Associated Press*," runs the article's opening paragraph. [...]

[...]

But this police-state nightmare bears no resemblance to the nuanced work of the Demographics Unit. The unit employed what is called a risk-basis model. In the three Islamist plots against New York between 1993 and 2001, the vast majority of the conspirators were from a limited group of countries: Egypt, Kuwait, Lebanon, the Palestinian territories, Saudi Arabia, the United Arab Emirates, and Yemen. The risk-basis model would therefore indicate that these countries could be deemed "higher risk" or "of concern" in relationship to terrorism.

Plainclothes officers of the Demographics Unit were deployed for this mission. They went into neighborhoods that had heavy concentrations of populations from the "countries of interest" and walked around, purchased a cup of tea or coffee, had lunch and observed the individuals in the public establishments they entered. This is an important point: Only public locations were visited. Doing so was perfectly within the purview of the NYPD, for, as the Handschu Guidelines say: "The NYPD is authorized to visit any place and attend any event that is open to the public." [Editor's Note: The Handschu Guidelines are a set of rules that a court imposed on the NYPD in 1985 to end NYPD spying on political groups. The rules were loosened following the 9/11 attacks.]

Here's what they did not do: Plainclothes officers did not conduct blanket ongoing surveillance of communities. Not only is that an impossible task, but it also would have been inefficient and had a low likelihood of identifying terrorist plots in their early stages. At its largest, during a brief period after the July 7, 2005, attacks in London, the unit had 16 officers—hardly enough to monitor a neighborhood, much less whole communities. Officers would take a first pass to familiarize themselves with luncheonettes, dollar stores, and other legitimate businesses and record what they saw. They would be very unlikely to return unless there was reason to believe that a location might be a "venue of radicalization."

How did the AP treat this? Its writers claimed that "the department has dispatched teams of undercover officers, known as 'rakers,' into minority neighborhoods as part of a human-mapping program, according to officials directly involved in the program." As mentioned above, individuals involved were not undercover officers. Undercover officers are provided with fake identities and misrepresent who they are. Plainclothes officers of the Demographics Unit carried no false identification and did not purport to be anyone in particular. This was a blatant error on the part of the AP. In addition, the AP claimed, "Police have also used informants, known as 'mosque crawlers,' to monitor sermons, even when there's no evidence of wrongdoing." As a matter of Police Department policy, undercover officers and confidential informants do not enter a mosque unless they are following up on a lead vetted under the terms of the Handschu Guidelines. The AP's description of "mosque crawlers" roving from mosque to mosque without express legal permission to enter that location is pure fiction.

Still, there was the collection of information, and that is really what troubled people. So why cover social and recreational sites to begin with? The answer: Radicalization frequently occurs in nontraditional locations, not only religious centers. [...]

[...]

For example, the Demographics Unit was critical in identifying the Islamic Books and Tapes bookstore in Brooklyn as a venue for radicalization. Information the unit collected about the store provided a predicate for an investigation that thwarted a 2004 plot against the Herald Square subway station. The unit also played a role in forming the initiation of an investigation that led to the 2008 identification of Abdel Hameed Shehadeh, a New Yorker who was arrested and is currently facing federal charges for allegedly lying about his plans to travel to Afghanistan in order to kill U.S. servicemen. [...]

[...]

## On Campus

*The AP Claim: The NYPD has investigated and infiltrated Muslim student groups without any legal basis to do so.*

At universities students are expected to explore new ideas, challenge themselves, and engage in robust debate involving multiple dissenting opinions. The NYPD has been especially sensitive in any operational work that risks infringing on this protected space. Allegations that police have been infiltrating Muslim student groups at colleges in the city and schools beyond city limits, including Yale and the University of Pennsylvania, are serious and need to be addressed.

But in covering this topic, the AP conflated two different elements of investigative work: open-sourced Internet searches and undercover officers. "Investigators have been infiltrating Muslim student groups at Brooklyn College and other schools in the city, monitoring their Internet activity and placing undercover agents in their ranks," reads an October 11 story. "Legal experts say the operation may have broken a 19-year-old pact with the colleges and violated U.S. privacy laws, jeopardizing millions of dollars in federal research money and student aid." This is a dramatic misinterpretation of the nature and scope of the department's actions.

The first investigative initiative involving students began in 2006 and involved the NYPD Intelligence Division's Cyber Unit. Officers reviewed Muslim Student Association (MSA) websites, all of which were publicly available, for a period of six months—and with good reason.

Consider the following stories from Great Britain: On March 30, 2004, British authorities disrupted an al-Qaeda plot to mount a bomb attack in the United Kingdom. [...] Four of the seven conspirators were either current university students, dropouts, or graduates of London Metropolitan University, the University of Hertfordshire, and Brunel University. [...]

The 2005 London subway plot killed 52 commuters, injured 700, and severe disrupted the city's transport infrastructure. One of the suicide bombers was a recent graduate of Leeds Metropolitan University, one a recent dropout from the same university, and one a university student at Thomas Danby College in Leeds at the time of the attack.

[...]

Most important, the trend is not limited to the U.K. Right here in New York, Mohammed Junaid Babar and Syed Fahad Hashmi, who were arrested in connection with the previously referenced 2004 plot in the U.K. and pled guilty to al-Qaeda-related terrorist activities, had been radicalized through the university-based New York branch of al-Muhajiroun, an Islamist student group in Britain to which several of the subway bombers were linked. The group actively recruited at the Muslim Student Associations of Brooklyn College, Queens College, and other universities in New York City. [...]

So what did the NYPD do about campus radicalization and recruitment? For a six-month period, beginning in November 2006 and ending in May 2007, Intelligence Division detectives conducted public-information Internet searches to determine if radicalization and recruitment to terrorism were occurring on local university campuses and, if so, to what extent.

Detectives visited publicly available websites of universities and colleges in and around New York City, catalogued what they saw, and assembled the information into 23 biweekly reports. (Once again, NYPD members investigating counter-terrorism activities are authorized by the Handschu Guidelines to search websites open to the public for the purpose of developing intelligence information to detect or prevent terrorism or other unlawful activities.) They were looking mostly at speakers, conferences, and events held at MSAs that might—even if inadvertently—support terrorism or provide a recruiting venue for extremist Islamist groups.

Fortunately, the vast majority of speakers, conferences, and events held at Muslim Student Associations in the tristate area were nonthreatening in nature, and in May 2007 the initiative was closed. The information from the biweekly reports was not entered into any database.

[ ... ]

Wholly separate from this initiative is the use of undercover officers in investigations that sometimes involved MSA-related activities. [ ... ]

[ ... ]

[ ... ] The Handschu Guidelines require written authorization from the deputy commissioner of intelligence when utilizing human intelligence. [ ... ] Moreover, an internal committee reviews each investigation to ensure compliance, and a legal unit based in the Intelligence Division evaluates every field intelligence report generated through an investigation. This committee meets regularly every month, and at one meeting at the end of my tenure, no fewer than 10 attorneys and five assistant or deputy commissioners were in attendance. It is important to note that investigations are discontinued unless they reasonably indicate that an unlawful act has been, is being, or will be committed.

As a matter of Police Department policy, undercover officers and confidential informants do not enter a mosque unless they are doing so as part of an investigation of a person or institution approved under the Handschu Guidelines. Likewise, when undercover officers or confidential informants have attended a private event organized by a student group, *they have done so only on the basis of a lead or investigation reviewed and authorized in writing at the highest levels of the department.*

Given my dual role as a former director of intelligence analysis at the NYPD and a visiting lecturer at Columbia University, I took a special interest in this issue and personally reviewed the documents in question to see the number of times that NYPD human sources were present on local campuses in the last five years. The numbers are very small and almost always involved intelligence-collection efforts limited to individuals who were under investigation, not the broader student body.

So, yes, in 2006, given the trends observed both here and overseas, the NYPD thought it prudent to learn more about what was occurring at Muslim Student Associations in the region via open sources, and the six-month initiative generated six months' worth of public-information reports. The NYPD did not send undercover sources to infiltrate MSAs throughout the northeast. Both the open-source initiative and the few investigations where undercover officers examined the activities of university students as part of an ongoing investigation authorized by Handschu Guidelines have led to a greater understanding of the relationship between terrorism and university organizations and have, as a result, kept New York City safer.

In total, the NYPD has helped to prevent 14 terrorist attacks on New York City and its surrounding areas and permitted exactly zero deadly plots to materialize in the 11 years since 9/11. Its success, based on the math alone, is indisputable. But in a free country, success is not enough. Civil libertarians are correct in asserting that safety at the cost of political freedom would betray the highest American ideals. And the unlawful targeting of New York City's minorities would constitute nothing less than a cultural and spiritual gutting of the greatest, most diverse city history has seen. But neither of those travesties have occurred, thanks to the genius of America's Constitution and the NYPD's exquisite adherence to it.

[...]

*Mitchell D. Silber was a member of the New York Police Department from February 2005 to May 2012. He served as a special assistant to the deputy commissioner from 2005 to 2007 and as the director of intelligence analysis from 2007 to 2012. He is the author of *The Al Qaeda Factor: Plots against the West.*

Silber, Mitchell D. "Who Will Defend the Defenders." *Commentary,* March 2012. http://www.commentarymagazine.com/article/who-will-defend-the-defenders/.

# PART 6

# Identifying Terrorist "Supporters"

In 1995, two right-wing American terrorists exploded a car bomb in front of a federal office building in Oklahoma City, killing 168 people, including 19 children under the age of six. In response, Congress passed the Antiterrorism and Effective Death Penalty Act of 1996, which made it a crime to provide "material support" for a terrorist act or for any organization that has been designated a foreign terrorist organization (FTO) by the secretary of state. In addition to providing cash, weapons, and other forms of logistical assistance, material support includes "training," "personnel," and "service." The PATRIOT Act added "expert advice or assistance." The material support statute has become the government's main weapon in fighting terrorism since 2001, accounting for more than 150 prosecutions.

Freedom of speech includes the freedom to associate with any group that we wish, even groups that may advocate violence. Civil libertarians argue that the material support statute limits free speech by preventing groups from providing humanitarian assistance to FTOs or in areas controlled by FTOs. In 1998, Robert D. Fertig, president of the Humanitarian Law Project, challenged the law in court, claiming that the statute is so vague that such groups might be prosecuted even when the "personnel" are providing food aid in regions of famine controlled by an FTO or the "expert assistance" is helping persuade the FTO to put aside its weapons. Fertig's case finally reached the Supreme Court in 2010 ("Right to Free Speech Collides with Fight Against Terror"). In *Holder v. Humanitarian Law Project,* the Supreme Court rejected the challenge to the material support statute, holding that even nonviolent assistance to an FTO could be used to advance its illegal activities. In his opinion for the Court ("Majority Opinion of the Supreme Court, *Holder v. Humanitarian Law Project*"), Chief Justice John Roberts insisted that Americans retain the right to advocate on behalf of any group, including an FTO, as long as their speech is "independent advocacy" and not directed to, coordinated with, or controlled by the FTO. After the decision was handed down, David Cole, the lawyer who argued the case for the Humanitarian Law Project, urged Congress, in "Chewing Gum for Terrorists," to amend the law to make clear that advocating lawful, nonviolent activities is not a crime.

The Tarek Mehanna case illustrates just how difficult it is to distinguish between speech that provides material support to terrorists and speech that simply endorses their views. In 2009, the U.S. attorney charged Mehanna with providing material support to Muslims who were fighting American forces in Iraq ("Massachusetts Man Charged with Conspiracy to Provide Material Support to Terrorists"). According to the prosecutor, Mehanna's crime was to translate extremist documents and post terrorist propaganda on the Internet. He was convicted. But many observers, Adam Serwer ("Does Posting Jihadist Material Make Tarek Mehanna a Terrorist?") among them, argue that Mehanna is guilty only of advocating ideas. At his sentencing hearing, Mehanna read a statement ("The Real Criminals in the Tarek Mehanna Case") insisting that he was only supporting the right of Muslims to defend themselves from foreign aggressors. He was sentenced to 17½ years in prison.

Critics of the Mehanna prosecution, including political scientist and philosopher Andrew F. Marsh ("A Dangerous Mind?"), assert that the judge did not understand Justice Roberts's opinion in the *Humanitarian Law Project* case, which upheld the right to advocate even violent acts as long as they constitute independent advocacy. But others, such as Peter Margulies, an expert on national security law ("Peter Margulies Responds to David Cole"), question this view. Whether the speech is protected or not depends on whether Mehanna was actively cooperating with terrorists. Margulies contends that the website Mehanna used is controlled by supporters of al Qaeda and that his speech was therefore not independent advocacy. This is disputed in a friends of the court (amicus curiae) brief ("*United States of America v. Tarek Mehanna*, Brief...") filed by a group of Muslim scholars, publishers, and translators in support of Mehanna's appeal of his conviction. They contend that neither the documents that Mehanna translated nor the website that he used to post them support terrorism.

Mehanna is appealing his conviction to the U.S. Court of Appeals. The American Civil Liberties Union and the ACLU of Massachusetts have filed an amicus brief supporting Mehanna. As you read the articles in this section, consider the following questions:

- Why is the right to associate with others considered to be free speech?

- Should assisting a terrorist group to pursue nonviolent goals be legal?

- Should advocacy of violent acts be permitted?

- Is Tarek Mehanna a terrorist?

# Right to Free Speech Collides with Fight against Terror

*by Adam Liptak\**

WASHINGTON—Ralph D. Fertig, a 79-year-old civil rights lawyer, says he would like to help a militant Kurdish group in Turkey find peaceful ways to achieve its goals. But he fears prosecution under a law banning even benign assistance to groups said to engage in terrorism.

The Supreme Court will soon hear Mr. Fertig's challenge to the law, in a case that pits First Amendment freedoms against the government's efforts to combat terrorism. The case represents the court's first encounter with the free speech and association rights of American citizens in the context of terrorism since the Sept. 11 attacks—and its first chance to test the constitutionality of a provision of the USA Patriot Act.

Opponents of the law, which bans providing "material support" to terrorist organizations, say it violates American values in ways that would have made Senator Joseph R. McCarthy blush during the witch hunts of the cold war.

The government defends the law, under which it has secured many of its terrorism convictions in the last decade, as an important tool that takes account of the slippery nature of the nation's modern enemies.

The law takes a comprehensive approach to its ban on aid to terrorist groups, prohibiting not only providing cash, weapons and the like but also four more ambiguous sorts of help—"training," "personnel," "expert advice or assistance" and "service."

"Congress wants these organizations to be radioactive," Douglas N. Letter, a Justice Department lawyer, said in a 2007 appeals court argument in the case, referring to the dozens of groups that have been designated as foreign terrorist organizations by the State Department.

Mr. Letter said it would be a crime for a lawyer to file a friend-of-the-court brief on behalf of a designated organization in Mr. Fertig's case or "to be assisting terrorist organizations in making presentations to the U.N., to television, to a newspaper."

It would be no excuse, Mr. Letter went on, "to be saying, 'I want to help them in a good way.'"

Mr. Fertig said he was saddened and mystified by the government's approach.

"Violence? Terrorism?" he asked in an interview in his Los Angeles home. "Totally repudiate it. My mission would be to work with them on peaceful resolutions of their conflicts, to try to convince them to use nonviolent means of protest on the model of Mahatma Gandhi and Martin Luther King."

Mr. Fertig said his commitment to nonviolence was not abstract. "I had most of my ribs broken," he said, after his 1961 arrest in Selma, Ala., for trying to integrate the interstate bus system as a freedom rider.

He paused, correcting himself. "I believe all my ribs were broken," he said.

Mr. Fertig is president of the Humanitarian Law Project, a nonprofit group that has a long history of mediating international conflicts and promoting human rights. He and the project, along with a doctor and several other groups, sued to strike down the material-support law in 1998.

Two years earlier, passage of the Antiterrorism and Effective Death Penalty Act had made it a crime to provide "material support" to groups the State Department had designated as "foreign terrorist organizations." The definition of material support included "training" and "personnel." Later versions of the law, including amendments in the USA Patriot Act, added "expert advice or assistance" and "service."

In 1997, Secretary of State Madeleine K. Albright designated some 30 groups under the law, including Hamas, Hezbollah, the Khmer Rouge and the Kurdistan Workers' Party. The United States says the Kurdish group, sometimes called the P.K.K., has engaged in widespread terrorist activities, including bombings and kidnappings, and "has waged a violent insurgency that has claimed over 22,000 lives."

The litigation has bounced around in the lower courts for more than a decade as the law was amended and as it took on a central role in terrorism cases. Since 2001, the government says, it has prosecuted about 150 defendants for violating the material-support law, obtaining roughly 75 convictions.

The latest appeals court decision in Mr. Fertig's case, in 2007, ruled that the bans on training, service and some kinds of expert advice were unconstitutionally vague. But it upheld the bans on personnel and expert advice derived from scientific or technical knowledge.

Both sides appealed to the Supreme Court, which agreed to hear the consolidated cases in October. The cases are Holder v. Humanitarian Law Project, No. 08-1498, and Humanitarian Law Project v. Holder, No. 09-89. The court will hear arguments on Feb. 23.

David D. Cole, a lawyer with the Center for Constitutional Rights, which represents Mr. Fertig and other challengers to the law, told the court that the case concerned speech protected by the First Amendment "promoting lawful, nonviolent activities," including "human rights advocacy and peacemaking."

Solicitor General Elena Kagan countered that the law allowed Mr. Fertig and the other challengers to say anything they liked so long as they did not direct their efforts toward or coordinate them with the designated groups.

A number of victims of McCarthy-era persecution filed a friend-of-the-court brief urging the Supreme Court to remember the lessons of history.

"I signed the brief," said Chandler Davis, an emeritus professor of mathematics at the University of Toronto, "because I can testify to the way in which the dubious repression of dissent disrupted lives and disrupted political discourse."

Professor Davis refused to cooperate with the House Un-American Activities Committee in 1954 and was dismissed from his position at the University of Michigan. Unable to find work in the United States, he moved to Canada. In 1991, the University of Michigan established an annual lecture series on academic freedom in honor of Professor Davis and others it had mistreated in the McCarthy era.

Mr. Fertig said the current climate was in some ways worse.

"I think it's more dangerous than McCarthyism," he said. "It was not illegal to help the communists or to be a communist. You might lose your job, you might lose your friends, you might be ostracized. But you'd be free. Today, the same person would be thrown in jail."

A friend-of-the-court brief—prepared by Edwin Meese III, the former United States attorney general; John C. Yoo, a former Bush administration lawyer; and others—called the civil liberties critique of the material-support law naïve.

The law represents "a considered wartime judgment by the political branches of the optimal means to confront the unique challenges posed by terrorism," their brief said. Allowing any sort of contributions to terrorist organizations "simply because the donor intends that they be used for 'peaceful' purposes directly conflicts with Congress's determination that no quarantine can effectively isolate 'good' activities from the evil of terrorism."

Mr. Fertig said he could understand an argument against donating money, given the difficulty of controlling its use. But the sweep of the material-support law goes too far, he said.

"Fear is manipulated," Mr. Fertig said, "and the tools of the penal system are applied to inhibit people from speaking out."

*Adam Liptak is the Supreme Court correspondent for the *New York Times*. He graduated from Yale Law School and has also contributed to *The New Yorker, Vanity Fair, Rolling Stone, Business Week,* and *The American Lawyer*.

Liptak, Adam. "Right to Free Speech Collides with Fight against Terror." *New York Times,* Feb. 11, 2012. http://www.nytimes.com/2010/02/11/us/11law.html?_r=1&.

# Majority Opinion of the Supreme Court, *Holder v. Humanitarian Law Project*

*by John G. Roberts, Jr.\**

[...]

In analyzing whether it is possible in practice to distinguish material support for a foreign terrorist group's violent activities and its nonviolent activities, we do not rely exclusively on our own inferences drawn from the record evidence. We have before us an affidavit stating the Executive Branch's conclusion on that question. The State Department informs us that "[t]he experience and analysis of the U.S. government agencies charged with combating terrorism strongly suppor[t]" Congress's finding that all contributions to foreign terrorist organizations further their terrorism. [...] In the Executive's view: "Given the purposes, organizational structure, and clandestine nature of foreign terrorist organizations, it is highly likely that any material support to these organizations will ultimately inure to the benefit of their criminal, terrorist functions—regardless of whether such support was ostensibly intended to support non-violent, non-terrorist activities." [...]

That evaluation of the facts by the Executive, like Congress's assessment, is entitled to deference. This litigation implicates sensitive and weighty interests of national security and foreign affairs. The PKK [Kurdistan Workers' Party] and the LTTE [Liberation Tigers of Tamil Eelam] have committed terrorist acts against American citizens abroad, and the material-support statute addresses acute foreign policy concerns involving relationships with our Nation's allies. We have noted that "neither the Members of this Court nor most federal judges begin the day with briefings that may describe new and serious threats to our Nation and its people." [...] It is vital in this context "not to substitute ... our own evaluation of evidence for a reasonable evaluation by the Legislative Branch." [...]

Our precedents, old and new, make clear that concerns of national security and foreign relations do not warrant abdication of the judicial role. We do not defer to the Government's reading of the First Amendment, even when such interests are at stake. We are one with the dissent that the Government's "authority and expertise in these matters do not automatically trump the Court's own obligation to secure the protection that the Constitution grants to individuals." [...] But when it comes to collecting evidence and drawing factual inferences in this area, "the lack of competence on the part of the courts is marked," and respect for the Government's conclusions is appropriate. [...]

One reason for that respect is that national security and foreign policy concerns arise in connection with efforts to confront evolving threats in an area where information can be difficult to obtain and the impact of certain conduct difficult to assess. The dissent slights these real constraints in demanding hard proof—with "detail," "specific facts," and "specific evidence"—that plaintiffs' proposed activities will support terrorist attacks. [...] That would be a dangerous requirement. In this context, conclusions must often be based on informed judgment rather than concrete evidence, and that reality affects what we may reasonably insist on from the Government. The material-support statute is, on its face, a preventive measure—it criminalizes not terrorist attacks themselves, but aid that makes the attacks more likely to occur. The Government, when seeking to prevent imminent harms in the context of international affairs and national security, is not required to conclusively link all the pieces in the puzzle before we grant weight to its empirical conclusions. [ ... ]

We also find it significant that Congress has been conscious of its own responsibility to consider how its actions may implicate constitutional concerns. First, § 2339B only applies to designated foreign terrorist organizations. There is, and always has been, a limited number of those organizations designated by the Executive Branch, [ ... ] and any groups so designated may seek judicial review of the designation. Second, in response to the lower courts' holdings in this litigation, Congress added clarity to the statute by providing narrowing definitions of the terms "training," "personnel," and "expert advice or assistance," as well as an explanation of the knowledge required to violate § 2339B. Third, in effectuating its stated intent not to abridge First Amendment rights, [ ... ] Congress has also displayed a careful balancing of interests in creating limited exceptions to the ban on material support. The definition of material support, for example, excludes medicine and religious materials. [ ... ] In this area perhaps more than any other, the Legislature's superior capacity for weighing competing interests means that "we must be particularly careful not to substitute our judgment of what is desirable for that of Congress." [ ... ] Finally, and most importantly, Congress has avoided any restriction on independent advocacy, or indeed any activities not directed to, coordinated with, or controlled by foreign terrorist groups.

At bottom, plaintiffs simply disagree with the considered judgment of Congress and the Executive that providing material support to a designated foreign terrorist organization—even seemingly benign support—bolsters the terrorist activities of that organization. That judgment, however, is entitled to significant weight, and we have persuasive evidence before us to sustain it. Given the sensitive interests in national security and foreign affairs at stake, the political branches have adequately substantiated their determination that, to serve the Government's interest in preventing terrorism, it was necessary to prohibit providing material support in the form of training, expert advice, personnel, and services to foreign terrorist groups, even if the supporters meant to promote only the groups' nonviolent ends.

We turn to the particular speech plaintiffs propose to undertake. First, plaintiffs propose to "train members of [the] PKK on how to use humanitarian and international law to peacefully resolve disputes." [ ... ] Congress can, consistent with the First Amendment, prohibit this direct training. It is wholly foreseeable that the PKK could use the "specific skill[s]" that plaintiffs propose to impart [ ... ] as part of a broader strategy to promote terrorism. The PKK could, for example, pursue peaceful negotiation as a means of buying time to recover from short-term setbacks, lulling opponents into complacency, and ultimately preparing for renewed attacks. [ ... ] A foreign terrorist organization introduced to the structures of the international legal system might use the information to threaten, manipulate, and disrupt. This possibility is real, not remote.

Second, plaintiffs propose to "teach PKK members how to petition various representative bodies such as the United Nations for relief." [ ... ] The Government acts within First

Amendment strictures in banning this proposed speech because it teaches the organization how to acquire "relief," which plaintiffs never define with any specificity, and which could readily include monetary aid. [...] Indeed, earlier in this litigation, plaintiffs sought to teach the LTTE "to present claims for tsunami-related aid to mediators and international bodies," [...] which naturally included monetary relief. Money is fungible, [...] and Congress logically concluded that money a terrorist group such as the PKK obtains using the techniques plaintiffs propose to teach could be redirected to funding the group's violent activities.

Finally, plaintiffs propose to "engage in political advocacy on behalf of Kurds who live in Turkey," and "engage in political advocacy on behalf of Tamils who live in Sri Lanka." [...] As explained above, [...] plaintiffs do not specify their expected level of coordination with the PKK or LTTE or suggest what exactly their "advocacy" would consist of. [...]

In responding to the foregoing, the dissent fails to address the real dangers at stake. It instead considers only the possible benefits of plaintiffs' proposed activities in the abstract. [...] The dissent seems unwilling to entertain the prospect that training and advising a designated foreign terrorist organization on how to take advantage of international entities might benefit that organization in a way that facilitates its terrorist activities. In the dissent's world, such training is all to the good. Congress and the Executive, however, have concluded that we live in a different world: one in which the designated foreign terrorist organizations "are so tainted by their criminal conduct that any contribution to such an organization facilitates that conduct." [...] One in which, for example, "the United Nations High Commissioner for Refugees was forced to close a Kurdish refugee camp in northern Iraq because the camp had come under the control of the PKK, and the PKK had failed to respect its 'neutral and humanitarian nature.'" [...] Training and advice on how to work with the United Nations could readily have helped the PKK in its efforts to use the United Nations camp as a base for terrorist activities.

If only good can come from training our adversaries in international dispute resolution, presumably it would have been unconstitutional to prevent American citizens from training the Japanese Government on using international organizations and mechanisms to resolve disputes during World War II. It would, under the dissent's reasoning, have been contrary to our commitment to resolving disputes through "'deliberative forces,'" [...] for Congress to conclude that assisting Japan on that front might facilitate its war effort more generally. That view is not one the First Amendment requires us to embrace.

All this is not to say that any future applications of the material-support statute to speech or advocacy will survive First Amendment scrutiny. It is also not to say that any other statute relating to speech and terrorism would satisfy the First Amendment. In particular, we in no way suggest that a regulation of independent speech would pass constitutional muster, even if the Government were to show that such speech benefits foreign terrorist organizations. We also do not suggest that Congress could extend the same prohibition on material support at issue here to domestic organizations. We simply hold that, in prohibiting the particular forms of support that plaintiffs seek to provide to foreign terrorist groups, § 2339B does not violate the freedom of speech.

[...]

*John G. Roberts, Jr. has served as chief justice of the United States since 2005.

*Holder v. Humanitarian Law Project.* 130 S. Ct. 2705 (2010), 2727–2730. http://scholar.google.com/scholar_case?case=3116082426854631219& hl=en&as_sdt=2,33.

# Chewing Gum for Terrorists

*by David Cole**

Did former Attorney General Michael Mukasey, former New York Mayor Rudolph Giuliani, Tom Ridge, a former homeland security secretary, and Frances Townsend, a former national security adviser, all commit a federal crime last month in Paris when they spoke in support of the Mujahedeen Khalq at a conference organized by the Iranian opposition group's advocates? Free speech, right? Not necessarily.

The problem is that the United States government has labeled the Mujahedeen Khalq a "foreign terrorist organization," making it a crime to provide it, directly or indirectly, with any material support. And, according to the Justice Department under Mr. Mukasey himself, as well as under the current attorney general, Eric Holder, material support includes not only cash and other tangible aid, but also speech coordinated with a "foreign terrorist organization" for its benefit. It is therefore a felony, the government has argued, to file an amicus brief on behalf of a "terrorist" group, to engage in public advocacy to challenge a group's "terrorist" designation or even to encourage peaceful avenues for redress of grievances.

Don't get me wrong. I believe Mr. Mukasey and his compatriots had every right to say what they did. Indeed, I argued just that in the Supreme Court, on behalf of the Los Angeles-based Humanitarian Law Project, which fought for more than a decade in American courts for its right to teach the Kurdistan

Workers' Party in Turkey how to bring human rights claims before the United Nations, and to assist them in peace overtures to the Turkish government.

But in June, the Supreme Court ruled against us, stating that all such speech could be prohibited, because it might indirectly support the group's terrorist activity. Chief Justice John Roberts reasoned that a terrorist group might use human rights advocacy training to file harassing claims, that it might use peacemaking assistance as a cover while re-arming itself, and that such speech could contribute to the group's "legitimacy," and thus increase its ability to obtain support elsewhere that could be turned to terrorist ends. Under the court's decision, former President Jimmy Carter's election monitoring team could be prosecuted for meeting with and advising Hezbollah during the 2009 Lebanese elections.

The government has similarly argued that providing legitimate humanitarian aid to victims of war or natural disasters is a crime if provided to or coordinated with a group labeled as a "foreign terrorist organization"—even if there is no other way to get the aid to the region in need. Yet The Times recently reported that the Treasury Department, under a provision ostensibly intended for humanitarian aid, was secretly granting licenses to American businesses to sell billions of dollars worth of food and goods to the very countries we have blockaded for their support of terrorism. Some of the "humanitarian aid" exempted? Cigarettes, popcorn and chewing gum.

Under current law, it seems, the right to make profits is more sacrosanct than the right to petition for peace, and the need to placate American businesses more compelling than the need to provide food and shelter to earthquake victims and war refugees.

Congress should reform the laws governing material support of terrorism. It should make clear that speech advocating only lawful, nonviolent activities—as Michael Mukasey and Rudolph Giuliani did in Paris—is not a crime. The First Amendment protects even speech advocating criminal activity, unless it is intended and likely to incite imminent lawless conduct. The risk that speech advocating peace and human rights would further terrorism is so remote that it cannot outweigh the indispensable value of protecting dissent.

At the same time, Congress also needs to reform the humanitarian aid exemption. It should state clearly that corporate interests in making profits from cigarettes are not sufficient to warrant exemptions from sanctions on state sponsors of terrorism. But Congress should also protect the provision of legitimate humanitarian aid—food, water, medical aid and shelter—in response to wars or natural disasters. Genuine humanitarian aid and free speech can and should be preserved without undermining our interests in security.

***David Cole** is a professor of constitutional law at Georgetown University. He is the legal affairs correspondent for *The Nation* and a fellow at Open Society Foundations.

Cole, David. "Chewing Gum for Terrorists." *New York Times,* Jan. 2, 2011. http://www.nytimes.com/2011/01/03/opinion/03cole.html?_r=2.

# Massachusetts Man Charged with Conspiracy to Provide Material Support to Terrorists

*by Michael K. Loucks**

BOSTON—A Sudbury, Mass., man was charged today in federal court with conspiracy to provide material support to terrorists.

Acting U.S. Attorney Michael K. Loucks and Warren T. Bamford, Special Agent in Charge of the FBI—Boston Field Division, announced today that Tarek Mehanna, 27, of 6 Fairhaven Circle, Sudbury, Mass., was charged in a complaint with conspiracy to provide material support to terrorists.

The complaint alleges that, beginning in or about 2001 and continuing until in or about May 2008, Mehanna conspired with Ahmad Abousamra, and others to provide material support and resources for use in carrying out a conspiracy to kill, kidnap, maim or injure persons or damage property in a foreign country and extraterritorial homicide of a U.S. national.

Specifically, the complaint affidavit alleges that Mehanna and coconspirators discussed their desire to participate in violent jihad against American interests and that they would talk about fighting jihad and their desire to die on the battlefield. The complaint further alleges that the coconspirators attempted to radicalize others and inspire each other by, among other things, watching and distributing jihadi videos.

It is alleged that, among other things, Mehanna and two of his associates traveled to the Middle East in February 2004, seeking military-type training at a terrorist training camp that would prepare them for armed jihad against U.S. interests, including U.S. and allied forces in Iraq. The complaint also alleges that one of Mehanna's coconspirators made two similar trips to Pakistan in 2002.

According to the complaint affidavit, Mehanna and the coconspirators had multiple conversations about obtaining automatic weapons and randomly shooting people in a shopping mall, and that the conversations went so far as to discuss the logistics of a mall attack, including coordination, weapons needed and the possibility of attacking emergency responders. It is alleged that the plan was ultimately abandoned, because of their inability to obtain the automatic weapons they deemed necessary to effectively carry out the attacks.

Mehanna was previously indicted in January 2009 for making false statements to members of the Joint Terrorism Task Force of the FBI in connection with a terrorism investigation.

If convicted on the material support charge, Mehanna faces up to 15 years in prison, to be followed by three years of supervised release and a $250,000 fine.

[...]

*Michael K. Loucks served as the acting United States attorney for the District of Massachusetts from 2009 to 2010.

Loucks, Michael K. "Massachusetts Man Charged with Conspiracy to Provide Material Support to Terrorists." Department of Justice press release. Oct. 21, 2009. http://www.investigativeproject.org/documents/case_docs/1095.pdf.

# Does Posting Jihadist Material Make Tarek Mehanna a Terrorist?

*by Adam Serwer**

Does posting militant videos on the internet make you a terrorist?

For Tarek Mehanna it just might. Arrested in 2009, Mehanna is a Massachusetts resident whom prosecutors describe as a longtime terrorist wannabe. He isn't just being prosecuted for trying (and failing) to acquire terrorist training in Yemen and lying to federal investigators. He's also being tried for posting pro-jihadist material on the internet.

Mehanna's indictment says that since the early 2000s, he and his friends watched extremist videos on the web and discussed going abroad to receive training in Pakistan and later Yemen. When Mehanna and his alleged accomplice finally reached Yemen in 2004, they were turned away by an old man who told them "all that stuff is gone ever since the planes hit the Twin Towers." Returning home, prosecutors say, Mehanna committed himself to battling the West by other means: spreading Al Qaeda's ideology to the masses by translating extremist documents and posting terrorist propaganda on the Internet, in the hopes of converting more to the cause.

"This case is being used by the government to really narrow First Amendment activity in dangerous new ways," says Nancy

Murray of the Massachusetts branch of the American Civil Liberties Union. "It might be speech that horrifies people, but it's the nature of the First Amendment to protect that speech, unless it's leading to imminent lawless action."

Civil liberties advocates say the case represents a slippery slope. In the 2010 case *Holder v. Humanitarian Law Project*, which decided whether or not providing nonviolent aid (such as legal advice) to terrorist groups constitutes material support for terrorism, the Supreme Court ruled that even protected speech can be a criminal act if it occurs at the direction of a terrorist organization. Based on that ruling, you could be convicted of materially supporting terrorism merely for translating a document or putting an extremist video online, depending on your intentions.

"If he's doing it on behalf of a designated group, he's providing a service, and that's the crime," says Georgetown University law professor David Cole, who argued against the government in *Humanitarian Law Project*. "It doesn't matter if the speech is itself violent or nonviolent." The question is whether Mehanna's actions were done at the direction of a terrorist group or whether his actions constituted "independent advocacy."

Convicting Mehanna on conspiracy charges stemming from his alleged attempt to seek terrorist training or lying to investigators is one thing. Convicting him based on his alleged pro-jihadist internet advocacy could establish a legal path to stamping out extremist propaganda on the web. At the same time, in the view of some civil libertarians, the case could narrow the right to free speech by allowing the government to successfully prosecute the expression of radical or unpopular views as a crime. The verdict could come as soon as next week.

The Mehanna prosecution followed a series of terrorist incidents, including the 2009 shooting rampage at Fort Hood in Texas, where the internet played some role in the individual's radicalization. In September, the Obama administration announced it had killed Anwar al-Awlaki, a radical US-born Imam whose ability to give sermons in colloquial American English made him the symbol of a new era of homegrown extremism. Though administration officials insisted Awlaki's activities in support of terrorism weren't merely rhetorical, he was never indicted—his death was approved by a secret national security panel.

"The dominant narrative right now among Western counterterrorism experts is that because Al Qaeda can't undertake a big attack in the United States, they're advocating these lone-wolf attacks, and a big part of that is pushing out that stuff online," says Will McCants, a former counterterrorism official at the State Department. For English-speaking extremists in particular, McCants says, the internet has been a crucial tool for finding kindred souls. Though "radicalization primarily takes place in the physical world," McCants says, "you can point to a few cases where someone has been radicalized solely on internet material."

Testifying before Congress in April, FBI Director Robert Mueller warned: "The increase and availability of extremist propaganda in English can exacerbate the problem. Ten years ago, in the absence of the internet, extremists would have operated in relative isolation, unlike today."

Mehanna's defense team has argued that his views have been misrepresented and that he doesn't share Al Qaeda's extremist worldview. Holding radical or abhorrent beliefs, however, is still protected by the Constitution. The basic legal standard for when speech becomes criminal is referred to as the "Brandenburg test." Stemming from a 1969 Supreme Court case, the rule essentially stipulates that speech can't be criminalized unless it is deliberately meant to incite "imminent lawless action" and there's a reasonable belief that action could take place.

---

*After all, if the government can kill someone for posting extremist sermons on the internet, why can't it put someone in prison for doing the same thing?*

---

"That's a very hard standard to meet," Cole says. "The court saw from experience that prosecutions for advocacy of illegal conduct often became politically motivated prosecution of dissenters where there was no actual nexus to crime."

But, as Cole points out, the decision in *Holder v. Humanitarian Law Project* created a key terrorism-related exception making even nonviolent, nonmonetary aid to a terrorist organization a crime.

The government has tried to argue that Mehanna's speech isn't protected for two reasons. One, that his actions reflect Al Qaeda's call for its followers to preach its twisted gospel to Westerners. The second is that Mehanna posted extremist propaganda and responded to requests to translate materials from individuals associated with terror groups.

Scholars of Islamic extremism, however, frequently translate and post jihadist material on the internet for the purpose of study—something Mehanna's attorneys have noted in their defense.

"The Supreme Court says the law makes a distinction between independent advocacy and advocacy at the direction and control of a group," Cole says. Prosecuting someone for obeying a "general call" for extremists to spread Al Qaeda's message, Cole says, seems like a reach.

The indictment alleges that Mehanna edited and translated materials at the request of known terrorists, saying of one video that he hopes it "leads to action." Whether Mehanna acted on the direct suggestion of a terror group or not could ultimately make a huge difference.

The government has tried to prosecute other people on the basis of online activities in the past—without much success. In 2003, a University of Idaho graduate student named Sami Omar al-Hussayen was prosecuted for administering a website that linked to extremist sermons and jihadist sites that solicited donations to extremist groups.

Hussayen's attorneys argued that he was a nonviolent man who wasn't responsible for the material. When it came time to offer up a defense, his attorney relied on one man's testimony—a former CIA official named Frank Anderson, who testified that people don't become terrorists just because of what they read on the Internet. Hussayen was ultimately acquitted.

"Recruitment is personal and requires the identification, assessment, and persuasion of 'candidates,'" Anderson told Mother Jones in an email. "Hussayen was involved in none of that... It's not that it can or can't be conducted over the internet." Mehanna's defense team is trying a similar gambit, calling former CIA official Marc Sageman to testify that Al Qaeda's ability to recruit people over the internet is overhyped.

The political landscape has shifted dramatically since Hussayen was acquitted. Since then, the United States has killed at least two American citizens abroad whose roles, it appears, were primarily as Al Qaeda propagandists. Administration officials convicted them in a court of public opinion rather than law, testifying not on the stand but through anonymous statements to reporters. If the prosecution manages to convict Mehanna over posting and translating extremist materials without showing that he was acting on directions from people he believed to be Al Qaeda members, it could open the door to prosecution based on actions that have traditionally been seen as protected speech.

"Is a propagandist for Al Qaeda someone who works with Al Qaeda, or someone who just says positive things about Al Qaeda, or anyone the government has said is furthering the ends of Al Qaeda?" asks the ACLU's Murray. In the post-Awlaki era, the line between "independent advocacy" and "direction or control" may not matter all that much to a jury. After all, if the government can kill someone for posting extremist sermons on the internet, why can't it put someone in prison for doing the same thing?

*Adam Serwer* is a reporter for *Mother Jones* and a staff writer for *The American Prospect*. His pieces have also been featured in the *Washington Post*, the *New York Daily News*, and *The Atlantic*.

Serwer, Adam. "Does Posting Jihadist Material Make Tarek Mehanna a Terrorist?" *Mother Jones*, December 16, 2011. http://www.motherjones.com/politics/2011/12/tarek-mehanna-terrorist.

# The Real Criminals in the Tarek Mehanna Case

*by Glenn Greenwald**

In one of the most egregious violations of the First Amendment's guarantee of free speech seen in quite some time, Tarek Mehanna, an American Muslim, was convicted this week in a federal court in Boston and then sentenced yesterday to 17 years in prison. He was found guilty of supporting Al Qaeda (by virtue of translating Terrorists' documents into English and expressing "sympathetic views" to the group) as well as conspiring to "murder" U.S. soldiers in Iraq (i.e., to wage war against an invading army perpetrating an aggressive attack on a Muslim nation). I'm still traveling and don't have much time today to write about the case itself—Adam Serwer several months ago wrote an excellent summary of why the prosecution of Mehanna is such an odious threat to free speech and more background on the case is here, and I've written before about the growing criminalization of free speech under the Bush and Obama DOJs, whereby Muslims are prosecuted for their plainly protected political views—but I urge everyone to read something quite amazing: Mehanna's incredibly eloquent, thoughtful statement at his sentencing hearing, before being given a 17-year prison term.

At some point in the future, I believe history will be quite clear about who the actual criminals are in this case: not

Mehanna, but rather the architects of the policies he felt compelled to battle and the entities that have conspired to consign him to a cage for two decades:

*Read to Judge O'Toole during his sentencing, April 12th 2012.*

In the name of God the most gracious the most merciful Exactly four years ago this month I was finishing my work shift at a local hospital. As I was walking to my car I was approached by two federal agents. They said that I had a choice to make: I could do things the easy way, or I could do them the hard way. The "easy" way, as they explained, was that I would become an informant for the government, and if I did so I would never see the inside of a courtroom or a prison cell. As for the hard way, this is it. Here I am, having spent the majority of the four years since then in a solitary cell the size of a small closet, in which I am locked down for 23 hours each day. The FBI and these prosecutors worked very hard—and the government spent millions of tax dollars—to put me in that cell, keep me there, put me on trial, and finally to have me stand here before you today to be sentenced to even more time in a cell.

In the weeks leading up to this moment, many people have offered suggestions as to what I should say to you. Some said I should plead for mercy in hopes of a light sentence, while others suggested I would be hit hard either way. But what I want to do is just talk about myself for a few minutes.

When I refused to become an informant, the government responded by charging me with the "crime" of supporting the mujahideen fighting the occupation of Muslim countries around the world. Or as they like to call them, "terrorists." I wasn't born in a Muslim country, though. I was born and raised right here in America and this angers many people: how is it that I can be an American and believe the things I believe, take the positions I take? Everything a man is exposed to in his environment becomes an ingredient that shapes his outlook, and I'm no different. So, in more ways than one, it's because of America that I am who I am.

When I was six, I began putting together a massive collection of comic books. Batman implanted a concept in my mind, introduced me to a paradigm as to how the world is set up: that there are oppressors, there are the oppressed, and there are those who step up to defend the oppressed. This resonated with me so much that throughout the rest of my childhood, I gravitated towards any book that reflected that paradigm—Uncle Tom's Cabin, The Autobiography of Malcolm X, and I even saw an ethical dimension to The Catcher in the Rye.

By the time I began high school and took a real history class, I was learning just how real that paradigm is in the world. I learned about the Native Americans and what befell them at the hands of European settlers. I learned about how the descendants of those European settlers were in turn oppressed under the tyranny of King George III.

I read about Paul Revere, Tom Paine, and how Americans began an armed insurgency against British forces—an insurgency we now celebrate as the American revolutionary war. As a kid I even went on school field trips just blocks away from where we sit now. I learned about Harriet Tubman, Nat Turner, John Brown, and the fight against slavery in this country. I learned about Emma Goldman, Eugene Debs, and the struggles of the labor unions, working class, and poor. I learned about Anne Frank, the Nazis, and how they persecuted minorities and imprisoned dissidents. I learned about Rosa Parks, Malcolm X, Martin Luther King, and the civil rights struggle.

I learned about Ho Chi Minh, and how the Vietnamese fought for decades to liberate themselves from one invader after another. I learned about Nelson Mandela and the fight against apartheid in South Africa. Everything I learned in those years confirmed what I was beginning to learn when I was six:

that throughout history, there has been a constant struggle between the oppressed and their oppressors. With each struggle I learned about, I found myself consistently siding with the oppressed, and consistently respecting those who stepped up to defend them—regardless of nationality, regardless of religion. And I never threw my class notes away. As I stand here speaking, they are in a neat pile in my bedroom closet at home.

From all the historical figures I learned about, one stood out above the rest. I was impressed be many things about Malcolm X, but above all, I was fascinated by the idea of transformation, his transformation. I don't know if you've seen the movie "X" by Spike Lee, it's over three and a half hours long, and the Malcolm at the beginning is different from the Malcolm at the end. He starts off as an illiterate criminal, but ends up a husband, a father, a protective and eloquent leader for his people, a disciplined Muslim performing the Hajj in Makkah, and finally, a martyr. Malcolm's life taught me that Islam is not something inherited; it's not a culture or ethnicity. It's a way of life, a state of mind anyone can choose no matter where they come from or how they were raised.

This led me to look deeper into Islam, and I was hooked. I was just a teenager, but Islam answered the question that the greatest scientific minds were clueless about, the question that drives the rich & famous to depression and suicide from being unable to answer: what is the purpose of life? Why do we exist in this Universe? But it also answered the question of how we're supposed to exist. And since there's no hierarchy or priesthood, I could directly and immediately begin digging into the texts of the Qur'an and the teachings of Prophet Muhammad, to begin the journey of understanding what this was all about, the implications of Islam for me as a human being, as an individual, for the people around me, for the world; and the more I learned, the more I valued Islam like a piece of gold. This was when I was a teen, but even today, despite the pressures of the last few years,

I stand here before you, and everyone else in this courtroom, as a very proud Muslim.

With that, my attention turned to what was happening to other Muslims in different parts of the world. And everywhere I looked, I saw the powers that be trying to destroy what I loved. I learned what the Soviets had done to the Muslims of Afghanistan. I learned what the Serbs had done to the Muslims of Bosnia. I learned what the Russians were doing to the Muslims of Chechnya. I learned what Israel had done in Lebanon—and what it continues to do in Palestine—with the full backing of the United States. And I learned what America itself was doing to Muslims. I learned about the Gulf War, and the depleted uranium bombs that killed thousands and caused cancer rates to skyrocket across Iraq.

I learned about the American-led sanctions that prevented food, medicine, and medical equipment from entering Iraq, and how—according to the United Nations—over half a million children perished as a result. I remember a clip from a '60 Minutes' interview of Madeline Albright where she expressed her view that these dead children were "worth it." I watched on September 11th as a group of people felt driven to hijack airplanes and fly them into buildings from their outrage at the deaths of these children. I watched as America then attacked and invaded Iraq directly. I saw the effects of 'Shock & Awe' in the opening day of the invasion—the children in hospital wards with shrapnel from American missiles sticking out of their foreheads (of course, none of this was shown on CNN).

I learned about the town of Haditha, where 24 Muslims— including a 76-year old man in a wheelchair, women, and even toddlers—were shot up and blown up in their bedclothes as the slept by US Marines. I learned about Abeer al-Janabi, a fourteen-year old Iraqi girl gang-raped by five American soldiers, who then shot her and her family in the head, then set fire to their corpses. I just want to point out, as you can see, Muslim women don't even show their hair to unrelated men. So try to imagine this young girl from a conservative village with her dress torn off, being sexually assaulted by not one, not two, not three, not four, but five soldiers. Even today, as I sit in my jail cell, I read about the drone strikes which continue to kill Muslims daily in places like Pakistan, Somalia, and Yemen. Just last month, we all heard about the seventeen Afghan Muslims—mostly mothers and their kids—shot to death by an American soldier, who also set fire to their corpses.

These are just the stories that make it to the headlines, but one of the first concepts I learned in Islam is that of loyalty, of brotherhood—that each Muslim woman is my sister, each man is my brother, and together, we are one large body who must protect each other. In other words, I couldn't see these things beings done to my brothers & sisters—including by America—and remain neutral. My sympathy for the oppressed continued, but was now more personal, as was my respect for those defending them.

I mentioned Paul Revere—when he went on his midnight ride, it was for the purpose of warning the people that the British were marching to Lexington to arrest Sam Adams and John Hancock, then on to Concord to confiscate the weapons stored there by the Minuteman. By the time they got to Concord, they found the Minuteman waiting for them, weapons in hand. They fired at the British, fought them, and beat them. From that battle came the American Revolution. There's an Arabic word to describe what those Minutemen did that day. That word is: JIHAD, and this is what my trial was about.

All those videos and translations and childish bickering over 'Oh, he translated this paragraph' and 'Oh, he edited that sentence,' and all those exhibits revolved around a single issue: Muslims who were defending themselves against American soldiers doing to them exactly what the British did to America. It was made crystal clear at trial that I never, ever plotted to "kill Americans" at shopping malls or whatever the story was. The government's own witnesses contradicted this claim, and we put expert after expert up on that stand, who spent hours dissecting my every written word, who explained my beliefs. Further, when I was free, the government sent an undercover agent to prod me into one of their little "terror plots," but I refused to participate. Mysteriously, however, the jury never heard this.

So, this trial was not about my position on Muslims killing American civilians. It was about my position on Americans killing Muslim civilians, which is that Muslims should defend their lands from foreign invaders—Soviets, Americans, or Martians. This is what I believe. It's what I've always believed, and what I will always believe. This is not terrorism, and it's not extremism. It's what the arrows on that seal above your head represent: defense of the homeland. So, I disagree with my lawyers when they say that you don't have to agree with my beliefs—no. Anyone with commonsense and humanity has no choice but to agree with me. If someone breaks into your home to rob you and harm your family, logic dictates that you do whatever it takes to expel that invader from your home.

But when that home is a Muslim land, and that invader is the US military, for some reason the standards suddenly change. Common sense is renamed "terrorism" and the people defending themselves against those who come to kill them from across the ocean become "the terrorists" who are "killing Americans." The mentality that America was victimized with when British soldiers walked these streets 2 ½ centuries ago is the same mentality Muslims are victimized by as American soldiers walk their streets today. It's the mentality of colonialism.

When Sgt. Bales shot those Afghans to death last month, all of the focus in the media was on him-his life, his stress, his

PTSD, the mortgage on his home—as if he was the victim. Very little sympathy was expressed for the people he actually killed, as if they're not real, they're not humans. Unfortunately, this mentality trickles down to everyone in society, whether or not they realize it. Even with my lawyers, it took nearly two years of discussing, explaining, and clarifying before they were finally able to think outside the box and at least ostensibly accept the logic in what I was saying. Two years! If it took that long for people so intelligent, whose job it is to defend me, to de-program themselves, then to throw me in front of a randomly selected jury under the premise that they're my "impartial peers," I mean, come on. I wasn't tried before a jury of my peers because with the mentality gripping America today, I have no peers. Counting on this fact, the government prosecuted me—not because they needed to, but simply because they could.

I learned one more thing in history class: America has historically supported the most unjust policies against its minorities—practices that were even protected by the law—only to look back later and ask: 'what were we thinking?' Slavery, Jim Crow, the internment of the Japanese during World War II—each was widely accepted by American society, each was defended by the Supreme Court. But as time passed and America changed, both people and courts looked back and asked 'What were we thinking?' Nelson Mandela was considered a terrorist by the South African government, and given a life sentence. But time passed, the world changed, they realized how oppressive their policies were, that it was not he who was the terrorist, and they released him from prison. He even became president. So, everything is subjective—even this whole business of "terrorism" and who is a "terrorist." It all depends on the time and place and who the superpower happens to be at the moment.

In your eyes, I'm a terrorist, and it's perfectly reasonable that I be standing here in an orange jumpsuit. But one day, America will change and people will recognize this day for what it is. They will look at how hundreds of thousands of Muslims were killed and maimed by the US military in foreign countries, yet somehow I'm the one going to prison for "conspiring to kill and maim" in those countries—because I support the Mujahidin defending those people. They will look back on how the government spent millions of dollars to imprison me as a "terrorist," yet if we were to somehow bring Abeer al-Janabi back to life in the moment she was being gang-raped by your soldiers, to put her on that witness stand and ask her who the "terrorists" are, she sure wouldn't be pointing at me.

The government says that I was obsessed with violence, obsessed with "killing Americans." But, as a Muslim living in these times, I can think of a lie no more ironic.

—Tarek Mehanna

*Glenn Greenwald is an American political journalist, lawyer, columnist, blogger, and author.

Tarek Mehanna is an American pharmacist convicted of conspiring with al Qaeda. The statement was read to Judge O'Toole during Mehanna's sentencing on April 12, 2012.

Greenwald, Glenn. "The Real Criminals in the Tarek Mehanna Case." Salon.com. April 13, 2012. http://www.salon.com/2012/04/13/the_real_criminals_in_the_tarek_mehanna_case/.

# A Dangerous Mind?

*by Andrew F. March\**

LATE last year, a jury in Boston convicted Tarek Mehanna, a 29-year-old pharmacist born in Pittsburgh, of material support for terrorism, conspiring to provide material support to terrorists and conspiring to kill in a foreign country, after a 35-day trial in which I testified as an expert witness for the defense.

On April 12, Mr. Mehanna was sentenced to 17 and a half years in prison. Hearing this, most Americans would probably assume that the F.B.I. caught a major homegrown terrorist and that 17 and a half years is reasonable punishment for someone plotting to engage in terrorism. The details, however, reveal this to be one of the most important free speech cases we have seen since Brandenburg v. Ohio in 1969.

As a political scientist specializing in Islamic law and war, I frequently read, store, share and translate texts and videos by jihadi groups. As a political philosopher, I debate the ethics of killing. As a citizen, I express views, thoughts and emotions about killing to other citizens. As a human being, I sometimes feel joy (I am ashamed to admit) at the suffering of some humans and anger at the suffering of others.

At Mr. Mehanna's trial, I saw how those same actions can constitute federal crimes.

Because Mr. Mehanna's conviction was based largely on things he said, wrote and translated. Yet that speech was not prosecuted according to the Brandenburg standard of incitement to "imminent lawless action" but according to the much more troubling standard of having the intent to support a foreign terrorist organization.

Mr. Mehanna was convicted and sentenced based on two broad sets of facts. First, in 2004, Mr. Mehanna traveled with a friend to Yemen for a week, in search, the government said, of a jihadi training camp from which they would then proceed to Iraq to fight American nationals. The trip was a complete bust, and Mr. Mehanna returned home.

Some of his friends continued to look for ways to join foreign conflicts. One even fought in Somalia. But Mr. Mehanna stayed home, completed a doctorate in pharmacology and practiced and taught in the Boston area. But the Yemen trip and the actions of his friends were only one part of the government's case.

For the government, Mr. Mehanna's delivery of "material support" consisted not in his failed effort to join jihadi groups he never found, nor in financial contributions he never made to friends trying to join such groups, but in advocating the jihadi cause from his home in Sudbury.

MR. MEHANNA'S crimes were speech crimes, even thought crimes. The kinds of speech that the government successfully criminalized were not about coordinating acts of terror or giving directions on how to carry out violent acts. The speech for which Mr. Mehanna was convicted involved the religious and political advocacy of certain causes beyond American shores.

The government's indictment of Mr. Mehanna lists the following acts, among others, as furthering a criminal conspiracy:

"watched jihadi videos," "discussed efforts to create like-minded youth," "discussed" the "religious justification" for certain violent acts like suicide bombings, "created and/or translated, accepted credit for authoring and distributed text, videos and other media to inspire others to engage in violent jihad," "sought out online Internet links to tribute videos," and spoke of "admiration and love for Usama bin Laden." It is important to appreciate that those acts were not used by the government to demonstrate the intent or mental state behind some other crime in the way racist speech is used to prove that a violent act was a hate crime. They were the crime, because the conspiracy was to support Al Qaeda by advocating for it through speech.

Much of Mr. Mehanna's speech on Web sites and in IM chats was brutal, disgusting and unambiguously supportive of Islamic insurgencies in Iraq, Afghanistan and Somalia. In one harrowing IM chat, which the government brought up repeatedly during the trial, he referred to the mutilation of the remains of American soldiers in response to the rape of a 14-year-old Iraqi girl as "Texas BBQ." He wrote poetry in praise of martyrdom. But is the government right that such speech, however repulsive, can be criminalized as material support for terrorism?

In the 2010 Supreme Court decision Holder v. Humanitarian Law Project, Chief Justice John G. Roberts Jr. declared that for speech to qualify as criminal material support, it has to take the form of expert advice or assistance conveyed in coordination with or under the control of a designated foreign terrorist organization. In that decision, Justice Roberts reaffirmed that "under the material-support statute, plaintiffs may say anything they wish on any topic" and pointed out that "Congress has not sought to suppress ideas or opinions in the form of 'pure political speech.'" Justice Roberts emphasized that he wanted to "in no way suggest that a regulation of independent speech would pass constitutional muster, even if the Government were to show that such speech benefits foreign terrorist organizations."

The government's case against Mr. Mehanna, however, did not rest on proving that his translations were done in coordination with Al Qaeda. Citing no explicit coordination with or direction by a foreign terrorist organization, the government's case rested primarily on Mr. Mehanna's intent in saying the things he said—his political and religious thoughts, feelings and viewpoints.

The prosecution's strategy, a far cry from Justice Roberts's statement that "independent advocacy" of a terror group's ideology, aims or methods is not a crime, produced many ominous ideas. For example, in his opening statement to the jury one prosecutor suggested that "it's not illegal to watch something on the television. It is illegal, however, to watch something in order to cultivate your desire, your ideology." In other words, viewing perfectly legal material can become a crime with nothing other than a change of heart. When it comes to prosecuting speech as support for terrorism, it's the thought that counts.

That is all troubling enough, but it gets worse. Not only has the government prosecuted a citizen for "independent advocacy" of a terror group, but it has prosecuted a citizen who actively argued against much of what most Americans mean when they talk about terrorism.

On a Web site that the government made central to the conspiracy charge, Mr. Mehanna angrily contested the common jihadi argument that American civilians are legitimate targets because they democratically endorse their government's wars and pay taxes that support these wars.

Mr. Mehanna viewed Muslim attacks on foreign occupying militaries as justified but rejected the Qaeda doctrine that the civilian citizens of a foreign country at war with Muslims can be targeted. His doctrine was that "those who fight Muslims may be fought, not those who have the same nationality as those who fight."

The centerpiece of the government's case against Mr. Mehanna's speech activities was a translation of a text titled "39 Ways to Serve and Participate in Jihad." The government described this text, written by a late pro-jihad Saudi religious scholar, as a "training manual for terrorism." It is nothing of the sort. It is a fairly routine exercise of Islamic jurisprudence explaining to pious Muslims how they can discharge what many of them believe to be a duty to contribute to wars of self-defense.

This text does explain that in Islamic law a Muslim may "go for jihad" or "collect funds for the mujahidin." But it also explains that, in place of fighting or sending money, a Muslim can assuage his conscience and take care of widows and children, praise fighters, pray for fighters, become physically fit, learn first aid, learn the Islamic rules of war, have feelings of enmity for one's enemies, spread news about captives and abandon luxury.

The act of translating this text is far from incitement to violent action. The text in fact shows Muslims numerous ways to help fellow Muslims suffering in their own lands, without engaging in violence. Instead of this common-sense reading, however, the government did something extraordinary. It used this text of Islamic law to help define for us what should count as a violation of our own material support law.

Everything Mr. Mehanna did, from hiking to praying, was given a number in the indictment based on this text as an act of material support for jihad. For example, his online discussion with a friend about working out and exercising should, in the government's words, be "placed next to the directives in 39 Ways (Step 25: 'Become Physically Fit')." Federal prosecutors, in effect, used a Saudi religious scholar to tell us what our "material support" statute means.

The Mehanna case presented an excruciating line-drawing exercise. How pro-Al Qaeda is too pro-Al Qaeda, legally speaking?

We have the resources to prevent acts of violence without threatening the First Amendment. The Mehanna prosecution is a frightening and unnecessary attempt to expand the kinds of religious and political speech that the government can criminalize. The First Circuit Court of Appeals in Boston should at least invalidate Mr. Mehanna's conviction for speech and reaffirm the Supreme Court's doctrines in Brandenburg and Holder v. Humanitarian Law Project. Otherwise, the difference between what I do every day and what Mr. Mehanna did is about the differences between the thoughts in our heads and the feelings in our hearts, and I don't trust prosecutors with that jurisdiction.

*Andrew F. March is an assistant professor of political science at Yale University. He focuses on contemporary political theory and Islamic jurisprudence.

March, Andrew F. "A Dangerous Mind?" *New York Times,* April 21, 2012. http://www.nytimes.com/2012/04/22/opinion/sunday/a-dangerous -mind.html?_r=0&adxnnl=1&pagewanted=all&adxnnlx=1359411940.

# Peter Margulies Responds to David Cole

*by Peter Margulies\**

Peter Margulies of Roger Williams University School of Law writes in with the following response to David Cole's recent article on the Tarek Mehanna case:

> While David Cole's passionate defense of the First Amendment is always welcome, David overshoots the mark in his recent post on the Mehanna case. [ ... ]

[ ... ] Tarek Mehanna was convicted in December, 2011 in federal court in Massachusetts of conspiring to commit violence in this country, go to an Al Qaeda training camp abroad, and furnish Al Qaeda with propaganda. David is right that this last charge has First Amendment implications, since propaganda is speech. However, U.S. courts have regularly permitted prosecutions of individuals, such as World War II's infamous Tokyo Rose, who knowingly provided propaganda to nations engaged in war against the U.S. In principle, the rule should be no different for DFTOs. For such groups, propaganda is inextricably linked to operations; terrorist plots are not random, but are carefully planned to maximize propaganda value. Propaganda spread by the group is not separate from, but indeed is crucial to, the group's operations.

Mehanna made two claims at trial to counter the government's charges. First, he claimed the material he provided consisted of translations into English of prominent texts justifying violent jihad. Mehanna said that these texts were of scholarly value, and had a merely abstract relationship to any particular acts of violence. Second, Mehanna said that he had posted these texts to an on-line chat room visited by individuals with a purely intellectual interest in these texts. Members or organizers of the chat room who had requested that Mehanna translate the documents were, according to Mehanna, acting independently of Al Qaeda. Mehanna therefore sought refuge in doctrine, ably unpacked by David, holding that the expression of abstract views supporting violence by someone acting independently of a DFTO is protected by the First Amendment, when those views happen to coincide with those of the DFTO itself. At least in the domestic setting, such views do not meet the test for incitement, which as David correctly noted requires the intent to cause imminent harm and the reasonable likelihood that such harm will result.

The government saw Mehanna's case differently. It successfully argued at trial that Mehanna knew that the chat room, sponsored by an entity called Tibyan Publications, was in fact run by persons from Al Qaeda's network, including the notorious Abu Qatada, who has long encouraged extremist violence from the United Kingdom while resisting extradition for past terrorist acts. American, Canadian, and British visitors to the chat room, which was password-protected, had sought to attend training camps or provide other assistance to Al Qaeda. Mehanna repeatedly lied to federal investigators about his role. The government took the reasonable position that terrorist networks are not hierarchical, but instead are widely dispersed. Organizations like Al Qaeda do not carry business cards, and security concerns mean that Al Qaeda's former leader, Osama bin Laden, or current leader, Dr. Ayman al-Zawahiri, rarely offer specific operational advice. Instead, most orders and advice come from a broad group of people around the world. Courts have never required the government to prove that conspirators in ordinary cases involving drugs or organized crime had contact with the kingpins of the organization. The government can prevail in such cases by simply showing that defendants were "spokes in a wheel," who had agreed with other conspirators to further the conspiracy's objectives. Proving conspiracy to provide material support to a DFTO like Al Qaeda should be no different, the government argued; the jury agreed.

Unlike the plaintiffs that David represented so ably in Holder, Mehanna clearly intended to spur violence. Indeed, he boasted to friends that he was part of Al Qaeda's media arm in the United States. David is right that independent speakers with extreme views should be protected by the First Amendment. But shills for Al Qaeda should not be. By assembling propaganda at Al Qaeda's direction to further the recruitment of new operatives, Mehanna placed himself in this category. The Constitution does not bar Congress from deterring Mehanna and those who would follow his example.

***Peter Marguiles** teaches immigration law, national security law, and professional responsibility at Roger Williams University School of Law. He is the author of *Law's Detour: Justice Displaced in the Bush Administration*.

Margulies, Peter. "Peter Margulies Responds to David Cole." *Lawfare,* April 21, 2012. http://www.lawfareblog.com/2012/04/peter-margulies -responds-to-david-cole/.

# United States of America v. Tarek Mehanna, Brief of *Amici Curiae* Scholars, Publishers, and Translators in the Fields of Islam and the Middle East in Support of Defendant-Appellant and Reversal

*by E. Joshua Rosenkranz\**

## Interest of Amici Curiae[1]

*Amici* are scholars, publishers, and translators who work on topics related to the Middle East, Islam, and Islamic militant groups. In the ordinary course of their academic and professional lives, *amici* engage in the same acts that the Government contends constituted material support for terrorism when undertaken by Tarek Mehanna: *Amici* conduct fieldwork in countries where foreign terrorist organizations ("FTOs") operate and might interact with FTO members (even if only inadvertently); *amici* visit FTOs' websites, or websites that express views sympathetic to FTOs, to access content, read documents, and watch videos pertaining to jihad and militant Islam; they translate jihadi materials into English; they disseminate these materials in articles, books, and Internet postings; and they discuss jihad and militant Islam in university classrooms, academic journals, and online. *Amici* have a substantial interest in ensuring that the material support statutes, 18 U.S.C. §§2339A and 2339B, not be interpreted or applied, as here, in a manner that exposes their work to potential criminal liability.

## Introduction and Preliminary Statement

*Amici* file this brief in support of Mr. Mehanna's request for vacatur of his convictions for conspiracy to provide material support to al-Qa'ida, in violation of §2339B (Count 1); and conspiracy to provide and attempted provision of material support to terrorists, in violation of §2339A (Counts 2 and 3). *Amici* wish to make two points of particular importance to them as scholars, publishers, and translators.

*First,* Mr. Mehanna's convictions will chill academic freedom and stifle public discourse. The Government's material support case against Mr. Mehanna depends on his "online activities of translating, editing, and distributing certain pro-jihadi materials"—that is, conduct that scholars undertake every day. [...] Academic and reference works that include compilations and translations of "pro-jihadi materials," including speeches and writings by the leaders of al-Qa'ida, Hizbullah, and Hamas, abound. So too do websites maintained by scholars, think tanks, consulting groups, and independent terrorism monitors (including the U.S. Military Academy at West Point) that collect, translate, and disseminate militant communications to a worldwide audience. The utility of such resources is self-evident: By illuminating the activities, ideologies, strategies, and organizational structures of terrorist groups, they make it easier to understand, and so to combat, global terror.

In the Government's view, the activities in which *amici* regularly engage were criminal when undertaken by Mr.

Mehanna because Mr. Mehanna intended his translations and Internet postings to benefit terrorist groups. But the way the Government proved Mr. Mehanna's intent—by piling in front of the jury evidence that Mr. Mehanna held disfavored political and religious beliefs—exerts a serious chilling effect on academic freedom. If the Government's view prevails, scholars who wish to translate and publish "pro-jihadi materials" will have to take care not to express beliefs that the Government could conceivably characterize as anti-American or "pro-jihadi," lest those beliefs supply the basis for an inference of unlawful intent in a material support prosecution. Conversely, scholars who have expressed or may wish to express controversial or disfavored views will have to refrain from translating or disseminating texts or undertaking fieldwork that the Government could portray as beneficial to or supportive of militant groups. In either case, the ability of scholars to carry out valuable academic work would depend on conformity with a preferred Government ideology. That would trench on " special concern of the First Amendment, which does not tolerate laws that cast a pall of orthodoxy over the classroom." *Keyishian v. Bd. of Regents of Univ. of State of N.Y.,* 385 U.S. 589, 603 (1967).

Separately, the expansive view of "coordination" with an FTO advanced by the Government and adopted by the district court—a view that does not require any degree of direct contact or activity in concert with an FTO—will discourage valuable research. Social scientists and anthropologists studying the Middle East, Islam, or Islamic militant groups must travel to countries where FTOs operate in order to conduct fieldwork. Such scholars may come into contact with members of FTOs—indeed, that may be the point of their fieldwork. Or researchers may be required to communicate with intermediaries of FTOs or media organizations sympathetic to FTOs in order to access primary sources. Either activity is, of course, completely lawful. [...] But if, as the Government contends, any interaction with an FTO or its affiliated entities that occurs during the course of research suffices to show coordination, scholars cannot publish the fruits of their research without fear of prosecution.

*Second, amici* are concerned about the way the Government portrayed the text Mr. Mehanna translated, *39 Ways to Serve and Participate in Jihad,* and the website to which he provided it, *at-Tibyan.* While the text and website contain certain material that many Americans would find offensive, *amici* do not believe that Mr. Mehanna's translation and dissemination activities can fairly be said to constitute material support. Contrary to the Government's characterization, *39 Ways* is not a manual for terrorist activity but theoretical treatment of a basic question in Sunni jurisprudence—how a Muslim may discharge his individual duty to contribute to wars of self-defense. If translating *39 Ways* satisfies the statutory definition of "material support or resources," then so too will translating or publishing innumerable mainstream theological texts—notwithstanding the statutory exclusion for "religious materials." [...] Likewise lacking in precision is the Government's depiction of *at-Tibyan* as a "radical jihadi website." In fact, *at-Tibyan* was primarily dedicated to the thought of Abu Muhammad al-Maqdisi, who is a theologian and a jurist—not the leader of an FTO—and has dissented from crucial aspects of al-Qa'ida's terroristic tactics. While Maqdisi's ideology endorses rebellion against what he sees as illegitimate Muslim regimes, *at-Tibyan's* library of publications contained many texts on such mundane religious topics as Islamic missionary activities and Qur'anic commentary. A person might go to *at-Tibyan* to discuss and consume unpopular views, but a reasonable person could not conclude that *at-Tibyan* was an outlet of an FTO and thus a vehicle through which to provide material support.

In light of these concerns, this Court should vacate Mr. Mehanna's convictions on Counts 1–3.

## NOTE

1. All parties have consented to the filing of this brief. See Fed. R. App. P. 29(a). No party's counsel authored this brief in whole or in part; no party or party's counsel contributed money that was intended to fund preparing or submitting this brief; and no person other than amici or their counsel contributed money that was intended to fund preparing or submitting this brief. See Fed. R. App. P. 29(c)(5).

*E. Joshua Rosenkranz is a partner at Orrick, Herrington & Sutcliffe LLP. He leads the firm's Supreme Court and appellate litigation practice and was named "Litigator of the Year" by *The American Lawyer* in its January 2012 issue.

Rosenkranz, E. Joshua. "Brief of *Amici Curiae* Scholars, Publishers, and Translators in the Fields of Islam and the Middle East in Support of Defendant-Appellant and Reversal." *United States of America v. Tarek Mehanna*. n.d. http://www.orrick.com/Events-and-Publications/Pages/United-States-of-America-v-Tarek-Mehanna-Amicus-Brief-Scholars.aspx.

Used by permission.